W9-CJD-154

3867

The
Best Friend
You'll Ever
Have

The Best Friend You'll Ever Have

BERNARD SLOAN

CROWN PUBLISHERS, INC.   NEW YORK

Inquiries should be addressed to Crown Publishers, Inc.,
One Park Avenue, New York, New York 10016

Printed in the United States of America

Published simultaneously in Canada
by General Publishing Company Limited

Library of Congress Cataloging in Publication Data
Sloan, Bernard.
The best friend you'll ever have.

1. Sloan, Dora. 2. Aged—United States—Psychology.
3. Conflict of generations. 4. Mothers—United
States—Biography. 5. United States—Biography.
6. Jews in the United States—Biography. 7. Cancer—
Biography. 8. Sloan, Bernard.   I. Title.

CT275.S52335S58   1980   973'.04'924 [B]   79–26523
ISBN: 0-517-540037

Book Design: Shari de Miskey

10   9   8   7   6   5   4   3   2   1

First edition

To my wife, Ethel,
and my sons, Steven and Paul,
whom I am proud to call my family

MY MOTHER WAS THE GRANDMOTHER who lived out West, an occasional voice on the telephone at odd hours when the rates were cheaper. "Funny," Steven, my older son, wisecracked, "she doesn't sound Western."

My mother would never be mistaken for John Wayne or Miss Kitty of "Gunsmoke." Instead of "Howdy pardner" and "Head 'em off at the pass," she cried "Oi vay" and "gevalt," a mystery I cleared up by explaining that she was Jewish—Eastern European Jewish—long before turning Western. She and my father migrated to the land of sand and cactus in the rush of '49—1949—fighting off porters attacking with extended palms in the sleeping car of the Southern Pacific. A far cry from a covered wagon, although both now equally historical in the minds of my children.

"How come my friends don't talk like her?" asked my younger son, Paul. "They're Jewish."

"They live in Larchmont," I said, explaining that as soon as people made it across the line into Westchester accents mysteriously evaporated and everyone spoke nice. Only those left behind in the Bronx, Brooklyn, and Queens were doomed to spend their lives talking funny.

As I grew up my mother and father issued regular warnings to me of the perils of a mixed marriage, reading me horror stories from the Yiddish newspaper *The Forward* of foolhardy couples rejected by all the families involved, driving their Jewish parents to an early grave, culminating with the Christian spouse screaming "dirty Jew" in the heat of the first argument.

So, naturally, I married a Protestant and discovered that religion was the least of our problems. No child ever ran screaming into the house demanding a religion. I never discovered hidden crosses— or phylacteries for that matter. Still, after twenty years, my mother remained convinced that our marriage was a shaky structure held together only by my refusal to admit I had made a mistake.

It was no rarity in Larchmont for people to have remote parents. If one generation did not move, the other did. And often. During the holidays the travel agencies burst into activity as families took off for Miami, San Diego, and Duluth to snap Instamatics at beaming grandmas and grandpas who rushed breakables out of reach and wheeled out cots.

The majority of absent grandparents had migrated to Florida— Jews in Miami, gentiles in Palm Beach and Sarasota. God only knows if there was yet a further division between Protestants and Catholics. My mother had to land in Arizona.

Not that it was her choosing. My father's asthma chose it for her. Selling their hardware store in Detroit, they fled to the dry desert air soon after World War II, expecting to be sustained by the "income property" they had acquired over the years by denying themselves everything else. Eight years later my father lay buried in the desert. "I had eight beautiful years," he said, slipping peacefully into death as the cells devoured his pancreas and his skin turned yellow. "Take care of your mother."

My mother required very little taking care of. She remarried three years later. Cy Raskin, owner of a chain of Indian souvenir stores, who went to the great reservation in the sky after a marriage that lasted, according to my mother, "twelve miserable years." She referred to him by his last name, Raskin. My father she called "my Saul."

Married or widowed, she hated all her thirty years in Arizona. "Who can stand such heat?" she complained steadily, as if she were a Gila monster sentenced by nature to spend her life there.

"Mom and Dad are having a ball," Al Russell said of his parents cha-chaing in their Miami Beach condo, freed at last from their Columbus Avenue candy store. Beach every day, concerts at night, loads of friends, love it.

But when Mom died of a heart attack, Al and Nancy were a thousand miles away. And three years later, when Al was wheeled into the hospital for a heart operation and came out a corpse at the age of forty-two, his father screamed at the grave that he had not been told his son was sick. Not that he would have made it in time. By the time they reached him on the beach . . .

Not all elderly parents had migrated. Many still hung in there—

Long Beach, Brighton, Sheepshead Bay, Manhattan. On the fourth Sunday of each month, unless saved by a downpour, Walter and Daisy Ryan and their three children returned drained from their pilgrimage to Wally's mother in Long Beach. "My mother," Wally said, "is firmly convinced the world was created to keep her comfortable."

Margaret Lazar hit the chocolate chip cookies after every conversation with her mother in Peter Cooper Village.

And there was the famous Sally Lianetti story: Sally turned a cup of tea upside down on her mother's dinette table when her mother insisted, once too often, that her thirty-eight-year-old daughter, mother of two, "drink it, it's good for you."

Jerry Neumann's father was found murdered in his Brooklyn apartment on his seventy-second birthday after failing to arrive at his son's house for a birthday dinner.

It was easy for me to feel superior to my fifty-year-old friends behaving like children with their parents. Pillars of the community, members of the school board, militants for political action shriveling at the sound of a parent's voice, paying duty calls to the far reaches of the city, fortifying themselves with a Scotch before dialing the phone.

I was safe. My mother was too far away to be a problem. She was working out her own destiny. A fighter, no serious illness would dare attack her. A perfectly reasonable attitude. After all, I was not going to turn thirty, then forty, then—whammo—fifty. Or be fired from the advertising agency where I had been the boy wonder for twelve years. Should she ever by some remote possibility age a little, she would be welcomed by the Arizona home for aged Hebrews to which she had contributed generously. There, where the mere mention of her name brought them to attention, she would be treated like a queen.

So there was really nothing to worry about.

Until very late one night when the phone rang.

2

"BERNIE ..." Her normally powerful voice was a thin, lonely wail. "I'm very sick."

Not now, I thought. Not us. It had to be part of her act. For all her fierce independence, she could be a pro at playing the part of the sufferer when it suited her. Given the proper motivation, she could recite symptoms with the best of them. Her pains could be more painful than anyone else's, her sicknesses sicker, a sore throat a national emergency. But she always triumphed. The worse the affliction, the sweeter the victory. Further proof of her indestructibility.

"Dr. Greenstone wants me to go to the hospital"—she choked back tears—"for tests."

That did not sound exactly terrifying. I had survived hospitals. Appendectomy. Kidney stone. My sixteen-year-old son Steven had lived to tell about his hernia operation. At our local hospital the meals were catered by Marriott, easily three star.

"It's my shoulder," she wailed.

"Still?"

"I can't raise my arm," she cried. "I thought it was getting better, but all of a sudden I can't move it." She broke into sobs.

Her shoulder had been going on for months. No, years. It started when she had visited us almost three years earlier on her way to and from long-lost friends in Argentina. She returned to Arizona with a pain in her shoulder that she attributed to flying with a cold caught in our unheated home. The last time she mentioned it was when Dr. Greenstone told her he wished he could raise his arm as high as she could. She had been going to Dr. Greenstone for years. He kidded around with her.

"So they'll find out what's wrong and cure it," I assured her. "That's what hospitals are for." But to a woman hovering around seventy a hospital was no rest stop.

"Bernie, I don't want to go to the hospital," she cried.

"There's nothing to be afraid of," I said, because that was what one said.

"You mean it?" she said.

"Look, they have millions of dollars' worth of equipment nowadays," I said. "Every doctor can't have his own. He needs the money for his pool and tennis court."

"I'll give you the hospital number. Call me."

I waited as she dug through papers, mumbling. "A curse on it!" she cried in Yiddish. "Everything keeps disappearing."

I told her I would look it up. It was long distance.

"St. Catherine's," she said. "Where did I . . ."

I asked if she had someone to take her.

"More than I want," she said. "Who needs them? Call me. I'll take a private room."

I suggested that she might like a roommate.

"To see my misery?" she answered.

"You'll be fine," I said.

"Of course I'll be fine," she said, her voice tightening. "It's only tests. Call me, Bernie."

"I'll call you," I said, the click snuffing out her crying.

I stared at the silent phone. It was nothing, I told myself. It was my mother being dramatic. So what else was new?

Downstairs Ethel was where women were no longer supposed to be—in the kitchen. But the goal was a worthy one—me. She was organizing my birthday party. What had begun as a discreet little get-together to inform a few friends I had made it to fifty, now loomed as a mass event with a cast of thousands. Why not let the world know, I decided. Having had three friends who died in their forties, for me reaching fifty was cause for jubilation. Especially when I knew I looked ten years younger.

Ethel asked who called.

"My mother," I said. "She's going to the hospital tomorrow."

She looked anxiously at me.

"For tests.

She looked puzzled. "More tests?"

It seemed my mother was always on her way to or from tests. It was one way to keep busy. Alone, financially secure, she tracked down the cause of every twinge. She had a social club going in Dr.

Greenstone's waiting room, none of whose members, of course, were as important to him as she. But this was the first time she was being sent to the hospital.

"You think it's serious?" Ethel frowned over her lists.

"No, it isn't serious," I said, as if I knew.

"She isn't young," Ethel said, taking inventory of nuts and crackers. Her exact age, like everything else in her life, was a state secret. She guarded not only the year of her birth but the month and date, as if, given that information, the enemy could extrapolate everything. To compute her age I simply added twenty years to mine, accepting her claim of marrying while still a child to escape from Aunt Sarah, who treated her like Cinderella.

"Maybe *The Merck Manual*," Ethel said, heading for her medical books in the TV room a step from the kitchen. If she had been born twenty years later, or in a family that prized education, she might have been a doctor. The shelves sagged with medical books and magazines to which she dashed at the first symptom and returned to prepare us for the worst. Ethel had a dark side to her personality that contradicted her perky manner, while my dispassionate exterior concealed a rosy outlook. While Ethel was "very concerned" over upset stomachs and fevers and appetite losses, I had to hear a death rattle before consenting to worry.

"It could be several things," Ethel announced. "Tendonitis. Arthritis."

"It's in her head," I said. "She wants attention."

"Or cancer."

3

IT WAS THE FIRST birthday party I'd been given.

Since my parents "slaved in the store" six days a week, every week of the year, scheduling birthday parties was not exactly top priority. Such things were indulgences for gentile families whose pork-cooking mothers had nothing better to do. My parents were building a future.

"In Europe," my mother said, "only the Czar and his family had birthday parties. Everyone else was sorry they were born."

I received only one birthday present as a child—an insurance policy that would provide me with a thousand dollars when I reached the age of thirty.

About three dozen senior citizens doddered in, friends who I realized were the same age as the parents of my friends when I was in high school, those balding paunchy fathers slumped in easy chairs in their undershirts, heavy gray-haired mothers forever stationed at the kitchen sink. Was it possible we were the same age? We lithe suburbanites who tore about the tennis courts, flew to the Caribbean, and followed the Scarsdale, drinking man's, grapefruit, Mayo Clinic, and Swami Krishna diets?

"Happy birthday!"

Being Larchmonters they brought clever presents. Glenn Miller and Andrews Sisters albums. A Lane Sisters poster. A trylon and perisphere. A cane. Along with more practical items such as seventeen cans of tennis balls (fifty and one to grow on, get it?) and a few bottles of Scotch to face senility. Everyone howled over a pinup photo of Betty Grable, a phony birth certificate, and a *New York Times* headlined SLOAN WINS WIMBLEDON, in honor of my prowess on the courts. A Manhattan couple drove up with their feverish child and stayed for twenty minutes just to present me with a figure of a man pushing a rock uphill.

I loved them all.

The Carvel cake reached the right temperature at the right time, the champagne popped without bulleting through the plaster, "Take the A Train" skimmed from the stereo, and my mother was a vague presence in the distance. I was not prepared to take on her illness. Steven was about to be a high-school senior; colleges had to be considered. I had just started a new job after a year of recovering from the trauma of being fired from the agency I was convinced could not function without me. Ethel was toiling in a local travel agency for less than a cleaning woman's wages, cushioning our future. Our family was no all-American TV family moving on

well-oiled tracks, each well-adjusted member fitting happily into a
comfortable slot. Steven, though doing superbly in school, had not
yet overcome the problems of being youngest in his class. Although liked and respected, he was still unsure of himself. Paul, for
whom the phone never stopped ringing, would barely get to college with his freshman grades. And I could get fired tomorrow.

Nor was my mother the sweet little storybook grandmother who
baked brownies and doted on her grandchildren. She was a scrap-
py woman who prided herself on fighting for what she wanted and
overcoming all obstacles to get it. After an automobile accident she
screamed a doctor out of her hospital room when he told her she
would never walk again. She walked. As a young woman she vowed
that the entire Bolshevik army would not stop her from getting to
America. She got to America. And when her Aunt Sarah and Uncle
Meyer advised her and my father to continue managing their hardware store rather than risk opening their own, my mother laughed
in their faces, saying, "We should work to make you rich?"

While pretending to be absorbed in Sally Lianetti's account of
her son's achievements in our high school's alternative program, I
caught Ethel's voice telling another voice that if my mother were
sick she would be welcome to live with us. In her family, Ethel said,
the young always took care of the old. She grew up in the same
house with her grandparents and great-grandmother, a woman
whose stories of the Civil War so fascinated Ethel she felt sorry for
children who had no great-grandmother at home.

Ethel and my mother had been together on exactly four occa-
sions; each time my mother treated her like an outsider in the
house. My mother first visited us when our younger son was a
baby. "Your baby is crying," she announced to Ethel when Paul
screamed, making no move to go to him. "It's hard to believe your
mother was ever a mother," Ethel said. She used our house as a
base for forays into New York, where countrymen, now in the gar-
ment center, provided her with bargains in underwear.

When we visited her and her second husband on our way to Australia, she sang Jewish songs to our children in the back seat of
their Cadillac—songs I'd never heard when I was a child. At the
pancake house she made a game of asking the children to share
their food with her, shrieking with delight when they gave her a

piece of their waffle or a frozen strawberry. "See how they love me!" she cried to her husband, neglecting to notice that they soon dreaded eating with her.

We saw her again on our way back from our two years in Australia. She was a widow once more. We drove to the Grand Canyon together. It was at the end of that visit that she fell in love with Steven when he told her on leaving, "We can't leave you here alone, Nana."

Her last visit, the stopovers on her way to and from Argentina, was made memorable by two incidents. As she carried a glass of water on her way up to bed one night she spilled it halfway up the stairs. She came down to the kitchen, refilled the glass, and spilled it once more on the stairs. As she returned to the kitchen for the second time, Ethel asked her why she did not fill her glass in the upstairs bathroom. "From where?" my mother answered. "The toilet?"

Another time my mother insisted that Ethel drive her to Saks; she could not arrive in Argentina without a new handbag. Buying a bone handbag on Ethel's charge account, my mother carried it, wrapped, to Argentina. Returning six weeks later, she handed it back to Ethel with the announcement that it was scratched and instructed her to return it for credit. At the same time, she presented Ethel with a beautiful hand-embroidered sweater, as well as sweaters for the boys and me, beaming as we modeled them for her. "Don't think they were cheap," she said.

Although Ethel offered my mother the use of our car, my mother insisted she would get lost unless Ethel chauffeured her to shopping centers, the beauty shop, and the subway stop twenty minutes away so she would save the train fare from Larchmont. When I suggested that Ethel was a fool for letting herself be used, she replied that it would be a short time and it was easier to accede than fight. I suspect that Ethel, sensitive about her religious background and part German ancestry, was really trying to win my mother's love. A love my mother had no intention of ever granting, while releasing just enough encouragement to keep her daughter-in-law trying. It was on that visit that my mother blamed her sore shoulder that would not heal.

"You know what'll happen to property values if the school budget doesn't pass!'' cried Margaret Lazar, the militant who spent her life handing out leaflets at the station and protesting at meetings.

"Who can afford to live here if it does?'' quipped Lenny Lazar, who was rewarded with a glare from little Margaret.

"I have a passion for older men,'' said Anthea Hopkins, Larchmont's near-famous writer, and kissed me. Her stories were published regularly in the top women's magazines, and she had an agent. She threw her blonde hair back and tilted her head when she talked, playing Faye Dunaway playing a writer.

Sally Lianetti continued babbling about how Martin felt so positive about the intercreative group dynamics of her son's alternative program.

And Ethel moved innocently to the dining room to lay out the cold cuts.

A FEW DAYS AFTER I RECOVERED from being fifty I called my mother in the hospital, expecting her to have passed her tests and be on her way home. The operator gave me the number of St. Catherine's instantly, as if it were the most asked-for number in the telephone system.

"I'm sick, Bernie''—her voice was weak and slurred, the sound of drugs.

For the first time I was alarmed.

"I'm so tired,'' her voice struggled. "Call me tomorrow.''

The next night she sounded no stronger.

Or the third.

"I'll call your doctor,'' I said.

"Don't,'' she cried. "What can he tell you?''

"Your mother,'' said Dr. Greenstone in a smooth, radio-announcer voice, "has multiple myeloma.''

Which was?

"Cancer of the bone marrow. Cancer cells move through the marrow, leaving the bones so brittle they can break at a touch. The pain," he said, as calmly as if he were describing dandruff, "can be unbearable." It was very common, he said, among older people, afflicting about half the people over seventy. (Other authorities later contradicted him, telling me that it was neither that prevalent nor the major cause of broken hips as he claimed. It was assumed I had not heard him correctly. What did it matter? It was just one of a maze of contradictions that lay ahead, sometimes from the same expert.) "It's invariably fatal," Dr. Greenstone said. "A patient can last anywhere from six months to three years. I'd give your mother a year at the outside."

I clutched the receiver.

"Your mother and I have been friends for a good many years," Dr. Greenstone said, delivering the commercial. "We had a heart-to-heart talk. I told her everything."

I'm not ready for this, I wanted to cry at him. Wait a year, a few months, give us time to organize our lives, decide what to do.

"Larchmont?" he went on. "I know the area well. We have friends in New Jersey. Englewood. Visit them every summer. Beautiful."

"Beautiful," I said.

Dr. Greenstone informed me that he had turned my mother's case over to a specialist. A hematologist. From the East, in fact; a very able young man. (Was he going to tell me he was unable?) He was sorry that our first conversation was under such unfortunate circumstances.

Closing the bedroom door, I bawled like a child. My mother did not get cancer. My father, maybe, but not my mother. Her family was strong, like iron. Unstoppable. Fighters. Of her two aunts in America, one died recently at ninety-five; the other was killed in an automobile crash at eighty. It took Hitler to kill her mother. No one I knew ever mentioned parents and lingering illnesses. Didn't it happen to other people? It never came up at dinner parties or the tennis courts. We concentrated on important things like school budgets and the crèche on town property. We went into the relative merits of Aruba, Jamaica, and Martinique. We compared plumbers, roofers, and pediatricians. Where, I suddenly wondered, were the sick parents? Did they discreetly withdraw from society, abandoning themselves to death on mountaintops like the Ainus of

Japan or on ice floes like the Eskimos? Was there a big trapdoor somewhere?

"What we have to watch out for," said able young Dr. Kraven, the hematologist, "is her falling. As the bones get brittle the slightest bump can cause a fracture. We don't want her fracturing her hip. She could be permanently crippled."

In spite of warnings she tried to get out of bed by herself on her first day in the hospital. Climbing over the bedrail, she slipped and struck her shoulder against the bed frame. To a normal person it would be a mean bruise. My mother fractured her collarbone. It would probably never heal.

"That's what's causing her distress now," Dr. Kraven explained. "But she's not as bad off as she makes out. Your mother's an actress. She likes to perform. Old people like to be the center of attention, but she needs it more than most. I tell her she's putting me on. I kid around with her. This morning I got a smile out of her. She knows I see through her."

His prognosis agreed with Dr. Greenstone's. Six months to three years; probably a year.

The handwriting was growing bigger.

"Does she have anyone out here?" he asked.

No one.

Only friends who came to her apartment by invitation. Only friends whom she thought she impressed with her Cadillac. "Even the closest friends vanish," a friend said when I asked him about the death of his mother, a subject in which I had little interest until I had to face my own mother's dying. "They visit at first, then they call, then the calls drop off. Pretty soon it's only the family."

And we were her only family. "Sixteen hours on the table," she used to say. How could she be expected to have more children? There was her twice-divorced brother Dave, in San Francisco, whom she had not seen in several years, and her brother Zach, in Detroit, with whom she had a tearful reconciliation after thirty years of not speaking. But now that they were inseparable (as long as there was two thousand miles between them), he was an old man with Parkinson's disease and not about to shelter his sister.

"The disease moves in waves," said able Dr. Kraven. "The patient feels better, then worse, alternately. But it's all relative. Feeling better one month was worse the month before."

Once the myeloma cells invade the bone marrow, Dr. Kraven explained, the marrow can no longer manufacture the blood cells the body requires. In addition to the pain, the patient develops acute anemia, chronic fatigue. Regular blood transfusions might be necessary, their frequency depending on the progress of the disease. Until, of course, the bones decay to a point where blood supply is irrelevant.

"I'm from the East," Dr. Kraven said. "Philadelphia. Arizona is great for raising children. I can get in a lot of skeet."

"I had a blood transfusion!" my mother announced joyously on the phone. "I feel so much better." Her voice was suddenly stronger, filled with energy. "What I have is anemia," she said. "A blood condition."

Had the doctors really leveled with her?

"Dr. Kraven says," she went on, "that the best place for my condition is near you. Teller. They have the best specialists there from all over the world.

The Teller Medical Center. A half-hour east of us on the thruway. We knew several Teller doctors who lived in Larchmont. All, I was happy to observe, deeply committed, reasonably nonmaterialistic, choosing the less lucrative path of pure research.

"Maybe I should go there," she said. "I'll get me a place near you somewhere."

"You can stay with us," I said.

"You mean it?"

"Of course," I said. "You can always get an apartment when you're better."

"Does Ethel want me?"

"Why shouldn't she?"

"I'll have to stay in your downstairs room," she said. "I can't climb stairs."

I told her we would figure something out. That was the advantage of an older home with spare rooms.

"You still keep your house freezing?"

"Only during the winter," I replied.

"I'll need someone to bring me," she said.

"I'll come and get you," I said.

The next day as I walked along Fifth Avenue on my lunch hour, trying to plan for what was happening, I passed St. Patrick's Cathedral. For the first time in my twenty years in New York I climbed the steps and went inside, standing in the rear, invisible in the vast spaces. A service was in progress. A robed priest spoke from the altar, his words spreading from speakers mounted on massive columns. People on their knees were scattered among the pews. "Please," I closed my eyes and whispered, "don't let her suffer." I was not so presumptuous as to ask that her life be spared in her seventies, but pain was something else. And God was reputed to be merciful, although his image had been dealt some pretty bad blows in recent years.

I felt relieved as I walked out to the sun-drenched avenue filled with shoppers. Maybe I had increased her chances.

5

I REMEMBERED A STORY we read years ago in elementary school. It seems that a Chinese peasant had stopped to fish on a riverbank, when he heard screams. He looked up to see a man clutching a log in the middle of the river, crying for help. "Throw me your line," cried the drowning man, "and pull me in." After squinting hard at the man to make sure he was not a relative, the peasant quickly packed up his fishing gear and scurried away—a reaction the teacher asked us not to judge until we knew the facts: In ancient China, if you saved a person's life that person belonged to you; you were responsible for him as long as either of you lived. And the peasant already had too many mouths to feed.

"The course of treatment for myeloma is pretty standard," said Dr. Kraven. A statement I did not believe for a second.

Maybe in Arizona it was standard. Maybe among doctors who spent their time shattering clay targets. The New York area was a center of medical knowledge. At Teller they came up with discoveries that doctors in the rest of the country only found out about when they read *Newsweek*. They were certain to be able to provide a doctor who would save my mother's life. A feat that would win her love, at last, not only for me but for Ethel.

I went immediately to a neighbor who was a doctor at Teller. A dedicated man who opted for the Teller clinic over private practice to avoid the issue of fees and office depreciation. A man who single-handedly threatened to make medicine an honorable profession again.

"Multiple myeloma?" Dan Green shook his head, the pruning shears suspended in his hand over his prized rose bushes. "Brutal. You're in for a rough time."

"That's what everyone keeps telling me," I said. "As if there's something I can do about it."

"I'm sorry," Dan smiled. "It's called 'being helpful.' " He said he did not know what else I could do other than what I was doing. If he were in my mother's situation, he said, he would want to be with his children and grandchildren. There was no other moral choice.

"Is Teller the right place?" I asked him. "Level with me."

"For myeloma it's more than adequate," he said, speaking doctor talk.

"Adequate?" I said, not exactly reassured.

"Most places are less than adequate," he said.

"What about outstanding?"

"When you're on the inside," he smiled, "no place is outstanding."

"What about a doctor in the city? New York Hospital? Sinai? Sloan Kettering?" If you lived in the middle of Nebraska you had no choice. But when you lived near New York you did not settle for a local suburban hospital. Not that Teller was local suburban. It was a prestigious medical center. Settling would be the nearby hospital famous for misread x-rays and postappendectomy infections.

"I can recommend a very competent hematologist at Teller," Dan said.

His choice of words would never get him into advertising.

"And I can also give you the top authority on myeloma in New York City."

Nothing was simple. It was a portent of things to come, the constant agonizing over choices.

He named a doctor at a famous hospital on the West Side of Manhattan. Getting to him was at least an hour's drive. It meant fighting through clogged streets, impossible parking, menacing youths on street corners.

"If you want someone at Teller," Dan said, "you can't do better than Jeremiah Gordon. We went through med school together. Jerry and I," he chuckled, "were the last of the old school."

"He's good?"

"I would say so."

Damn, why wouldn't he tell me he was superb? Brilliant? Unequaled?

"What would you do if it were your mother?" I asked Dan.

Deep in my heart I felt I should take her to the New York doctor. But it was Ethel who would be doing the taking. Fair or not, it was my job that paid the bills. Even though Ethel was working full time at the travel agency, taking care of the house and the boys' needs, my mother would become *her* burden.

"Jeremiah's a fine doctor," Dan said. "I don't think anyone is more dedicated." He knew what was on my mind. "Convenience has to be considered too," he said. "The impact on the family. She might have to be taken to the doctor every week. You have to do what's reasonable for everyone."

The rich did live differently from you and me, and probably longer. A million dollars in tax-free municipals and there would be no question. A housekeeper, a driver, and the top specialist in Manhattan. But when your wife has a job that is an investment in future security, not to mention present satisfaction, and you have two boys on the verge of college, you make compromises. Especially—and it's a painful thing to say—when your mother has not been a part of your lives, but an intrusion, the drowning stranger.

"If you're unhappy with Jerry"—Dan said what I wanted him to say—"you can always consult with Kesselring."

"It won't be too late?" I asked.

"I hate to say it," Dan said, "but it probably won't matter."

Suddenly everyone I spoke to knew all about multiple myeloma, and it was all contradictory. It could go on forever. It went fast. If you were old it might take years. The young had better chances of survival. There were remissions, there were no remissions. Tremendous advances had been made. Yet nothing had saved Martha Mitchell. Remission meant years of agony. It meant a fairly healthy life. A man in Larchmont was living a normal life after reportedly being struck by myeloma five years ago at age forty-five. A friend's mother was said to have lived for ten years with myeloma, in her own apartment, checking into the hospital for a transfusion whenever she felt weak. Both turned out to have different forms of cancer.

On one thing there was total agreement: "You don't know what it's like until you live through it," said a friend at work. "All those great social services you read about, they don't exist. When you need them they're always someplace else or for other people. You're on your own. There is no help."

An article in the *New York Times* reported a total leukemia cure at Mt. Sinai—a college president who knew a senator who managed to have a forbidden drug flown in from England. Not all of us knew senators.

When we lived in Australia, where I was assigned to "Americanize" the Sydney office of my former company, we knew an American couple whose son's asthma attacks were ended by an English drug not allowed in the United States; but Americans were apparently incapable of making decisions for themselves. The very drug that might save my mother her agony, if not her life, was very possibly being kept from her by a bureaucrat's fear of making a decision.

"Chemotherapy works wonders nowadays," people said. "It isn't worth the torture," said others. "You throw up, your hair falls out, it tears your insides to shreds, it drives you crazy. And you die just as if you'd never had it."

Yet the papers were filled with stories of cures. A school run by the New York Board of Education in the children's ward of a cancer hospital had graduates for the first time. A boy at the Cleveland Clinic was cured of liver cancer, hopeless until now. A famous

movie star had apparently survived. As had the child of a famous
senator. Another senator was under treatment, the prognosis
"hopeful."

"If it ever happens to me," said the lady at our local bank, "I
don't want them to do anything. No radiation, no chemotherapy. It
leaves you so weak you can't do anything. That's no way to live.
And I don't want them cutting my body apart a piece at a time. I'd
rather just say so long. We've all got to go sometime."

Easy to say when your greatest concern is the Umbrella Account.

By shifting beds and bureaus we turned our downstairs TV room
into a room for my mother. Originally a maid's room when the
house was built in the thirties, it now had built-in shelves and cabinets and mocha walls, from which hung aboriginal artifacts we had
brought back from Australia. It connected with a full bathroom
meant to serve that maid. We·cleared the lower shelves of books,
emptied the cabinets and the closet, replaced one of the aboriginal
masks with a mirror, and placed a picture of the boys on top of the
bureau—the grandchildren she would be coming to know.

"She needs life around her," I told my family. "She needs to
hear Paul play the guitar. She needs people in the house."

"What you're doing is admirable," said Kevin O'Gorman, a
neighbor who took his Catholicism seriously. "These days so many
people do what's convenient for *them*. If their parents don't fit in
with their plans they shove them in some home and forget about
them. Nobody knows the meaning of doing onto others anymore."

"Thank you," I said, "but I have no choice."

"You've made your choice," he said, adding, "Your boys will remember what you're doing when your turn comes."

"Thanks."

I flew to Arizona.

6

"ST. CATHERINE'S? Hope no one's sick," said the driver.

Why the hell did he think I had flown from New York and was on my way to a hospital? There was something to be said for the glass partitions of New York cabs.

"Nothing serious?" he said, determined to be friendly in his folksy Western drawl.

Was I supposed to tell him that my mother was dying of cancer? I mumbled something and looked out the window at the dreary succession of gas stations, used-car lots, and motels. I loosened my tie, wishing I could throw it away. I wished I could take off all my clothes. I was the only man in the blazing city wearing a suit and tie. Stepping off the plane was like stepping into a blast furnace. In seconds I was drenched. It not only felt the 110 degrees it was, it looked it. Searing sun, patches of scrubby vegetation—the only trees were palms—not an inch of shade except an occasional awning. And the air conditioner in the cab was broken.

The uniformed woman behind the desk practiced nondiscrimination. She ignored me equally with everyone else. It was not of the slightest interest to her that I had just flown two thousand miles or that my mother lay dying. The world was not about to stop, or even pause, because I had a problem. People died all the time. How many was it every second? Not a moment passed that somewhere in the world someone wasn't grieving, coping, facing death. Why was I special? Only when she was ready did she look up from her file cards and raise her eyebrows.

"How do you spell that?" she asked when I told her my mother's name.

I spelled "Sloan."

"Are you sure she's a patient here?" she challenged as she squinted through half-glasses at her file cards.

Had I landed in the wrong city? Or was it all a nightmare, after all?

"We don't have a Floan," she said.

"Sloan," I cried, "S like in, . . ."—and all I could think of was "Sloan."

She found my mother.

And so did I.

I tried to hide my shock at the sight of the shrunken doll with the wizened face and wild gray hair slumped in the hospital room chair, a nurse hovering over her while she clutched a carton of juice, sucking at a straw. As the sunken eyes met mine we threw our arms around each other and burst into sobs. I could not dam the spasms; the pain was unbearable. The nurse slipped out of the room and waited outside the door.

"She likes to hear everything," the withered face hissed in my ear as the nurse left the room, jolting me back to reality. She might have been totally transformed physically, changed from a hearty, stout woman to a shriveled straw doll, but her inner demons had not shrunk.

"What's there to hear?" I asked, angry at her for not letting me feel the pure anguish I wanted to feel.

"Plenty," she said.

Her voice was not the faint telephone whine but oddly powerful, too powerful for the wasted body.

"Don't I look gorgeous?"—she smiled as if reading my mind. "See how thin I am? I could be a model." Never smaller than a size sixteen (she claimed), she always envied the thin and the tall on whom "everything looks good."

"I'm so glad you came," she said. "I can't stand hospitals. They can kill you."

Her tray was untouched. "Who could eat the food?" she asked, "everything was drowned in gravy."

"I found you a doctor connected with Teller," I said, praying that she would like Jeremiah Gordon, whose receptionist had been delighted to inform me that the doctor could not possibly see my mother on the first day after her arrival, no matter how urgent or who sent her. "This isn't an emergency room," she said, letting me know that all of Dr. Gordon's patients considered themselves urgent. "They think they're the only ones," she said. She "put my mother down" for later in the week. An appropriate phrase.

"All they know here is how to take your money," my mother said. "Dr. Kraven comes in and smiles like Carter and charges twenty-five dollars." She opened her mouth and made a toothy smile. "He maybe spends thirty seconds. They're so rich, the doctors. And you know what did it? Medicare. At first they were against it. It made them millionaires."

She was wearing her nightgown. Garments hung in the closet. Things were on the table next to the bed. Nothing was packed. Sweltering in my New York suit, desperate for a shower, I seemed to be the only person concerned about leaving.

Her private nurse told me I had to get a release from the nurses' station. At the nurses' station I was told I had to get a release from her doctors, neither of whom had left any clue that she was departing today, although they both knew I was arriving. After some searching, a nurse surrendered the phone numbers of her doctors, whose answering services informed me that neither worked on Saturday. A backup would call. Sometime soon. A half-hour later a doctor with a new name and a Western twang recalled hearing something about my mother checking out today. No, Dr. Kraven was skeet shooting, but this doctor would instruct the nurses' station. My mother was to continue taking whatever pills Dr. Kraven had given her for her blood condition, a buffered aspirin for pain, and milk for the ulcer they had discovered while discovering her other problems. Would I please transfer his call to the nurses' station? Twenty cents was twenty cents.

Returning from the cashier's office, I found two women in her room helping her dress. One of them, a small birdlike lady with round glasses and pursed lips, flew out to intercept me in the doorway. "Is it leukemia?" she asked eagerly, pulling me into the corridor.

As I started to answer, angry at her prying, feeling the need of a stick to beat her off, tears welled up and I cried in front of her.

She introduced herself. Pearl Robins. Her son, Marvin, may he rest in peace, had been my mother's dentist. "Passed away at thirty-six," she said, "left a wife and two little ones. Believe me, I've lived through plenty." She paused and shook her head. "Mother looks terrible. Her skin is gray. It's leukemia, isn't it?"

"I don't know," I said, not wanting to turn my mother's sickness into gossip and not wanting to brand it with a name when there was still hope, when the wizard of Teller might prove it a mistake.

"You don't know?"—she cocked her head at me. "I kept telling her, 'Dora, see my doctor. Can it hurt to have a second opinion?' But she wouldn't listen. That Dr. Greenstone, I wouldn't give you a penny for him. She was sick for months. She kept going to him and going to him and he could never find anything. She said he was so successful. I told her, 'Success is one thing, good is something else.' "

I told her I was taking my mother to a specialist near us.

Her eyes bulged up at me through her round, metal-framed glasses. "There aren't specialists here?" she asked.

"She should be near her grandchildren," I said.

"Of course," Pearl chirped. "She loves them so. She talks about them all the time. I hear they're exceptional."

"They're children," I said.

She smiled. She knew better.

"You have a place for her to stay? A big house?"

"We have a spare room," I said.

"Then you must have a big house," she said with a smile, adding, for no particular reason, "Only three months ago I buried my second husband."

The private nurse appeared and announced that my mother was ready to leave and that her bill was twenty-five dollars for the day. From inside my mother cried that she would send her a check, let her leave her name and address. "Everybody wants money," she cried in Yiddish.

"If there's anything I can do," Pearl said. "Don't be like your mother, don't be afraid to ask."

A nurse arrived with a wheelchair. Suddenly I realized that she was about to become entirely my responsibility. Like the Chinese peasant, I wanted to flee.

"Are you serious?" I asked Pearl.

"Why wouldn't I be?"

"Can you drive us to my mother's apartment?" I asked.

"Who needs a ride?" my mother protested. "Bernie has two cars."

"And they're both in Larchmont," I said. But my mother had made her point. Her son was affluent enough to own two cars.

Pearl insisted that she would be glad to drive us if we did not mind waiting while she trudged in the heat to her car a half mile away in the Penney shopping center. She could always shop tomorrow for her grandson's birthday gift—where was it written he had to have something exactly on his birthday? She would gladly brave the sun even if her doctor did say to be careful. She was having another checkup in a week, and she was sure the fluttery feeling around her heart was nothing.

As Pearl flew off, the rest of us formed a procession through the hospital corridors. The other visitor (a big woman with a leonine face), me, a nurse following my mother in her wheelchair, her shriveled face staring like a puppet over a lapful of totebags stuffed with hospital supplies—lotion, talcum, tissues, toilet paper. "Look how they're looking at me," my mother laughed. "Like Queen Elizabeth."

Placed on the front seat of Pearl's car, she slumped like a rag doll, unable to move. To close the door I had to hold her up with one hand through the open window. As soon as I let go, she slumped against the locked door.

"Are you all right?" Pearl asked.

"Wonderful," my mother said. "I couldn't be better."

As I took my place in the back, the big-faced woman rapped on the front window. She was carrying a huge pot of plastic flowers.

"Give Goldfinger a ride," my mother said, miraculously managing to unlock the door.

Pearl leaned across her and locked it again, asking the identity of the rapping woman.

"Goldfinger," my mother said, unlocking the door once more. "She needs transportation."

"So let her find it," Pearl said, leaning over and locking the door once more.

"How will she get home?" my mother asked.

"The same way she got here," said Pearl, driving away and leaving the big woman standing with her plastic plant under the blazing sun.

"My seat belt!" my mother cried.

"Forget it," I said. Neither Pearl nor I had buckled ours. "It's dangerous," my mother cried, groping determinedly for her seat-belt buckles at the risk of toppling headfirst into the dashboard. Pearl had no choice but to stop the car while I leaned over the front seat and belted my mother, straining my back and bumping my skull against the roof of the car.

If we crashed, my mother would be the sole survivor.

7

HER APARTMENT BUILDING, like all Sunbelt apartment buildings, looked like a motel. As if the occupants were on a perpetual vacation or in transit, on the way to a permanent residence.

The three-story building consisted of "units" connected by a covered walkway that horseshoed around an inner courtyard containing the mandatory postage-stamp-size pool the residents were too feeble to use. Beyond the courtyard, separated by a low wall and a squeaky gate, was a carport filled with mastodons slumbering in the heat.

The building was always deathly quiet, even in the middle of the day. There were no children or animals. The tenants, elderly couples or the widowed, burrowed inside their air-conditioned apartments, emerging at dusk with garbage and dirty laundry or for trips to shopping centers. Stray supermarket carts stood abandoned in the alleyway behind the building like tanks in the Sinai, but I never caught anyone pushing one. They just appeared.

Checking my mother with Pearl on the lobby sofa, I hauled suitcases and totebags up the stairs to the second floor, too anxious to wait for the elevator.

Her door would have done San Quentin proud. Secured with three locks, each was designed not to open until I tried every key on the ring she handed me—a ring with enough keys to break a wrist.

Stepping into her sea of possessions was like stepping into the deep end of a pool. Not just furniture, not just a mile of sofa, love seat, chairs, piano, home entertainment center, floor-to-ceiling breakfront; but objects everywhere—breakable, fragile objects. Candy dishes, ashtrays, bowls, vases, music boxes, figurines. There was not an empty surface in sight. Not even on the walls. They were covered with reproductions of idyllic landscapes submerged in massive rococo frames, along with sconces, plaques, and brass "decorative" objects, such as a fountain spewing plastic ivy. The breakfront that filled a wall was swollen with stacks of dishes, goblets, china cups and saucers. Every lamp was a colossus. Big flouncy shades, satin bows and ribbons. A gigantic cherubic shepherdess lamp smiled coyly and lifted her porcelain skirt at a cherubic shepherd lamp on the opposite end of the sofa. All remaining space was filled with artificial flowers. In small bud vases, big flower vases, planters, and urns. Everywhere artificial flowers.

And that was just the living room.

There was still a dining area, kitchen, two bedrooms, two bathrooms, and packed closets.

"Get rid of everything," Monty Bliss said blithely, when I told him why I had to be away for a week. "Tell her, 'Mom, we love you and want you to be with us.' Don't ask her what she wants to keep; old people want to keep everything. Call up a dealer and sell everything."

Easy for Bliss to say. Aggressive, razor-thin man, who cut an unhesitant swathe through a fainthearted world. Anyone who failed to produce rarely lasted more than two weeks, sometimes two hours, at Bliss Advertising, a twenty-person shop that served as a starting point for the young and a haven for the aged. "You can tell pretty quick who's going to work out and who isn't," Monty said. "Why fuck around?"

In a tender moment before I left, Monty came into my office, closed the door (sending rumors flying through the agency), and told me how he had taken his sick mother from doctor to doctor, city to city until, all hope gone, she told him, "Monty, you've been a good son." A recollection that choked his voice and brought tears to his eyes.

"Let me know," he urged, "if there's anything I can do."

What he did was deduct a week's pay from my check. Perfectly understandable, of course, since I had been there a mere three months. He would have many later opportunities to show his generosity.

Monty or not, I was not about to say to my mother, "Look, you've got cancer and you aren't likely to live more than a few months, so you might as well stop pretending and sell your furniture."

It would certainly have made life easier. For me.

But she was the one who was dying.

What she wished to believe remained her privilege.

Maybe this is what is called "failure to talk it out," "hiding from reality," or "conspiring with the victim's denial"; but since it was my mother's life, I felt it was her right to believe whatever she chose. I was not about to deprive her of hope in order to avoid moving furniture.

Yet, as I stared at her possessions, I realized that she belonged exactly where she was. Thirty years in Arizona. Thirteen in the same apartment. A collection of Pearls undoubtedly. The Raskin family nearby. "They treat me like their own," she never tired of saying.

Maybe I should seek other doctors in the area. But I hadn't a clue about how to find them, nor the time. I had a new job. Three months. And jobs, I learned the hard way, were not easy to come by at my age, no matter how special my mother thought I was. If she, with all her intelligence, had failed to find proper medical attention in thirty years, how could I do it in a week?

Even if I could find her a doctor remotely as good as those at Teller, she could not be left alone. There were too many horror tales about housekeepers and the elderly. She might be no joy to have around, but how could I leave her to die at the mercy of paid help, thousands of miles away from her only family? She should know her grandchildren before she died. She should see Paul ski, Steven debate. She needed people who cared. Didn't I owe her at least that much?

"Did you get lost?" she asked as I returned to the lobby, jolting me back to reality. She might be sick, her body emaciated, but her personality was unyielding. It was still the kind of personality that could ask "What took you so long?" to someone who had just staggered up and down stairs, hauling suitcases in 110-degree heat.

"You see that building across the street?" Pearl said as I walked her to her car. "For twelve years we lived across from your mother and Cy Raskin. You know how many times we were in their apartment? Exactly twice." She looked up at me and smiled sadly. "I tried to be close with her, but she doesn't let you."

I knew, I knew.

"But lately"—the tiny woman squeezed my hand—"I felt we were beginning to be more like sisters."

I choked back tears.

"If you want I'll come and cook dinner," she said. "Just ask. I know your mother. She doesn't want favors from nobody. She's afraid she'll be obligated." Pearl gave me a slip of paper with her phone number. "I'll call later, but if you need anything, call me."

"What did she tell you?" my mother asked suspiciously as I came to claim her.

"She wants to help, she said."

"I don't need anybody's help!" my mother cried as I reached behind her and, pushing on her back with one hand, pulling on her unaffected arm with the other, raised her to her feet. As she leaned on her cane I walked behind her, holding her by the waist to keep her from falling. "Pearl's given plenty of parties since her husband died," she said as we crept toward the elevator. "The first thing she did was buy a condominium."

"She offered to come and cook dinner," I said.

"And leave a mess to clean up?" my mother cried. "Why doesn't she invite us to her place if she wants to help?"

Good question, but wasn't there an adage about beggars not being choosey?

Getting her into the elevator was an intricate procedure involving wedging the door open with a totebag, walking her into the elevator, and holding on to her while snatching up the totebag; getting out required the same maneuvers in reverse.

As we inched along the corridor, she in front, I holding her waist from behind, a voice cried out a cheery, "Hi ya, Mrs. Sloan!" It was the manager's wife swimming in the pool below, like a lobster in a pot. "Have a good trip?" she called up.

"It's so good to be back in my apartment," she sighed as I propped her in the one chair with the right shape to keep her from slipping out. Gazing lovingly at her objects, she suddenly let out a shriek. "My bedroom set!"

She tried to force herself to her feet, knowing I would rush to help her. Once more I held her waist and walked behind her, the two of us inching, train fashion, through the endless hallway to her bedroom. The closed door was locked.

"Whoever heard of locking a bedroom door!" I cried, shaking the knob as if that would help.

"The manager has a key to the apartment. She doesn't have to know what I have."

"You think she cares?"

"And how she does."

As a child I remembered her constantly trying doors or sending me or my father running out of the car to try them for her. Sometimes we drove back for blocks because she was positive someone had failed to lock the door. She was years ahead of her time.

The key to her bedroom door was on a special keyring that was either in her red or her white totebag, both of which were in the living room. It was back to the living room and back with the bags, while leaving her propped against the bedroom door. Weren't things hard enough? Did she have to make everything harder?

"Twenty thousand dollars I could get for it," she said as the door opened on an explosion of inlaid woods, gold claws and heads, gold griffins scaling crowned mirrors and headboards. There were curves, swirls, and whorls, shadings and striations— nothing left unornamented. I remember my parents buying it in the Depression, a closeout, thrilled at the coup of owning a Grand Rapids interpretation of the bedroom set in which Marie Antoinette had laid her head before it was summoned elsewhere. The original, she informed the world, was in Versailles. "Let them prove different," she said, in a day when very few people made it to French palaces.

The set was kept in one bedroom, while my parents slept in another. Occasionally my mother opened the door and gazed at it as she did now. "It gives me a lift just to look at it," she said as she said then. "It will make me well."

Nothing about her changed as she grew older except her condition. Her view of the world was exactly the same as when I was a child.

I helped her change into her nightgown, a long, tedious process, since she could barely move her left arm. "The slightest touch is like sparks," she said. Instead of wishing to go to bed as I had hoped, she asked to be returned to the living room so she could look again at her beautiful things, which were "better than the best medicine," an expression I could hear coming.

As we retraced our steps through the hallway I felt like the eternal newsreel refugee, the stooped ragged Oriental scurrying along the dirt road with his ancient mother tied to his back, planes strafing overhead.

"Hold me," she commanded. "I feel wobbly. The slightest breeze could blow me over."

"It takes time," I said. "You'll get stronger."

"Dr. Kraven said to exercise. I should take a walk every day to build up my strength."

"So we'll walk."

"Not now," she cried, as if I were about to force her out into the street. "Later, when it's cool. The heat could kill a healthy person."

"Later, fine."

I wanted only to set her in a place where she could stay on her own so I could shower, change, consider the next moves.

"On top of everything else," she said, "they found an ulcer. You'll have to buy milk."

I would buy milk.

"Maybe I'll take an aspirin," she said. "It's in one of the bags."

Which were, of course, back in the bedroom.

"The chain!" she cried as we inched past the front door. "You didn't put the chain on!"

It was four o'clock in the afternoon. The door was secured with three locks. I hooked the chain in its slot and began my sentence.

8

PLUCKED FROM MY COMFORTABLE suburban existence and locked
up in a strange apartment in a strange city with a sick old woman
requiring constant attention, I felt like a Kafka character serving a
sentence for an unknown crime, or a law-abiding German Jew wak-
ing up one morning and finding himself in Auschwitz.

There was no reason for it, no logic.

But the world, I kept learning again and again, was hardly reasonable.

Let alone logical.

I had the uneasy feeling that if I looked up I would find myself
eyeball to eyeball with a mad scientist recording my twitches as I
struggled to escape.

I was given two weapons—a telephone book and a telephone—
and a week's time to find a mover, sort out what should be saved or
thrown out, find a way to get her car to Larchmont, place an ad in
the newspaper to sell furniture (after finding the right newspaper),
sell the furniture, decide whether to move or store the remainder,
argue with the building manager, plead for cartons, shop for food,
make an attempt at feeding us, pick up x-rays at the hospital and
prescriptions at the drugstore (Dr. Kraven could not be bothered
háving them sent and the druggist could not promise delivery for
the remainder of the year), call the airline to confirm seats, ask for
a wheelchair at both ends and one kosher meal, graciously termi-
nate the callers who inquired after her health but offered no help,
engage in lengthy negotiations with insurance agents (car, furniture), take her to banks to empty safe-deposit boxes, all the while
battling the constant frustration of opening the wrong drawer for a
fork.

I helped her dress, I helped her get in and out of bed, I helped
her get to and from the bathroom, living room, kitchen, bedroom.
I cooked her oatmeal, which she claimed tasted raw if cooked less
than twenty-five minutes, and I warmed her milk to go with the oat-

meal. I was constantly running to fetch her glasses, lock a door, bring her milk, tea, ice cream. Evenings I took her for walks to build up her strength. And at least once each day, pulled to the snapping point, I screamed at her. It was always followed by regrets and by another outburst the next day.

I went to bed every night (rather, every morning) with my head filled with the sound of dialing, busy signals, recorded announcements, taped music. My hands ached from tying knots and smelled of packing tape.

Neither of her doctors offered any help or suggested that we meet and talk. No suggestions were offered about visiting nurses, homemakers, meals on wheels—any form of aid that might be available. As far as the local medical profession was concerned, her case was closed, except for the bills that would be forthcoming.

None of her myriad friends appeared with a pot of chicken soup or a casserole. They called to inquire about her health and that was all. Not a peep from any of the Raskin family, who "treat me like their own." Pearl called daily with suggestions of where to pick up packing boxes and how much to ask for furniture.

Although neither of us uttered the word "cancer," it was accepted that she was sick enough to give up her apartment and come to us in Larchmont. But this was for the purpose of being treated by the magicians of Teller, certainly not to spend the remaining months of her life.

We danced around the truth like sparring boxers.

"What did Greenstone tell you?" she asked.

"The same thing he told you," I answered.

"He neglected me!" she cried, shaking her fists, the backs of her hands blue-black from the needles. "I kept telling him I was sick; he said it was nothing. 'You're fine, Dora,' he kept telling me. 'I should be as healthy as you.' He should get his wish." Her fists trembled, her wizened face tightened. "The best doctor in the world, I thought. A home like a palace. Queen Elizabeth doesn't have it better. Medicare made them millionaires. They don't care anymore. If one patient departs this world, another is waiting to take his place."

Another time she said, outraged, "How do you like what he told me? He gave me a death sentence."

I shook my head, agreeing with her at the gall of Dr. Greenstone.
Dora Sloan die?

It would hardly be the first time in medical history that a doctor
was wrong.

In my mind danced the fantasy of finally proving, by saving her
life, that I was the tall, brilliant, successful son she always wanted
me to be. And recognizing that, she would turn into the loving, appreciative mother I always wanted her to be.

"I had to get sick to come to Larchmont," she said.

"You could have come before," I said unconvincingly.

"It isn't that I wasn't ready," she said. "I got no response."

What kind of response did she expect after her past behavior?
Did she expect Ethel to be desperate to be abused by her? Why was
it *our* lack of love that kept her from living near us, and not hers?

"You always talked about moving to California," I said lamely.
"Santa Monica."

"They want so much for me to come there," she said quickly.

Where were "they" now, I wondered.

Maybe her sickness would change her. The articles on dying that
now seemed to fill the newspapers claimed that the dying gave up
false values and pretense; they craved openness and honesty and
truth. Perhaps grateful for care, she would return love with love.
Even Christian love.

I plunged into a week of making decisions, at least half of which I
knew would be wrong. I could store everything in Arizona but that
would mean giving it all to the moving company if she died. I could
store everything in New York, but that would cost half again as
much. I decided to ship valuables to our home—the piano, breakfront, dishes, silver, kitchenware that either we could use now or
the boys could use later. It was one of the advantages of an older
home—big attic, lots of wall space—for which we finally had a use
after fourteen years. The rest would be stored in Arizona. I told my
mother the split move was saving storage costs. "Good," she said
as if she believed me, "let Paul have the piano."

After picking the moving company whose "counselor" assured
me they did not charge extra for moving on Saturday, they added
on another fifty percent after everything was on the truck. When I
protested I was told "the office will take care of it." With all the

scribbled numbers and mysterious charges, I never knew if they really did, but who could launch an investigation?

Something I would never do again is collect boxes at liquor stores and supermarkets and spend days packing. My advice—let the movers do it. They are going to get you no matter what you do. They insisted on repacking half of what I had packed "or the insurance won't cover it." And I ended up with a hodgepodge of boxes impossible to count when the shipment arrived at our house. Later, when I discovered boxes missing, too late for a reimbursement, I realized it would have been far cheaper to use the uniform size boxes from the moving company.

In one week I became an expert on matters I never wanted to become an expert on.

I learned that the movers would take the car on the van for $1,000, a company would send it by train for $600, and a "bonded responsible driver" from a drive-away company would handle it for $125, and you were allowed to fill the trunk. Deciding nervously on the "bonded responsible driver," I filled the trunk with the heaviest things possible, and the car actually reached our house in perfect condition.

I learned that my mother's automobile insurance covered the car when driven by the drive-away company and her tenant insurance covered her furniture during moving and in storage—information that seemed to surprise the moving "counselor," as he recommended extra insurance.

I learned that the telephone company suggests you cut the cord if you are concerned about leaving a working phone behind.

I learned that airlines provide wheelchairs and kosher meals on request.

And I learned that the folksy West was no more compassionate than the cold East. The manager's wife demanded $150 for cleanup expenses, three days after I had broken down sobbing in front of her while trying to explain the nature of my mother's illness. As I handed her a check, she asked what my mother's plans were for her reclining lounge chair.

And I vowed, after filling boxes with papers and possessions she had clutched over the years, to get rid of anything in our house we had not used in two years.

Her closets were swollen with clothes that went back decades. Dresses, robes, coats—both worn to tatters and untouched. Stacks of boxes held yellowed shoes and hats. Shelves sagged with piles of towels, bedspreads, blankets, and sheets in their original wrappers. There were bank gifts in sealed cartons—chafing dishes, teakettles, alarm clocks, an electric frying pan, dishes, glasses, flatware. I found two GE coffeemakers in unopened boxes—bought at a good price twenty-five years ago, my mother explained, in case they had to give a gift.

Cupboards were crammed with boxes of aluminum foil, paper towels, napkins, toilet tissue—enough to last years. One cupboard was filled with empty jars. Jars of pennies turned up in cupboards, closets, and drawers. She had four sets of china, yet ate and drank from chipped plates and jelly jars.

I remembered the Winchester House that I saw when I was going to college in California. Believing that she would not die as long as her house remained unfinished, the widowed Mrs. Winchester kept making additions to her house. What began as stately rooms deteriorated into a frenzy of cubicles, corridors leading nowhere, stairways ending at ceilings, and a maze of secret rooms, secret closets, dummy walls. Fearing murder, she slept in a different secret room each night. Her body was found by her servants on the morning after the San Francisco earthquake. All night long they heard her screams as they tried to find her room.

I spent days and nights going through boxes of opened envelopes marked "Save for Record." They filled closets, suitcases, drawers. Opened envelopes going back decades. Letters, bills, invoices, company reports, receipts, junk mail. Deep into the nights while she moaned in her bed I filled bag after bag, occasionally discovering something of value. A forgotten bankbook. Ten crisp two-dollar bills. Unused stamps. I found old photographs of my mother and father and of a wistful pudgy child, and a dozen naked baby pictures.

There was a photograph of a little boy on a pony, my mother and father beaming alongside while I smiled gamely. Those were the summers when the pony man came around, his appearance sending children rushing into their houses to plead for money for a ride. Photographs cost extra. My parents must have had a particularly good week in the store.

There were snapshots of the three of us, two at a time. I sat on the hood of our new car, my mother holding me. It was our Studebaker in the mid-thirties, black because "no other color looks so distinguished." Not a speck of dust was allowed to accumulate on its shiny finish without an immediate washing. It was perpetually Simonized. Sunday drives were our major recreation. To Belle Isle, Detroit's island park, for picnics. To a farm to buy fresh eggs, still warm from the coop. To the west side, pungent old-world blocks teeming with foreign aromas, accents, clothing, from where we carried home fresh-baked rye bread and bagels and freshly killed chickens for the week. As a special treat, there was a stop in the world's best delicatessen for incomparable corned beef on crusty rye with juicy dill pickles.

There was a sepia photograph of a chubby little boy wearing a knicker suit, white shirt, and tie, and holding a cane, posing with his beaming parents in front of a studio backdrop—a scenic mountain view. Oh, the preparation that had gone into that picture. Weeks of discussion followed by a trip downtown on the streetcar with my mother to buy that suit and, finally, the nervous arrival at the photographer's on a Sunday, the only day my parents were free from the hardware store. And, afterwards, studying the proofs. Debates and computations over quantities and prices, and which relatives would be honored.

All were saved in envelopes in boxes in suitcases in closets. My graduation pictures from elementary and high school. Out of focus pictures I had taken of my mother at the 1939 New York World's Fair in front of the Italian Pavilion with its waterfall wall. Even though it meant leaving my father alone in the store, and money was Depression-tight, my mother took me to New York. They had promised. It was the year after we had moved from a private home with a backyard to a flat above our store, and they wanted to make it up to me somehow. Nothing was too good for their son. I always had the best bicycle, the best sled, more of everything than any other child in the neighborhood.

And there were snapshots of my mother beaming proudly in the

Spanish courtyard of their Arizona home, elegance at last. At last, parties, friends, important affairs, important people, a life it had taken years to gain. But she had succeeded, and the triumph illuminated her smile. Succeeded as she had always succeeded in spite of a world determined to stop her.

But that was a long time ago. And now, during the days, I held up clothes as she lay in bed and decided what to keep and what to give away, "to Goodwill, and get a receipt."

She was distressed at abandoning her partially used, giant-size bags of sugar, flour, rice. When I suggested simply leaving them for the manager and his wife, she cried, "Poison I'll give them!"

After they asked for the $150, I was ready to help her mix it. After they complained that I was leaving too much junk outside her door, I was ready to administer it.

Occasionally the phone rang. Women who did not want to bother mother but did not mind bothering me to find out about mother. Drowning in packing, my mind torn apart with assignments, desperate to get on with it, I cut them short.

"You talk to her," my mother said, when I announced a caller. "I'm too tired."

"So am I," I said. "I only talk to the moving company, the car-moving company, your insurance men, doctors, drugstores, airlines—I don't talk to your friends."

"They want to talk to you," she said. "I've told them how exceptional you are."

"I'm not on a personal-appearance tour," I said, thrusting the phone into her good hand.

Whereupon she turned on either a thin wail or a bright peppy voice, depending on the caller. If there was an offer to help, I never heard it. Once I heard her say that "we have a woman here." What woman? I was the woman.

"You see how much people like me?" she said.

"Anybody can call," I said. "I don't see anyone coming over with a roast."

"Who can cook in this heat?" she said.

"I'm packing in this heat."

"Poor Mrs. Salt," she said after a call from a temple lady. "She'll miss me. They're all going to miss me. But," she added with a proud smile, "I won't miss them."

In the middle of the night, as I was sorting through envelopes, filling more bags, I started as I heard her call my name.

I dashed into the bedroom. She was not there. I turned to see her in the bathroom on the far side of a long dressing room. She was sitting on the toilet, grabbing for her cane on the floor.

"What are you doing there?" I called.

"What do you think?" she said.

It was the first time she had made it by herself to the bathroom, or anywhere, since the hospital. Employing the cane, the wall, furniture, anything, she managed to reach the toilet. Looking away, I stepped in and handed her the cane and ran out.

I watched her slowly maneuver herself through the dressing room and back into the bedroom, where she climbed back into bed and fell with a sigh on the pile of pillows. She had moved a mountain. If she lay flat she could not push herself up; her shoulder exploded into pain. Only by sleeping propped up in a nearly seated position could she crawl out of bed unaided.

Miraculously she appeared to be getting stronger—a testimony to the restorative powers of yogurt, cottage cheese, eggs, oatmeal, orange juice, pumpernickel bread, and ice cream. That was the range of our diet, since she insisted she was not hungry, and I was no cook, and no one appeared with anything more substantial.

What helped her most was a bank-gift heating pad. It quelled the sparks in her shoulder not snuffed out by the aspirin. I tied the pad around her shoulder with a towel and connected it to a long extension cord. She walked about the apartment with the cord trailing behind her as if she were personally powered by Arizona Electric.

As the pain eased she began to walk more briskly, aided only by the cane. In the evenings we took walks, first a few feet, then a block, then around the block. She held my arm and her cane as we promenaded past the identical apartment buildings that she said looked like barracks. Since dressing meant twisting her arm and shoulder, she settled for a housecoat over her nightgown. The star who would never be caught by her public without the right outfit, her hair bouffanted and makeup applied, had turned into a sick old lady with wild gray hair and a housecoat. But each night she walked a little steadier, a little faster. "Soon you won't be able to catch me," she said.

Selling her furniture was her miracle drug; it brought her back to life. Her eyes sparkled, her cheeks glowed as people surged into the apartment to take advantage of the unfortunates "Moving to New York Saturday. Sacrificing apartment full of furniture. Bed $25, home entertainment center $75, dishes, etc." Combing her hair and putting on lipstick for the first time since leaving St. Catherine's, she presided in her wing chair, playing the part of the sweet helpless old lady while she fleeced them.

Turning on the charm like a politician, she beamed proudly as she told potential customers of her devoted son taking her to his home in Larchmont to bring her back to health. She emphasized "Larchmont," making sure everyone got the message that she was being taken to no ordinary community. She joked with people, inviting anyone who bought anything to be sure to visit her when they came East. She promised to make her famous potato pancakes for the black army sergeant and his wife who bought the home entertainment center, while whispering to me in Yiddish to watch they shouldn't steal something.

Pictures, figurines, candy dishes she pronounced antiques, priceless art objects, gifts from her grandmother in Europe. A painting she bought in Israel she declared the work of the most famous artist in the country. "Surely you know Katz?" she said to an impressed young lady, a Baptist, and sold Katz for a hundred dollars. "I always hated that picture," she said when the lady left.

"I can see you appreciate art," she beamed, getting twenty-five dollars for a picture of a bowl of fruit for which she had paid a dollar. She sold a bank-gift set of dishes for fifty dollars. And a vanity lamp she bought in Woolworth's, proclaimed to be a gift from her grandmother, went for five times what she had paid. A Grant Wood couple from a church group made off with a vacuum cleaner for twenty-five dollars, "because you're religious and I like all religions." My mother disclosed afterward that the thing was thirty years old and never did work properly.

What hurt was the arty couple in their thirties who pounced on my old schoolbooks, squealing over their quaintness. I had become nostalgia.

A young woman from Iowa, captivated by my mother, made lunch for us and answered the phone while I helped people carry out furniture. She asked my mother if she was Italian; she had a girlfriend with an identical charming mother in Iowa. Months later, when my mother was in our home, a letter arrived from the young woman asking my mother about her health. She could not get us out of her mind, she said. After making sure we all read it, my mother threw it out; one letter she did not bother to save.

At the end of the second day, when the last of the buyers departed with an armload of folding chairs that would probably collapse at the first sit (I was glad we were skipping town), my mother glowed as if she did not have a single cancer cell in her body. I felt more alive too. After dreading the people, I was delighted to see new faces and rediscover life outside of our own solitary confinement.

By the end of the week she was able to dress and take me to close out safe-deposit boxes. At her first try she took me to the wrong branch. "It's because they remodeled it," she cried, bewildered. "I was sure it was here." When we finally found the right branch on the other side of the city she accused them of confusing her, as if they had moved the bank to fool her. "It's not my fault," she insisted. "They did it."

Another day she could not find the cemetery where my father was buried, although she went regularly. We drove for miles in the fiery heat, thwarted by swarms of trucks, roads under construction, detours, trains blocking crossings. "God will forgive me," she cried, begging me to turn back as the pain boiled up inside her body.

In the eight nights that I was there we were invited to dinner twice. Once by the big-faced lady, who spent the evening denouncing the woman who refused her a ride as "worse than a gentile." The last night we spent at the gentile's—Pearl fed and sheltered us after the furniture went, drove us to the airport, and turned my mother's car over to the drive-away company the following week.

"We can stay at a motel!" my mother cried when she heard I had accepted Pearl's offer.

"You stay at a motel," I said, "I'll stay at Pearl's."

"I'll never hear the end of it," she said. "I don't like favors."

"Maybe she wants to help," I said. "Maybe it gives her plea-sure."

"She wants plenty," my mother said. "Watch, she'll empty out my kitchen."

"Your open bottle of salad oil? Your open bag of sugar? Your open box of detergent?"

After dinner, while Pearl played the piano for us, my mother slipped out of her chair and fell to the floor, where she sat as help-less as a rag doll. "I don't know what happened," she said. "I just fell."

Early the next morning Pearl slipped me a sheet of paper on which she had written the name of the rabbi, the Jewish mortuary, and the cemetery where my mother had the plot next to my father.

9

"THE CHILDREN WILL FIGHT over who takes grandma for a walk," Pearl said as we drove to the airport. It was eight o'clock on a Sunday morning, the sun already singeing the empty streets.

My mother smiled.

I hoped reality would come just a little close to the fantasy. My sons had no reason to fight to do anything for her. And Ethel certainly did not. She would be a virtual stranger disrupting their lives, displacing them from the TV room, stationed downstairs where her presence would have to be considered when they spoke, ran, lived.

I expected no one to turn on love out of obligation. I could only hope that we had given our boys enough love to make them thoughtful enough, caring enough, to offer her affection and kind-ness. Anything more would be a bonus. I hoped they would be ma-ture enough to overlook her oddities and give of themselves even if her own concept of giving was writing a check to "go buy yourself something."

The wheelchair was waiting, as promised. From it my mother watched with the deepest mistrust the skycap slamming our suitcases on his trolley and reminded me every few seconds to make sure he didn't take the silver. In addition to checking four bulging suitcases ahead, we were carrying an assortment of totebags as well as her silver service aboard the plane.

As Pearl flew off with tears and kisses, and I was left with my mother once more, I felt like a recaptured prisoner brought back to serve his sentence.

I was rescued by a uniformed airline official who wheeled my mother up the ramp and into the plane before the other passengers were allowed through the gate. A pair of solicitous stewardesses installed us in the first seat of the coach section—the bulkhead seat—saved for invalids, mothers with babies, and other special cases because of its extra floor space. They propped my mother on pillows, covered her with blankets, pampered her with sweetness, and offered me the privilege of moving to another seat so that she could stretch out across all three seats, which they would save for her. Smiling sweetly, my mother asked for a deck of cards.

"Are you planning a canasta party?" I asked. I had found a kitchen drawer overflowing with decks of cards, most of them unopened.

"For the children," she said.

"We have plenty," I told the stewardess.

My mother glared.

The airline turned out to be much better at tender loving care than at flying. As the engines tuned up they emitted an ominous clunk, followed by the voice of the pilot announcing a slight delay while they replaced the broken part. An hour later his Western drawl returned to tell us they were flying the part in from Los Angeles. Three-hour delay.

"We aren't going?" my mother asked.

"They're flying in a part from L.A.," I said, irritated. Why did she always require a personal explanation?

"We aren't taking another plane?"

"If they had another plane we wouldn't have to wait three hours." Didn't she hear anything?

"How should I hear?" she said. "I wasn't listening."

A Sunbelt city terminal is no three-hour terminal, unless you are fascinated by squash-blossom necklaces and dioramas of desert retirement communities. The gleaming steel-and-glass complex, straight out of the airport school of design, is no match for the shed it replaced with its fat Indian women squatting under overhangs selling blankets—my first view of the region when I came to my parents' retirement world for the first time thirty years ago, a Stanford graduate and a grievous disappointment. I had landed no heiress or lucrative job. I had not even received much of an education. No corporations came begging for English majors, no one seemed awed by my insights into Chaucer and Donne. Now, at fifty, I was back and still a disappointment. Dismissed over a year ago from my big, but not big enough, job at a giant advertising agency after twelve eager-to-please years. A copywriter once more, back where I started, in a small agency, but with one important difference. Before I was on the way up.

"Don't tell anybody," was the first thing my mother said when she learned I lost my job.

"I wasn't planning to announce it on television," I said.

"Just wait, they'll beg you to come back," she said.

Her son did not get fired. Just as she did not get cancer. Just as she and my father were years younger, inches taller, pounds lighter than the calendars, rulers, and scales said. She altered her birthplace; she told people she was born in an important city instead of her village with chickens in the streets. Her father, the proprietor of a general store, she transformed into a rabbi; her mother into a beauty.

When she came to our home she would come face to face with truth. Her "exceptional" grandchildren were simply boys with their own particular problems. Ethel and I argued a lot lately. Arguments that began when she went to work after I lost my job. Ethel was growing into a successful travel agent and, having tasted achievement, was fighting any suggestion of reverting to being a housewife again. Gone forever was the PTA, tennis group, and scouring the *New York Times Cookbook* for the dinner-party recipe to beat all dinner-party recipes.

My mother would not be coming to a neatly organized family with a convenient niche into which she could fit. Daddy was not pleased as punch with his job, mommy was trying to find herself, and the boys had their share of problems. Much of the time we had a hard enough time getting along with each other—how could we be expected to absorb my mother painlessly into our lives? Especially a mother who prided herself on being a problem to prove that she was important—and alive.

Another thing I learned that week—thanks to our grounded plane: Look for the unobtrusive phone at the end of an airline counter, pick it up as if you know what you are doing, and you can dial anywhere in the country.

"We just got back from the pool," Ethel panted.

"Sorry to inconvenience you," I said, an edge in my voice I vowed during the past week never to let appear again. Life was too short. No more anger, no more bickering. Yet there it was—anger—triggered by a word, an inflection. Who cared where she was? I was bringing my mother home and the world had to stop.

"Why aren't you on the plane?" she asked.

"Because the plane is still on the ground." I told her about the flying part.

"Three hours," she moaned. "That's all you need. Where's your mother?"

"On the plane."

"By herself?"

"She won't fly away."

"What about dinner?"

Why was it that life always seemed to zero down to the next meal? As if the greatest catastrophe that could befall a person would be to miss a feeding. I told her I was sure the airline would not let us go hungry, or even go. She and the boys were all coming to meet us, thank God. Moving my mother required a staff. We needed someone just to guard the silver.

Aboard the plane I found my mother chatting animatedly with a chic woman across the aisle who told me not to worry, she was looking after her. "Your mother is such a sweet lady," she said. My mother smiled sweetly, almost winking at me. See how I impress people, her look said. See how I can get people to like me. Watch my performance. As sick, as drained as she might be, she recharged at the challenge of turning a stranger into an admirer. "What a beautiful dress!" she would suddenly exclaim. Or, "I've never seen such a lovely pin. Is it Indian?" Very few strangers could resist this sudden outpouring of seemingly spontaneous admiration from this pretty woman with a smile that beamed with apparent sincerity. For all her prejudices, she was an equal opportunity conversationalist—the conquests in her address books ranging from a woman who had been a famous movie star's maid to a New Jersey couple who manufactured eyeglasses for chickens. All people were fair game for her wiles, her ability to charm being proof of her worth.

As the plane took off a deck of cards fell from my mother's seat.

When the kosher meal arrived my mother made a face at it. "Fat," she said, "who can eat it?"

When the stewardess hovered over her with orange juice, my mother eyed her as if it were the milk in *Gaslight*. "They can drown you with their orange juice," she said.

When drinks were served my mother whispered to me to watch the passengers get drunk. "Without whiskey they can't survive," she said. Gentiles got drunk; Jews read the Talmud and made fortunes in scrap metal.

I had two Scotches.

It was the one time in my life I felt a desperate need for a drink.

I retreated several seats behind my mother while the nice lady joined her. She plumped her pillows, took her to the lavatory, and, most important, listened to her. I heard words like "prominent, executive, Larchmont, remarkable grandchildren."

"Isn't she striking?" my mother said when we were landing. "I think she's married to a producer."

I recognized the name.

Porn films.

10

NEW YORK.

We were instructed to wait until all the other passengers left the plane. Whereupon a sullen attendant appeared, grumbling about the difficulty of getting a wheelchair up the ramp.

Try having cancer, I thought.

He failed to intimidate my mother, who insisted on checking every inch of the bulkhead area before vacating it. Only when she was satisfied that nothing had escaped—not any of the sugar, salt, ketchup, or hard rolls she had craftily sneaked into her totebag—did she agree to let me help her into her sweater. A process that brought renewed grumblings from the wheelchair man as I worked it carefully around the pain still flashing in her shoulder. While he glared I transferred my mother to the wheelchair and buried her under totebags and the silver.

He informed me that it would not be easy pushing all of that.

"It's easier than carrying it," I replied.

This was the airline whose commercials featured ferociously smiling employees eager to make travel euphoric for the world, and wildly ecstatic passengers being treated like royalty.

At the sight of my family I could feel the tears welling up inside me. By the time I shook hands with Steven I could hold them back no longer. I threw my arms around his shoulders and burst into uncontrollable sobbing, embarrassing the sixteen-year-old boy, who, like me, was not famous for displaying emotions.

I could feel my mother watching from her wheelchair. What was my crying telling her?

"It's because he missed them so," Ethel said quickly, kissing my mother who offered her cheek.

"I see," said my mother.

Muttering that he did not have forever, the attendant who had angrily halted the wheelchair so that I could have my breakdown resumed pushing. In the middle of the terminal a smile surfaced on his face for the first time as he suddenly stopped and announced that he went no further. Rules. We were not near an exit, an entrance, or the baggage pickup. The only means of escape was an escalator going somewhere. No problem if you were not dying.

"Don't know what you do from here," he shrugged, grinning, waiting for a tip as he watched us transfer my mother to a bench. Desperate to get rid of his hostility, I gave him a dollar, an act of cowardice I regret to this day. But it hardly ranks with my major regrets.

With the precision of a general staff preparing an invasion, the four of us coordinated the movements of my mother, the baggage, and the car, finding ramps and exits in spite of every attempt of the airport to foil us. I dreaded to think of a handicapped person essaying it on his own. The simple act of getting my mother to the car required negotiations with policemen manning a barricade which seemed to have been erected for no other reason than to block the exit and make it hard for people.

Screaming over the din of jets, automobile horns, and bus exhausts, we squeezed the baggage and silver into the trunk and my mother into the front seat. It was a hot, acrid day, the air as thick with fumes as a chemical plant, gusts of litter and soot swirling angrily in the carbon monoxide.

"Don't I look beautiful?" my mother asked, while Ethel was watching for an opening in the angry traffic. "Not like the last time you saw me."

"Soon you'll be gorgeous again," Ethel said, darting into an opening while a horn blasted.

"With such good care, of course," my mother said. She turned slightly to look at Steven. "Steven," she said, "I don't like your face. What's wrong?"

Steven shrank. He smiled uneasily. He did not exactly love his acne either.

"Can't your parents afford a doctor?" she asked.

I told her he was using a cream. Prescribed by the doctor.

"See a specialist," she said. "I'll pay."

I repeated the information about the doctor and the cream.

"Is he a good doctor?" she challenged. "Plenty of doctors don't know what they're doing."

She should talk about doctors.

Ethel said it was too bad about the long delay.

"It had to happen to me," my mother said.

"It happened to everyone on the plane," Paul mumbled.

"What?" my mother asked.

"Forget it," said Paul, a conversational gambit of my blond fourteen-year-old that drove me up walls.

"Paul," my mother said, "why are you so skinny?"

She had an incredible ability to zero in on the area of most vulnerability. Zap!

"My parents don't feed me," Paul said.

"Now that I'm here, I'll feed you," she said.

Following the signs, Ethel swept out of the airport and into the rush through Queens.

"It's a lot different from Arizona, isn't it?" Ethel made conversation.

"What a comparison," my mother said. "Arizona is beautiful."

11

LIKE A WHALE flanked by pilot fish, my mother edged up the flagstone walk to our house, one hand on her cane, the other on Steven's arm, the rest of us scurrying about her collecting baggage and opening and closing doors.

My family led her eagerly to the TV room, now furnished with a bed, bureau, and rocking chair. On the table next to the bed Ethel had placed a dish of sunflower seeds, remembering my mother's favorite delicacy. Awaiting her in the kitchen were borscht, farmer's cheese, matzo, and Levy's unseeded rye. Ethel had cleared our things from the adjoining bathroom. Fresh towels hung on the racks.

"Simply beautiful," my mother said. "Brown. Like a coffin."

The smiles snapped off our faces.

"I like bright colors," she said. "Something cheerful."

"When you get your own apartment," I said, "you'll have bright colors."

She shot an angry look at me. "I just arrived. Don't be so anxious to get rid of me."

Paul looked at me, baffled. Steven smiled uneasily, cracking his knuckles. Ethel quickly asked my mother if she would like something to eat.

"Who can eat now?" my mother snapped, as if only a lunatic could make such a proposal. She frowned angrily as the boys attempted to squeeze into the room with suitcases and totebags overflowing with packets of airline sugar and ketchup. "Not now," she cried as if she were being attacked. "Don't bring me suitcases now."

The boys backed away as if from a wounded animal. I told them to leave the suitcases in the dining room, which would look like a refugee camp for months.

"I learned Dr. Zhivago," Paul tried.

Once, on the phone, she had asked him if he could play Dr. Zhivago on the guitar. She was referring to "Lara's Theme," which she declared was the most beautiful piece of music ever written. Painfully, Paul, the jazz lover, spent hours that could be devoted to real music capturing "Lara's Theme," which he categorized as "dentist music."

"Some other time," Nana said, lowering herself carefully to the bed.

We stood around her awkwardly, waiting for clues as to how to minister to her needs. No one was quite sure what to do with this semistranger who was like no one else they knew. They could not understand why she found everything wrong. Nothing anyone said or did pleased her. She was sick, in pain; allowances had to be made. But how many?

If only she had been a part of our lives so that we knew and understood her and knew how to react to her oddities. Even though they had met her before—even though *I* had met her before—we were jolted by her personality, which was nothing like the "grandmother" we expected, the one in our minds. My family was suddenly confronted with a very unusual lodger, with whom they were expected to be close. A stranger making no attempt to reach them. The strain showed. Awkward silences. Tension. It was a relief when she said she was tired and wanted to get into her nightgown.

Which was impossible because the suitcase was locked.

Somehow the dying woman had managed to get to her suitcases and spin the cylinders that locked the built-in combination locks. A deed she stoutly denied. "Who locked them?" she cried, feigning surprise. "They must have turned by accident." Since she could not be expected to recall the combination in her condition, it was up to Ethel to provide her with a nightgown and everything else.

"She doesn't seem so sick," Steven whispered, as we huddled in the dining room while Ethel helped her change.

"Does she always talk that loud?" Paul asked. "She gives me a headache."

"She isn't as bad off as she makes out," Dr. Kraven had said. "She overdramatizes. She wants attention. More than most old people."

"He tells me it doesn't hurt," my mother said in Arizona, imitating Kraven's Jimmy Carter smile. "I have the pain, and he tells me it doesn't hurt. He should have one tenth my pain. And the Arabs all of it."

"Ethel, you should be a nurse," my mother said as the door opened, revealing her in Ethel's nightgown, propped up in bed against a pile of pillows. Paul, his all-too-expressive face registering disapproval at the goings-on, brought her a dinner bell from the kitchen to keep next to her bed, while Steven brought a bedrail down from the attic. It would both keep her secure and provide something she could pull on with her unaffected arm to get out of bed.

The next crisis was the TV.

It had no remote control. How could she watch?

"I had such a good television," she shook her head. "Bernie gave it away."

"I gave it to the moving company," I said. "It's in storage. When you have your own apartment . . ."

"Again my own apartment!" she cried.

"What's so hard about changing a channel?" Paul asked.

"When you don't have pain," she said, "nothing's hard."

"You weren't always in pain," Paul said.

She gave him an angry look. Paul was not her favorite grandson. Steven, her prince, the scholar, looked like "the family." A handsome, olive-skinned boy with big brown eyes and a smile that lit up the room, he exuded concern and understanding. But Paul, the fair-skinned athlete with shoulder-length hair, who had no intention of playing anyone's game but his own, was not what she had in mind in the exceptional grandchild contest.

"Maybe you'd like an aspirin," I said.

"I don't want an aspirin," she said tensely.

"But if you're in pain . . ."

"I'll survive," she said. "And how I'll survive! Longer than anybody wants me to." She sank back on the pillows, the strength suddenly running out of her as if a plug had been pulled. "Maybe I *am* tired," she said. "Maybe I would like an aspirin."

Steven brought her the aspirin bottle and water. He removed the childproof cap for her, a feat requiring the "strength of Samson." While Paul edged out of the room, Steven lingered, ready to meet needs, his face drawn with concern. I closed the shutters, leaving the slats open for the moonlight to seep in. As Ethel switched off the dimmer, my mother screamed that she did not want to be left in the dark. "Don't leave me in a grave," she cried, insisting that the door be left partly open, a hall light on.

As Ethel started up the stairs that passed outside the TV room, my mother called her. "Ethel," she said weakly, "do you think maybe you could put more water in my glass? My mouth is so dry, like someone filled it with cotton."

After Ethel replenished her water, my mother stopped her once more halfway up the stairs and asked if she could put a robe over her feet; they were like ice. After Ethel tucked in her feet, already under two blankets (it was the last week in June, seventy-five degrees), my mother called to her as she reached the stairs to ask where I had put her silver. Ethel's assurance that it was safe did not satisfy her. She insisted that Ethel find it and put it in the TV room closet.

Late that night while the boys watched TV in our bedroom, Ethel and I huddled in a corner of the living room, speaking in the guarded tones that would become our standard form of communication.

"She doesn't look so sick," Ethel whispered.

"I know," I agreed, baffled. "A week ago she looked like a corpse. She couldn't stand up without help. She couldn't change her position in a chair."

A very peculiar thing had happened. In spite of the haphazard meals in her apartment, in spite of the strain of moving, packing, selling, flying, she had improved remarkably. While I was too busy to notice, she had progressed from the wizened doll who could barely sit upright in Pearl's car to a booming-voiced woman who walked with only the aid of a cane, sat down and stood up on her own, and managed to tell everyone what to do.

"She doesn't look much different than when she was here three years ago," Ethel said. "It's her hair that makes her look old. A little Loving Kindness and she'd look twenty years younger. She has fewer lines in her face than I have."

What happened to the deep lines that looked etched in acid a week ago?

"If she put makeup on," Ethel said, "she'd look terrific."

My God, I thought, what if it were all a mistake? What if Ethel took her to Jeremiah Gordon and he informed her that the diagnosis was wrong? A misread blood count. A blurred x-ray. A mixup at St. Catherine's. Those things happen, sorry. What if her illness turned out to be nothing more deadly than the anemia for which Dr. Greenstone had been giving her iron pills up to a few weeks earlier? Why hadn't I checked with another specialist, insisted on a second opinion, instead of rushing to pack her possessions, a truckload of which was roaring on its way across the country.

12

IT WAS NO MISTAKE.

My mother, Dr. Gordon told Ethel, not only had multiple myeloma, but it had probably been going on for months. Much of her marrow was already cancerous, the cells replaced by myeloma cells, the bones brittle, easily fractured, and susceptible to terrible pain. The affected marrow could no longer produce the red blood cells the body needed.

He was surprised, he said with surprising candor, that it had not been detected earlier, especially since she saw a doctor regularly. The blood count must have made it very clear that something was wrong, although it might first have appeared to be anemia.

I recalled my mother mentioning that she had gone to Dr. Greenstone over a year ago with a pain in her backside that would not go away. It was caused, she said, by sitting down improperly on the edge of a hard chair.

Another time it was her shoulder. Her hand.

The symptoms of myeloma. But also, unfortunately, the symptoms of arthritis.

He could not explain her apparent improvement. It was simply the nature of the disease. Often when the patient felt best the disease was advancing most rapidly. Other times it sent out pain signals. It was a malicious, taunting disease that kept giving you hope and yanking it away.

My mother's mind, he said, seemed fuzzy. He was not sure if it was senility, the myeloma, or pills she had been taking. She told him she had lived in Arizona for a few years instead of thirty, that she had been in St. Catherine's a few days instead of weeks, and that she had never been in a hospital before, although her x-rays showed a hysterectomy years earlier and the scars from an automobile accident.

Or it could have been my mother giving answers to create the right impression. "You have to know what to tell people," she taught me.

"I'm fine," she insisted to Dr. Gordon, as if it were a stigma for Dora Sloan to be less than perfect. "It's just that something got into me. It's nothing."

"Have you ever been hospitalized before?"

"Of course not," she said.

"But your records say you had a hysterectomy."

"Well, if it says so."

She had nothing more than a blood condition, she said. A blood condition for which she had come all the way from Arizona especially to see him. He was famous across the country, she said.

"You're putting me on, Mrs. Sloan," he smiled at her.

"So help me," she said. "They all talk about you like God. They're waiting to hear my report, so be careful."

"I hope you give me a good one," he grinned.

"If you give *me* a good one," she laughed.

Was there hope?

Dr. Gordon said that the prognosis for myeloma given by Dr. Kraven might have been given ten years ago; it appeared to ignore the tremendous advances of the past decade. With the right treatment she could live for eight or nine years. "She could outlive us all," he laughed.

It was unfortunate, he told us, that it had not been detected earlier. The more time they had to find the right treatment, the greater her chances.

He gave Ethel prescriptions for a multitude of pills, which my mother was to take in massive quantities—as many as twenty a day, tapering off to a few at the end of a three-week period, then beginning again. He warned of reactions. Hair loss. Upset stomach. Depression. Irrational behavior. Or nothing might happen. Each person was a unique chemical formula; each reaction was different.

So this was chemotherapy. No esoteric treatment, as I had always believed, but simply a combination of chemicals, either swallowed or injected. The trick was to find the right combination of chemicals that would destroy the cancer cells while miraculously ignoring the good cells. The chemotherapy drugs were surprisingly common—Alkeran, prednisone. Paul had taken prednisone for poison ivy.

To protect her insides from the conflagration of chemicals, my mother was to take Mylanta, a popular viscous stomach-coating sold over the counter. Astonished to hear that with her ulcer she was told to take an aspirin product for pain, he immediately prescribed Tylenol with codeine, a painkiller that would not sear the stomach.

It was clear from my mother's behavior, Dr. Gordon told Ethel, that she did not know she had cancer. Either she had not been told or, like many people, she screened out the information. And she refused to hear what drugs she was to take, or how many, diverting him to Ethel. "Tell my daughter-in-law," she said, "my mind is too confused."

My mother always managed to be looking the other way when the word "chemotherapy" was mentioned.

Fair or unfair, like it or not, Ethel became responsible for my mother. It was accepted that she had the dispensable career, the disposable ambitions. Since she worked nearby and took care of the house, she automatically accepted the role of my mother's keeper. At first.

"We'll get to know each other," Ethel said. "Maybe she'll find out I'm not so terrible."

My mother seemed to do everything possible to frustrate her. Each time she visited the doctor, she insisted on wearing an outfit that required a dozen healthy hands to assemble. When Ethel suggested that a dress might be more practical than an elaborate pants suit with a blouse that buttoned up the back, my mother answered, "It doesn't cost you anything, does it?" When Ethel, who was taking time off from the agency, said that she would like to save time, my mother replied, "What's the rush? Is Prince Charming waiting for me?" My mother was adamant about transferring the contents of one enormous bag to another and could spend what seemed like an eternity debating the wisdom of taking a sweater in July. Once in the car she blamed Ethel for not telling her how hot it was; another time she cried that she had forgotten her reading glasses, sending Ethel back in the house to find them. My mother promptly dropped them into her bag among the crumpled tissues, torn envelopes, dry ballpoints, and hard candies bleeding through stuck wrappers. Each time they reached the doctor's building, no ordinary parking space would do; my mother demanded that she be driven to the entrance. "For you this is close," she said. "Germans are strong."

"So many blacks!" my mother exclaimed the first time they entered the waiting room, not bothering to lower her voice. "You would never see them at *my* doctor's in Arizona."

Perhaps, Ethel wanted to tell her, they were smarter at picking doctors.

"It shows he must be very charitable," my mother said.

Ethel could have kissed the bleached-blonde receptionist when, on the very first visit, she produced without hesitation a folder on which was already typed the name of Dora Sloan. She very efficiently took the x-rays I had given Ethel and proceeded to question my mother, who fought over every answer.

"Ask my daughter-in-law," she frowned. "She'll tell you everything."

"But I don't know everything," Ethel said.

Every question invariably turned into intricate negotiations as my mother devised answers that would present the proper picture of herself. "Diabetes?" she said indignantly. "In *our* family?" And she smiled at the woman as if she were retarded. She was equally enraged at the suggestion that she might be allergic to any medication or have any problem other than a touch of constipation.

"You think I don't know why the doctor himself isn't asking me?" she smiled knowingly. "So he can see more patients and make more money. Who can blame him?"

Her age she declared at first to be sixty-six, glaring when Ethel reminded her that I was fifty. "He isn't," my mother snapped, finally settling for sixty-nine.

"May I see your Medicare card, Mrs. Sloan?"

"You don't trust me?"

"Show her your card," Ethel said.

"Now?" my mother said.

"Not Christmas," said the receptionist.

"If I can find it," said my mother. "Hold me," she commanded Ethel, thumping her bag on the receptionist's desk, sending papers flying.

While my mother searched, Ethel looked nervously at the clock. Each visit, it was clear from the first one, would consume an entire day. And not a day passed that another anxious woman did not step hesitantly into the travel agency to offer her services in hopes of launching a midlife career. Ethel had worked free for three months, "interning," as the Southern lady who owned the agency sweetly put it. Now Ethel was making money. She was just reaching

the point where she had her own following, where she felt the possibilities of opening her own agency. The pieces of our lives were
just beginning to fall back into place again when—zap!—who said
lightning did not strike twice in the same place?

"A curse on it!" my mother cried, unzipping and unsnapping little purses and wallets, some old and frayed, others new and glossy,
of which she seemed to have hundreds. "In the West all they have
to hear is my name," she laughed as she finally produced her Medicare card.

Catching Ethel looking at her watch, my mother said, "You're in
a hurry? Don't worry, the agency will manage without you."

Ethel felt like hitting her with her purse. She had clothes to buy
for Paul, she had postponed her own dental appointment twice,
she had a pyramid of wash to do and a refrigerator that ached with
emptiness.

When the receptionist called her name a few minutes later my
mother walked through the waiting room, head upraised, nodding
and smiling, a queen among the commoners who had been waiting
far longer than she. "You see?" she whispered. "It's because I'm
from Larchmont."

It was because the receptionist sent her for a blood test, requiring Ethel to take my mother down an elevator to a laboratory,
where she was told that Dr. Gordon would see my mother after
seeing the results. In two hours. It was a procedure that would be
repeated each time she saw the doctor.

At the end of the first visit, when Dr. Gordon asked my mother
to come over to his desk after the examination, she hopped down
from the table and hurried over to him, forgetting her cane. Only
when he asked her with a grin if she had not forgotten something
did she jump up, crying, "My cane!" and rush back to retrieve it.

"Why don't you leave it here?" Dr. Gordon grinned.

"Why? Do you need it?" my mother asked.

"Are they all as clever as you out West?" he laughed.

"Not as clever, or as beautiful," she laughed back.

While the nurse was dressing my mother, suggesting that next
time she wear something simpler (a suggestion she made at every
visit), Dr. Gordon told Ethel that my mother was neither well

enough to be by herself, nor sick enough to be in a nursing home. If she already had her own apartment, a housekeeper would do. Too bad she had lived so far away, he said. But it was more common than not these days. He was constantly seeing patients from Florida, brought in by their children. His own parents were in Indiana, still alive and well, but . . . he dreaded to think of the possibilities.

"You're very lucky to have such a nice daughter-in-law, Mrs. Sloan," he said, raising his voice and carefully enunciating each syllable. "I don't know if my wife would do so much for my mother."

"Very lucky," my mother said, adding as she noticed the photograph on his desk, "Is that your wife? Such a beautiful woman. And what beautiful children! Someday when you come West I'll show you such a wonderful time, believe me. I'll introduce you to all the prominent people."

All the way home my mother told Ethel how everyone loved her, how she wished her wonderful nieces could be with her now, how they treated her like a queen. But how could they help her, they had their own families? Distinguished husbands, exceptional children.

It was after five when they finally returned home from the first trek to Dr. Gordon. Steven, surrounded by a floor full of index cards he was organizing for a debate, reported that the agency owner had called. My mother said that she was starving. "There's nothing they wouldn't do for me," she said, following Ethel into the kitchen. She sat at the table and watched her rush to prepare dinner.

"She sat there telling me what good cooks her nieces were while I was cooking her dinner," Ethel said. "She told me what beautiful lives they led—after I'd spent the day taking her to the doctor."

But she actually liked Dr. Gordon! She whose personality standards were not easy to meet. For that we could forgive her anything. We were saved from more searching, spared from still more anxiety, the threat lifted of driving weekly into New York.

"The best!" my mother cried. "Such an examination. Better than the Mayo Clinic."

"He gave her special attention," Ethel winked.

"Two hours he spent with me," my mother beamed. "I'm sure he doesn't do it with everyone."

"It's because Bernie knows Dan," Ethel smiled.

"What else?" my mother glowed. She loved connections. For her alone, she was convinced, he charged a mere seventy-five dollars for the first visit, twenty dollars for follow-ups. It was less than Kraven, who charged a hundred. "And there's no comparison."

Maybe things would start to go right, I hoped. Maybe her delight with Dr. Gordon would make her happier, easier to live with, a little appreciative of what we were doing for her. She might not like a mocha room, Steven's acne, or Ethel's religious heritage, but she liked Dr. Gordon, and maybe that would make her like us all.

Maybe.

"He doesn't look like a doctor," my mother said. "What I mean is, he isn't exactly handsome."

"You already had handsome," I said.

"Greenstone should have my sickness!" she cried.

After hearing what Dr. Gordon said, I shared her feelings.

13

ETHEL CREPT DOWN THE STAIRS and hurried past the half-open door of my mother's room as if a troll were lying in wait. She managed to unload the dishwasher, put a pot of water on the stove, count out my mother's pills, and get halfway through her Special K before my mother's surprisingly strong voice boomed out her name.

Ethel froze.

Only three more minutes and she would have finished her cereal. Another five and she would have had her coffee and been out the door.

"Ethel," my mother called again.

Abandoning her cereal to a mushy fate, Ethel forced herself up from the table and into my mother's room, a step away. The non-stop sound of the television engulfed her like a wind as she pushed the door all the way open. The sound of "The Today Show" and a slightly rancid smell. My mother lay sprawled, as usual, on top of the sheet, her diaphanous nightgown pulled up to her crotch. A seventy-year-old flasher.

"Do you think," my mother squeezed out a feeble smile, "you could get me a little prune juice. I hate to bother you."

They played the same scene every morning. It could have been on tape like her TV shows. My mother playing helpless, and Ethel, made powerless by guilt and sympathy and resentment, yielding to her requests, the anger piling up daily like dry twigs destined for a match.

First prune juice, then a smiling plea for oatmeal, and milk, warm milk. All of which she was perfectly capable of getting for herself—a woman who managed to get to the mail before anyone else and make a mess in the kitchen when she was alone in the house.

"I'm so constipated"—my mother squeezed out the words—"I can't move."

Her constipation would kill her, Ethel thought, long before the myeloma did. It certainly meant more to her.

Ethel hurried back to the kitchen whose cupboards were now bulging with vat-sized bottles of prune juice, just as the bathroom shelves were sagging with milk of magnesia. She filled a glass from the bottle in the refrigerator. As she tried to sneak a mouthful of cereal, my mother called her, as if she saw through walls.

"Like ice"—my mother shuddered as she tried the prune juice, spilling some as she thumped the glass on the bedside table that had disappeared under envelopes, newspapers, magazines, tea-stained cups and saucers, packages of airline sugar and napkins, sunflower seeds spilling from a bowl. "Everything comes from your refrigerator like ice," she accused. "Who can drink it?"

Any warmer, Ethel knew, she would charge that it tasted like bath water. Not that she would recognize the taste, having made no attempt to bathe since her arrival. Or, judging from the odors, even making a pass with a washcloth. It took her a week to unpack her toothbrush, and only with prodding. She wore the same nightgown every day, removing it only when she dressed to see Dr. Gordon. Which was the only time she dressed.

"You're going to work?" my mother asked, registering the same surprise each morning as Ethel started for the door. Deep down my mother could not accept the fact that Ethel continued to work, actually chose to work, when her duty was to stay with her. "Do you think maybe you could fix a little oatmeal before you go?" my mother asked as she asked every morning, employing her thin "sick" voice. "With a little warm milk? Cold is torture for my stomach."

Although Ethel survived on cold, mushy Special K, her mother-in-law had to have endless oatmeal and warm milk. Anything that took time and dirtied pans. She was late to work every day. No matter how early she got up and dressed, her mother-in-law always managed to give her enough assignments to make her a half-hour late. There was no beating her.

"If you're in a hurry," my mother said, "don't bother. So I won't eat. Maybe Steven . . ."

No, not Steven, Ethel thought. Steven was already spending too much time with her. Handling her bank accounts, her stocks, taking her for walks, preparing her tea. She had his afternoons, she could not take his mornings, too. He was too acquiescent, too kind, too ready to fit into her picture of the devoted grandchild. He was going to a three-week debate workshop at Harvard at the end of the summer; he needed time to prepare, not oatmeal.

My mother would not think of asking Paul, who managed to disappear for the greater part of every day, dashing out to get in shape, he said, for his hosteling trip in Vermont. She and Paul understood each other. They had a truce.

"I'll make it," Ethel said.

"But you'll be late," my mother expressed concern.

"I'll make your oatmeal," Ethel repeated.

"I don't know why you want to work anyway," my mother called after her. "Why do you need it? You don't need the money. Stay home."

And take care of you? What an opportunity, Ethel thought, not to be missed. It was a quarter to ten. Already fifteen minutes late. The one time she left my mother to make her own oatmeal, Ethel returned to a cyclone of burnt pots that required endless scouring, as if my mother had used every pot in the kitchen. "I couldn't find a decent pan," she claimed.

"What are these?" Ethel pointed to the ones she was scouring.

"Not like mine," she answered.

Nothing was like hers.

While the oatmeal was cooking, Ethel brought my mother her pills, a glass of water, a tablespoon, and Mylanta. Sunflower seeds crunched under her feet. We stepped on them everywhere, we sat on them everywhere—clues to her whereabouts during the day, along with hardened puddles of milk of magnesia on counters, cracked eggs oozing in the refrigerator. The kitchen table was perpetually sticky with strawberry preserves and matzo crumbs. Often the toilet was not flushed. She required a personal attendant, yet she was not sick enough to need one and had made no offer to pay for extra help. Why should she? She had Ethel.

How, my wife wondered, would her mother-in-law manage without her? Would she just lie in bed and rot? Cling to her bed, watch TV, ignore Dr. Gordon's urgings to exercise; and never bathe, never brush her teeth?

Ethel watched her squint at the pills through her half-glasses. "Are you sure these are the right ones?" my mother asked, as she asked each time.

Ethel assured her, as she assured her each time, that they were exactly what the doctor ordered, the ones she took every day, three times a day.

"I'm supposed to take so many?" she asked, as if she did not take so many every day.

"Yes."

"Are you sure?"

"Yes."

It was ten o'clock. How many mornings could she be late? How many mornings would she let herself be trapped?

She watched my mother take the pills, followed by two tablespoons of Mylanta, which left a chalky white ring around her mouth, making her look like a minstrel performer, and which she managed to spill, as usual, on her nightgown and the sheet and the table.

Each day Ethel told herself she had to make allowances, turn anger into forgiveness, turn the other cheek. It would help, ironically, if my mother looked like she was suffering; if she really were helpless. Then rudeness could be forgiven, demands satisfied. But she seemed to enjoy her "condition."

"It's a brutal disease," Dr. Gordon said. "The pain is diabolical. The chemotherapy can alter behavior. I admire what you're doing. It takes a lot of patience to deal with it."

If only Ethel knew how to stop being admirable.

"It's raw, who can chew it?" My mother spat the oatmeal back into the bowl. "You didn't cook it long enough."

"Twenty minutes," Ethel said, taking the bowl away. A hundred and twenty minutes would not be long enough.

"Who can eat oatmeal anyhow in such heat?" my mother called after her. "When I think of my beautiful air-conditioned apartment Bernie took me away from . . ."

"You can always go back," Ethel cried, slamming the front door.

"You should hear how she talks to me," my mother would tell me later. "I swear I didn't do anything to deserve it."

14

"TOLSTOY!" my mother's voice shouted through the half-open door, followed by a burst of applause and a squeal of delight. "I told you!" she shrieked to the TV.

She called out to anyone who might be within earshot, "Such a good program, kids. It's educational. Put me on it, I would make a fortune. Dostoevsky!"

Paul stepped hesitantly into our bedroom where I was changing and asked if he could watch TV, promising to keep it low. It was no easy request to make; all the world knew I demanded tranquility after a day at work and had made my feelings clear about television noise following me from room to room. Commercials drove me berserk, the result of twenty-five years of writing them.

"It's a jazz concert from Wolf Trap," Paul said, explaining his act of courage.

"Anna Karenina!" her voice shrieked up the stairwell.

I would learn to love having music to change by.

In a matter of weeks her room had become *Her* Room, the TV her TV. She kept the door half closed when she was in, closed when she was out. ("The manager has a key. She doesn't have to see what I have.") I insisted that she leave the door open when she was not in—it needed air—but she always "forgot."

At first eager to have her grandchildren watch TV with her ("anything you like as long as I have company"), she began to fight with them over which shows to watch, trying to convert them to game shows and Merv Griffin. Steven retreated to his room to study, but Paul resisted at first. "Just because I'm a kid"—he fought her—"doesn't mean I don't have as much say as you."

"My grandchildren are exceptional," she told friends who called. "Just being with them will make me better." Sometimes she added, surprisingly, "It's their mother. You should see how beautifully she raised them."

"Try to understand her, Paul," I said to the kid lying across the bed, tuned in to the Wolf Trap guitarist. As if I were so great in the understanding department. I was constantly exploding at her. Not a day passed that there was not at least a skirmish.

"She thinks she's the only one who counts," Paul said.

"I know," I said.

Paul did not think of her as living or dying, but as a person who was trying to avoid following the rules that applied to everyone else. Perhaps his was the right point of view. Why should the fact of her dying give her more rights than anyone else? Why should dying give her the right to be a tyrant?

"I wish she'd stop talking about how everybody loves her," Paul said. "I don't know why they would."

"She thinks if we believe it, we'll love her too."

"If she'd only act human," Paul said.

"She can't help it"—I tried to be the reasonable, mature, wise father. "She's afraid. People who don't think much of themselves have to keep announcing how terrific they are. If she really believed it, she wouldn't keep saying it."

Understanding, unfortunately, did not make it any easier.

Paul pushed his hair out of his eyes and turned back to catch the guitarist. He could talk about his grandmother anytime. There was too much talk about his grandmother.

One call from a friend in California or Arizona, a relative in Detroit, picked up her spirits for a day. "You see how people love me?" she said. "You see how they miss me? I'm so lucky to have such wonderful friends. They'll do anything for me."

"It's easy to make a phone call," I said.

"What else can they do?" she asked. "Larchmont is on the moon." A dear friend in Santa Monica, she said, was furious with her for not notifying her at once of her illness. She would have brought her to California where the climate would cure her. How awful that she had to be subjected to a New York winter.

"It isn't too late," I said. "Planes are still flying. We aren't keeping you in chains."

"Don't aggravate me," she cried.

We all knew the truth—that she had no place else to go—and she hated us for knowing it. No one else was going to find her a doctor, count her pills, cook for her, clean for her, give up their days for her. Only Ethel. And she hated her for it. She could talk and talk about her devoted friends, but she knew it was talk, we knew it was talk, we each knew the other knew it was talk.

I watched Paul absorbed in the performance. Talk about neglected children, we hardly had time for ours anymore. My mother, fighting for our attention, was like having another child in the house. Everything was my mother. Ethel had to postpone a conference with Paul's advisor—my mother. She could not go shopping with Steven—my mother. Anything she required took precedence over anybody else's needs. Which was only logical. We could wait; she could not.

We were fortunate with our children. They cared, they were thoughtful. Steven was always cheerful. He found the humor in life. And Paul could be a charmer when he wanted to. Friends moaned about children on drugs, getting drunk in the village, dropping out of school. The Lianettis' older son was seeing a psychiatrist. The Lazars' boy was big on Arab rights. Anthea Hopkins's daughter had not spoken to her mother in two years, other than a yes or a no. We were lucky with our boys. We had forced them into no molds, handed them no ready-made ambitions and failure traps. Our feelings had been to let them grow and reach for the sun in their own fashion. And enjoy discovering the results. The result was that they were far more adult than I when it came to dealing with my mother.

Ethel came into the bedroom, carrying a glass of orange juice and a book. She tensed as she saw Paul on the bed. "There isn't any place in this house I can be," she said. "Except in the kitchen. Working." She was still in her travel agency pants suit, having rushed, as she did every day, straight from work to the kitchen to prepare dinner while my mother criticized.

She had earned the right to bathe, to lie in bed, to close a door on demands and assignments. And Paul was entitled to watch television.

"I get the message"—Paul shut off the TV.

"Can't you watch downstairs?" Ethel asked.

"Her dumb game shows?"

"Tell her you want to watch something else."

"Are you kidding?"

"She's lonely," I said. "She might appreciate company."

"Not my company," Paul said. "She hates me."

"Nobody could hate you," I said.

"She does," Paul said.

My mother and Paul fought constantly as she tried to run his life—something for which he considered his parents unqualified, let alone this person claiming to be his grandmother.

"Paul, when are you getting a haircut?" she would ask regularly.

"When are you going to stop telling people how to live?" was a typical answer.

"I'm not telling you how to live," she would reply innocently, "but how can you see me with such long hair?"

"Maybe I don't want to see you."

"Paul, you have to treat me with respect," she would shake her finger. "I'm your grandmother."

"Then act like it," he would reply fearlessly.

She had made it clear to Paul "with the light Christian hair" that he fell disappointingly short of being the princely scholar type she admired. She liked types, not people.

"I'll watch at John's," Paul said, heading out of the bedroom.

"What time will you be back?" I called after him.

"Bernie!" my mother's voice boomed from below.

Paul shrugged and mumbled something.

"Bernie!"

"Don't stay too late," I said, heading anxiously toward the stairs to quell the voice.

"Bernie!" her voice singsonged through the house.

"What do you care how late I stay?" Paul said as he hurried down the stairs. "You don't care about anything else I do."

"Paul!" I shouted after him as he bolted out the front door.

15

"STEVEN!"—her voice caught him the moment he stepped through the front door. "A letter from Israel!"

She waved an envelope at him from her bed.

He smiled at her childlike eagerness. He enjoyed her. He would miss her when she left. A sensitive boy who knew the pain of being a stranger as we moved from community to community, and to another country and back, he understood her plight. Without being asked, Steven looked for ways to make her life easier. He had a friend with a live-in grandmother, but she had just been rushed to the hospital. He asked around but failed to find other people her age. Not that she would have rushed to meet them. "The way I look?" she would say. "Wait, wait till I'm a somebody again."

"From your cousins"—she held the envelope toward him.

Noticing the telephone receiver off the hook, dislodged again by the pile of debris on her table, he quickly replaced it, thankful for catching it before I did, preventing another reign of terror. It was one of the things she did that happened too often to be accidental. She dropped things, she spilled things, she upset things without the slightest concern.

"What difference does it make?" she glanced at the phone. "They'll call back."

He took the letter and the snapshots that fell out of the envelope.

"My glasses!" she cried. "A curse on them!"

She poked wearily at her bedding and the chaos on the table, shrieking with delight as Steven produced them from somewhere. "You're a regular detective!" she cried. "If I ever get lost I'll know who to ask to find me."

Patient to the point of saintliness, Steven spent more time with her than anyone else in our family. He found her comical. Her two names (Raskin and Sloan), her two Social Security numbers (wasn't that illegal?), her tangled bank accounts, her indifference to rules and forms, her constant battle against a world trying to bend her to its desires rather than accommodate itself to her. She might not like the idea, he thought, but she was very much like Paul, the two of them liking not liking.

Steven, who was born wise, accepted the fact, as I could not, that there was no changing her. She had no intention of giving an inch, no matter how weak, sick, or dependent she was. Nothing was going to change her conviction that it was we who should be adjusting to her, not she to us. She was Mother and Grandmother, she was *Entitled*.

She promptly sabotaged the file cabinet he had painstakingly set up for her, jamming the drawers with her boxes of opened envelopes, continuing to stuff new mail into more boxes, which she stuffed under her bed. It drove me wild. He found it funny.

Without Steven, she declared, she would be lost.

So would we all.

The exact opposite of his younger brother, who thrived on being surrounded by his peers, Steven grew up preferring the company of adults to children. As a child he opted for a good discussion with grownups over the giggles and screams of moppets. There was always a mature quality about him. Once at a birthday party for four-year-olds, as the two finalists were about to circle the last remaining chair in a game of musical chairs, Steven called out for them to stop and shake hands and both be winners. Four years old.

One of Steven's close friends had been Mr. Barry down the

block, a man in his eighties. The two had long discussions. "He's a remarkable boy," Mr. Barry told me not long before he died. "He has more brains than most adults. You don't find many youngsters who would spend time with an old man. He's my best friend in Larchmont."

Although Steven never displayed the slightest interest in candy or toys, he did his part and went out trick-or-treating, providing me with a bagful of candy to raid during the months after Halloween.

"See how they want me?" Nana beamed. "Isn't it a beautiful letter?"

Steven found his grandmother from afar an endless source of surprise—a novelty in Larchmont where the few available grandmothers lived in stately apartment buildings and went on cruises. Suddenly his grandmother was the most important person in the house. A word from her could send his mother into tears, his father into rage. And, he suspected, she knew it. A look from her could turn on the juice that would get them all screaming at each other. "You have to argue sometime," she joked with him, "or life would be boring."

It intrigued him that she could talk without the slightest hesitation about all the people who loved her, as if it were an acknowledged fact that she was the most fascinating topic in the world. He wished he felt that positive about himself.

"Read it," she urged. "Your cousins."

They were people who had invited him for dinner on his trip to Israel, the trip Nana sponsored and now regretted. "Other boys go to Israel," she said, "they can't wait to go back. Some want to live there."

He made the mistake of saying he preferred Rome, a part of the youth tour. Tact was not his strong point. Truth was. He had not developed the art of saying the right thing.

"Isn't it a miracle," she cried, "what the Jews did? They took the desert and made it bloom, did you see?"

Everything she did, he learned, had a motive. She sent him to Israel so he would return a Jew. It was an investment, like her stocks.

"Isn't it beautiful how they miss me?" she said as he struggled to read the handwriting. "I can't wait to go back to Israel. I know all the important people there. They're counting the days till I come."

According to his psychology class, people who had to keep telling you how much they were liked really believed they were not liked. Yet she received letters from everywhere. People really did write that they loved her and missed her. "To know you is to love you, Dora darling," a friend wrote from California.

"If people don't like you," she lectured Steven, the only member of our household to take her words seriously, "you're a nobody. You have to use psychology with people. Tell them what they want to hear even if you don't mean it. Believe me, I know people. I have experience."

Which was not, unfortunately, her attitude in our house. But she had to take a break from performing. And we did not count. As she said, "Your family has to take you in whether they like you or not." Which gave us the privilege of hearing her real feelings. Feelings her "condition" allowed her to express with impunity.

She told Steven that he was exactly like me when I was young. Serious. Quiet. Handsome. The best grades. Won every award. "And look what he did with his life," she added.

Steven got the message.

"I sent him to Stanford, the best college . . ."

It occurred to Steven that if I had done anything different with my life, he would never have been born. A sacrifice Nana was more than willing to make in exchange for other benefits.

She told him of all the heiresses I dated at Stanford. "He could have had any one of them by snapping his fingers," she said. "And now I would have a place to lay my head."

But she had a place, Steven told her.

"What are you talking about?" she replied, taking back her letter. She told him how hard it must be for me to associate with Ethel's parents; I with my Stanford education merited the great and the powerful, not mere people. He told her that he never heard me complain. "He's too refined," she answered, "but, believe me, inside it's eating his heart out."

She told Steven what personality changes she would like to see him put into effect. She knew people, she knew what was best for them. "I used to tell your father, and I'm telling you—I'm the best friend you'll ever have."

"Your father never listened to me either," she said. "I kept telling him what to do—to smile, stop being so serious; people don't like someone who's always serious. You think he listened? He wouldn't change if you killed him. No matter how much I told him. Maybe just because I told him."

Steven smiled. At seventy, or whatever her age was today, she was beginning to learn a few facts of life.

"Look what happened to me," she said. "Like the atom bomb hit. You work, you slave, you try to save a little something so you can enjoy life someday, and what's the result?"

The future. She was always saving for the future.

"I was on top of the world. I ask you, does it pay to be born? When you see all the suffering in the world? We used to hide from the Cossacks. You could hear them coming on their horses maybe a hundred miles away, like thunder. They came through like a tornado and did whatever they wanted. They killed, they stole, they tortured—who was going to stop them? I saw their horses jump on a Jewish baby; they smashed its head, a Jewish baby, and they made the parents apologize for letting the baby make the horse stumble. What was a Jewish baby—nothing!

"Who knows," she laughed, "maybe they were right. In Europe nobody made a fuss over children. Another mouth to feed. I was on my own from the time I was born. Toys? Who had toys? Doctors? You had to be ninety-percent dead before anyone would spend the money. Five years old I was working. I fed the chickens, I picked berries, I milked cows. Late at night I used to go into the woods all alone and pick berries, and I wasn't scared. And if I was, would it make any difference? Was I going to refuse? When I was a little girl, maybe six years old, I used to go to the market and sell what we grew—all around me they were big people, but I knew how to weigh and how to figure out so nobody could take advantage of me. Six years old, did you ever hear of such a thing? Here at six they play with twenty-dollar dolls. If they can read a few words people think they're geniuses. I read, I counted, I did business, and nobody ever praised me for it.

"Six brothers, and I had to take charge. I was the businessman in the family. They left it all to me. They knew I would get the best price."

A story she loved to tell and tell again was the time she took a basket of eggs to sell to the German officers during the occupation of her town in World War I.

"People warned me not to go. 'They'll kill you, the Germans; who knows what they'll do to a little girl?' But I went anyhow—what could I do, we needed the money."

She went straight to their headquarters.

"The Germans started to laugh when they saw me. 'Don't you know we're the enemy,' they said. You know what I told them? 'I don't have any enemies,' I said, 'and if you want to be my friends you can buy my eggs.'

"They took me right to the commanding officer," she laughed. "He asked if I wasn't afraid of him. 'Why should I be afraid of you,' I asked him. 'You aren't going to hurt me.'

"They could have taken the eggs from me," she said. "Who was going to stop them? But they took a liking to me. You know how much they gave me for the eggs? Maybe a hundred times what they were worth. It was enough to buy food for a week for our whole family. Would you believe it? Maybe I was ten years old."

To the Jews, she said, the Germans were like the Messiah had come. After the Czar and the pogroms, they wished the Germans would stay forever. It was when they left that their problems started. "We ran from our house, we hid in the forest. One day we were hiding from the White Russians, the next from the Bolsheviks. We didn't know who to hide from next.

"Hungry? I know what it's like to be hungry. People would murder you for a piece of black bread. My brother's belly was swollen like he was pregnant."

And we were upset that she hid stale bread in napkins in her drawers, behind books on the shelves, in her suitcases.

Her father, she shook her head sadly, came to America and went back. To Hitler's ovens. He tried being a pedlar, she said, but it wasn't his line. Every time he started up the stairs in a building he met another pedlar already coming down. Other pedlars worked hard, built department stores, they became millionaires. Barry Goldwater's grandfather. "But your great-grandfather was too refined.

"You have to push a little if you're going to get anywhere," she said. "There's such a thing as being too polite. Polite people went to the gas chambers."

She could not understand why everybody was so anxious to go to Europe. "I was already there," she said. "I couldn't wait to get out. There isn't any place in the world like America. America has everything. Anybody can become something. You have to come from someplace else to appreciate it."

All her life she would not let anyone stop her from doing what she wanted to do. The Bolsheviks. The people who ran the steamship lines. The inspectors at Ellis Island. One wrong word, they sent you back. You had to know how to answer their questions. They tried to trick you. Who was going to be responsible for you? How old were you? Was anyone ever sick in the family? Tell them the truth, they shipped you back like defective merchandise, rotten potatoes. It wasn't true only on Ellis Island, she said. It was life. The world was full of people who tried to trick her and send her back. But she was smarter than every one of them.

Her stories were better than school history. She was there. She saw German soldiers. Cossacks. And she survived. Steven loved hearing them. All her stories had a common moral: success in spite of all obstacles. She had learned to listen to no one but herself. "Everyone is quick to tell you not to do something," she said. "But you have to listen to yourself. It looks like I could do whatever I decided," she smiled proudly.

He listened thoughtfully to her words. She was clearly no ordinary grandmother—she was a fighter. He admired her. She might be crude, she might have the wrong values, but she knew how to fight for herself.

"I'm not ready to leave the world yet," she told Steven. "I have to see you graduate from high school, and college, and get married to a nice girl. I have to dance at your wedding."

Steven shifted nervously. A scientist, he had read about myeloma—he knew her chances. "Steven is the only one who understands my condition," she often said. He seemed to know what she was going to say before she said it. He anticipated her reactions. It was understandable that *I* might, but Steven? Between them there was an unspoken connection, a mystic bond that went far back into genetic history. People used to say he looked like me, but handsomer. Now they said he looked like her.

"So how about taking me for a walk?" she said. "Wait, I'll put something on so I'll look beautiful."

Steven stepped to the kitchen to grab a quick yogurt. He had a mountain of work to do. Taking three advanced-placement courses was no breeze. And he had to compile a stack of evidence for the next debate—Bronx High School of Science. Whoever said New York schools had collapsed ought to tackle that one. He noticed an undetermined liquid on the floor. Grabbing a sponge, he quickly cleaned it up. One thing less to provoke an argument later.

"Is it all right to go like this?" she asked, standing in the doorway in her housecoat over her nightgown. She asked the same question each time they set forth. "Who'll see me?" she answered herself. "Nobody comes out of their houses in Larchmont. It's too high class."

Taking his arm, she beamed up at her prince as they inched out the door.

"You're walking a lot better," Steven said. He could always have the yogurt later.

"I have to dance at your wedding," she said.

"You will," he answered.

"We're just like the Odd Couple." She laughed as they shuffled along the sidewalk, she in her dressing gown, clutching his arm, he guiding her gently.

16

MONEY.

How did you bring it up?

In our case, with guilt.

Money was very important to my mother. Spend money on her, it meant you loved her. Lavish anything else on her—your time, your labor, your concern—it meant nothing.

Expenses leapt with her arrival. We hired Angelina, our weekly cleaning woman, to come a second day a week to clean my mother. That was an extra thirty dollars. Bathing my mother took hours. With the boys' help, Angelina managed to get my mother in and out of the tub, a procedure involving much shrieking and covering with towels. "Like a hippopotamus," my mother described the event. "She needs a crane to lift me." In the time left over, Angelina took care of my mother's other personal needs and scoured her room and bath, once easy rooms that were now desperate for attention. My mother's bathroom habits were not the most hygienic (was it age, illness, or indifference?), and her room with its hidden crusts of bread and sticky dishes had begun to attract ants.

Not even two days of Angelina was sufficient once my mother captured her. When Ethel appeared unexpectedly on either day she found Angelina preparing tea for my mother or brushing her hair.

"She insisted," my mother said. "I told her not to bother with me, your house needs attention, but she said she couldn't neglect me. It shows what a fine character she has. She says she wants to come and work for me when I get my apartment. But don't worry," she smiled slyly, "I won't take her from you."

My mother had a number of bank accounts, all in Arizona or in California, where she formerly summered. Steven took her into town to transfer her accounts into local banks. The moment she received a dividend or Social Security check she rushed Steven with the money into the savings bank so as not to lose a minute's interest. "What do I need with cash?" she said. "Where am I going?"

At the doctor's office she never had cash or the right checkbook. Ethel paid, and my mother made no offer to reimburse her, telling her not to worry, "I'm good for it." Prescriptions from the drugstore were charged to our account, and I paid for her drugs that I picked up in a discount store in the city (the five-dollar pills at our folksy local pharmacy cost two dollars on Forty-sixth Street). She kept telling us of friends whose children were so devoted they would not take a penny from their parents.

Another standard to meet in the love-thy-parent department.

It was not that we were poor. I would have supported her gladly if she needed it, but she hardly needed it. She had stock dividends, bank interest, and $445 a month of untaxed Social Security after

Medicare fees. She had no rent to pay, no expenses. Ours went merrily on—mortgage payments, climbing taxes, food bills, utilities—and two sons destined for college. It had not exactly helped to be unemployed for a year.

Not that she had not been generous. Savings bonds for the boys, bank accounts tucked away "for college." But the expenses were *now*, the struggle with the bank account was now.

One day, as the bills mounted, I asked if she would like to pay her expenses.

"I didn't know you were so broke," she said, her face tightening.

"If you can't," I said, after explaining our expenses, "you don't have to."

"Who needs Angelina for an extra day?" she said. "It's Ethel who needs her."

"Bathing you takes three hours," I said.

"I suppose you don't need her to clean your house?"

"We managed for years with once a week."

"Still, it's nice to have her twice a week."

"Look, if you can't pay . . ."

"Don't put up such a show," she said. "I know why you brought me here."

"Why did I bring you here?" I bit, knowing she was provoking another fight, unable to resist the red handkerchief.

"Don't act so innocent," she cried.

"Why do you think I brought you here?" I demanded.

"I think plenty," she answered, shaking her head from side to side. "Too much."

Often I wished she had nothing. It would have been one less issue. I would rather have a mother than a queen. I would rather have a mother who became part of our home than "royalty" standing apart, to whom we were expected to pay homage. But she did have money and, like it or not, it was a factor that never left the relationship. It managed to come up in some way every day, always with an implied threat—displease her and the sword would drop.

She was big on royal terminology. Steven was her prince, Raskin a king, and when someone plumped her pillows she said a queen did not have it better. Among the few non–Jewish-centered books she owned were *The Woman I Love* and an autobiography of Rose

Kennedy, of the American royal family. It did not occur to my mother that queens paid for royal treatment. The palace staff did not work for free.

"How much do you want?" she cried. One of the players had stopped playing her game. "I only sent you to the best school in the country. I only sent thousands of dollars into this house. But parents to children aren't like children to parents. A child can always go to his mother, but let a mother go to her child . . ."

Where did she think she was?

Who did she think was fighting to save her life?

Wasn't she supposed to help?

"Look," I said, "if you don't want to, if you can't, it really doesn't matter. We have more than enough."

"I'll write you a check!" she cried. "Don't worry, I'm good for it. But not now. Not now. I don't have the strength to pick up a pen."

"Anytime," I said.

She smiled grimly, her eyes narrowing. In spite of everything, her face was still pretty, still surprisingly sparkling. "Why did I let you take me away from Arizona?" she said. "Why did I let you bring me here?"

What had we done to her, I wondered, that was so awful?

"You want to go back, I'll take you," I said.

"How can I? You gave away everything."

"You have more than enough. I'll take you back, back to Dr. Greenstone."

"That murderer!" she screamed. "He ruined my life!"

"Maybe your friends can find you a better doctor and someone to stay with you."

"I don't need anyone," she screamed.

"All the better," I said, wondering why a woman who needed no one required a staff to serve her day and night. Why a woman who needed no one was unable to pour herself a glass of milk or make a sandwich or wash a dish.

"Don't be in such a rush to get rid of me," she cried.

"You were the one who said you were sorry you came."

"Don't aggravate me!" she cried.

"Then stop telling us how you're sorry you left all your devoted friends. I don't see your friends taking care of you now. I didn't see any of them doing anything for you, except Pearl. Let's see them take you into their house and find you a doctor and take you every other week. Let's see them provide you with the special foods you can't live without. I'll be happy to give them the chance."

"Don't aggravate me!" she howled. "I'll give you the money."

I wanted to apologize. I was ashamed. Our anger was tearing the house apart. Somewhere my boys were listening. But I was helpless. The simplest discussion, the most reasonable request always turned into a raging fight. Finally she agreed to give us a monthly check for Angelina and living expenses. She still managed to be penniless at the doctor, finding it sweeter to show "them" that Ethel was paying for her. Later she reimbursed us, always paying me, never Ethel. She liked to make everything involving money complicated, giving it the importance it deserved.

One day she said she wanted to make a will. She had one in Arizona, but the rules changed from state to state. I took her to a friend who was exactly her kind of lawyer. Tall, lean, distinguished. Cal Lipson and his wife, Leah, lived a few blocks from us in a white colonial with powder blue rugs, hutches, dry sinks, and a mezuzah on the door.

"Such a lovely home," she smiled at Cal and Leah, giving them her royal nod. She made a great fuss over lamps and vases, praising their good taste, which she never did in our house.

Her chief concern was that Ethel receive nothing, her second that her grandchildren get something, her third that some money go to a worthwhile organization in Israel that would put up a plaque in her memory, her fourth that taxes be avoided. Cal solved everything.

She would leave half her estate to me, the other half as a trust to the boys with the income going to me as long as I lived. The trust would be taxed only once, now, but not when it passed completely into the boys' hands later. Cal and I would be the executors of the boys' trust, satisfying the legal requirement that there be two executors, one not related to the boys. My mother named a distant cousin in the Bronx to succeed me as co-executor if I died before the boys were of age. She was adamant that Ethel have no part in managing the boys' trust. "Who knows," she said, "she could take their money and buy herself another husband."

After investigating, Cal reported that the tax problems of a gift to Israel would be so complex, it would be wiser to give the money to a Jewish organization in the United States. She settled on Teller. Provided, of course, she got her plaque.

Cal asked, tactfully, if she would like to give me what was known as power of attorney, which was the authority to sign checks for her and handle her finances on the remote possibility that she was unable to. It was a matter of signing a form, which he could notarize, and submitting copies to banks and brokers.

Quick to detect the suspicion in her face, he hurriedly said that he had it for both his "mothers" but, knock wood, never had to use it. She liked that. He gave "knock wood" a Jewish inflection, giving the impression he was uttering a Jewish phrase, of which he knew none.

He suggested alternatives to the foreboding power of attorney, such as bank forms that would give me access to her account at that bank only. It might also be a good idea to make me a co-owner of her safe-deposit box. He spoke very cautiously, as if sizing up a judge, aware that he was venturing into dangerous waters.

Giving me some form of power of attorney would have made her life infinitely easier. I would have taken on her banking, her books, her tax records, sparing her the effort that grew more burdensome as her illness grew worse—torture when the drugs simmered inside her. But I was not about to run to her to have every check signed, studied, questioned. I had another life.

She went so far as to have Steven get forms from the banks but signed nothing. "What's the rush?" she asked. "I'm not going anywhere."

Did she really think I was going to cash in her stocks and fly to Bimini? Did she have so low an opinion of herself as a mother, and me as a son, that she believed I brought her to our house for her bank accounts? Did she honestly believe she had raised an unfeeling stranger?

Me? Her son? The boy who ran home from school eager to show her his report card and see her face light up? The boy who worked gladly in the store, the three of us, together? We were not one of those families whose father disappeared all day, his function being to bring back money for the rest of the family to spend. From an early age I knew exactly what my father did to earn a living. And what my mother did. It was what we all did. It was something we shared. Our store. Even when I was a child my opinions were given serious consideration. I had an artistic sense—I became the window decorator. Our lives wove in and out of the store. I knew when the store was doing well, and when it was not, and adjusted my needs to it. As a child I made deliveries in a wagon, which I proudly pulled up and down the neighborhood blocks. Later I graduated to a panel truck.

And after all that, she trusted me no more than she did the rest of the world.

I told her I wished she spent every penny of her money on herself.

"There would be nothing left for you," she said.

"Worry about yourself," I said. "I'll manage."

"I know bettter," she said, and smiled knowingly.

She always knew better.

Cal sent her the will, which she read carefully and put in her safe-deposit box. She never opened the bill he sent her, stuffing the sealed envelope in one of her shoe boxes.

17

PRISS SAILED OUT OF THE AGENCY for her lunch-hour tennis game, Marlene sped over to Bloomingdale's, and Ethel rushed home to give my mother her chemotherapy pills, stopping on the way to pick up a few things my mother required for survival—farmer's cheese, rye bread, borscht.

"Can't you just call her to remind her?" Priss asked. "Set the pills out for her in the morning in a saucer."

"Like a cat," Marlene said.

Ethel had tried that route. But my mother either did not answer the phone (why should she, she knew it was not for her, not during prime time) or, if she did, she moaned that the pills confused her and without Ethel she would not know what to do first.

"If she didn't have you running over there," Marlene said, "you can bet your sweet ass she'd know what to do."

But what if she didn't, Ethel thought. What if she really was confused and made a mistake? Or spilled them all and missed a treatment? The woman had cancer; it was not too much to ask.

In Ethel's family the young always looked after the old, not as an onerous duty but as part of the natural course of life. Parents looked after children; children looked after parents. Ethel grew up in a big house in Brooklyn that included four generations who gave to each other. Only when her great-grandmother's eyesight failed in her nineties did she cease to do the family's sewing.

Ethel's great-grandmother, also named Ethel, kept a trunk in her room filled with treasures from which she gave Ethel gifts. When the trunk was opened after the old woman's death, they found a letter written two days before she died. She asked them to love one another.

And now there was another old woman lying in bed in her house. A woman who reacted to kindness with anger. Ethel understood, perhaps too much. She felt for her. Alone, in pain, once fiercely independent, now almost helpless, her rage was understandable. It was also understandable that in time it would subside, as she learned to trust us.

Unlike so many people, Ethel was accustomed to the old, and she was not afraid of sickness. So what if she missed a few tennis games or a Bloomingdale's sale? She had a human life on her hands. And no ordinary life, but the life of her husband's mother, her children's grandmother. She owed the woman something.

"All pills are poison," said Flora-Jean Sweet, the agency owner, an avid Christian Scientist who, nearing seventy, bicycled to work and swam daily laps at the town pool. "All they do is prevent the body from healin' itself," she said. "Why, I'd love to take your mother to church with me sometime. It's faith that heals. You have to let the Almighty do his work without interference."

"I'll tell her, Flora-Jean," Ethel said, dashing out—her quick shopping trip turning into a serious expedition, as usual, as she replaced provisions that disappeared at an alarming rate. Cancer victims supposedly lost their appetites, but my mother was ravenous. She regularly devoured the contents of the refrigerator while claiming that she ate nothing—how could she, there was never anything in the house.

If Ethel was a minute late for lunch, my mother called her at the travel agency, where she might be working with a client on a trip, building up a crucial following.

"Why do you have to work?" she screamed over the phone. "You aren't rich enough? I'll give you the money."

So far, Ethel thought, she was the only one who had done any giving. She had stopped going to travel seminars and to airline and tourist-bureau presentations. She turned down a chance to go to ticketing school. And she regularly rejected "fam" trips—the familiarization trips given travel agents—declining Bermuda, Barbados, and Aruba in order to take care of my mother.

If only once, Ethel wished as she entered the house, my mother would be dressed and out of bed, her teeth brushed, hair combed. But the sound of the television told her exactly where she would find her.

My mother looked up from the bed where she lay, as always, on top of the covers, showing everything through her nightgown to anyone passing through the hallway. At first Paul introduced his friends to her on the way to the kitchen, but now he took the alternate route through the dining room.

"Are you keeping busy, Mrs. Sloan?" Dr. Gordon asked at a recent visit. "I imagine you help do the shopping and help around the house."

"In my condition?" she asked.

"Why, I think you're doing quite nicely," he said. "You've gained weight. That's a good sign. It isn't good to lie in bed too much. You have to build up your muscles."

"Who says I lie in bed?" she glared at Ethel. "Don't worry, I do plenty."

"Make sure she keeps busy," Dr. Gordon told Ethel, privately. "Give her jobs to do."

My mother would die, Ethel knew, before working in her house.

At the sight of Ethel my mother pressed the button on the re-

mote control, shutting off the TV that we had rushed out to pur-
chase on the Saturday when, to my mother's relief, our former TV
died. Her major exercise, next to her occasional walks, was changing channels.

"Did you eat lunch?" Ethel asked from the doorway to the room.
She was supposed to eat before taking her pills; food helped arm
the body against the ravages of the chemicals.

"How could I eat?" my mother asked. "You don't have any food
in the house."

It was what she said every day, and every day Ethel knew from
the trail of sunflower seeds, crumbs, and spilled prune juice that
my mother had spent the morning eating.

As she did every day, Ethel opened the refrigerator and pointed
to the abundance of cottage cheese, cold cuts, eggs, yogurt, sour
cream, vegetables, fruit, milk, juices. And in the cupboards she
showed her again where to find the tuna, salmon, soup. Not to
mention the rye and the pumpernickel bread.

"But you don't have any farmer's cheese," my mother said.

When Ethel offered to share her tuna salad, my mother grimaced
at the thought of mayonnaise and announced she would fix something for herself. Banging, clanking, and dropping, she managed to
stand in front of the drawer when Ethel needed a fork and in front
of the sink when Ethel needed water. She finally expressed a desire
for cream of mushroom soup, but she lacked the strength to open
the can. And she would like it made with milk, if Ethel did not
mind.

When Ethel asked if there had been any calls, my mother said
that the phone had rung but she had not been able to get to the
kitchen to answer it. On being reminded that she had a phone next
to her bed, she cried, "It's a disease!"

Her phone was a raging issue in our house for a week, far out-
weighing in importance my work, Ethel's work, Paul's need for a
tutor for biology, and Steven's concern about colleges.

After she paid eighteen dollars to have a jack installed next to
her bed, I brought up a rarely used phone from the basement,
bought and attached the proper connections, and plugged it in,
saving her a monthly rental fee. "Filthy," she said.

For a week she spoke of nothing but the filthy phone we had given her. It would kill her, she said, before her blood condition. How, she wailed without letup, could we give her such a thing? She was afraid to speak into it.

"So get a rag and clean it!" I cried one night.

She looked at me as if I suggested that she strangle herself with the cord.

"I suppose you want me to scrub your floors too?" she cried.

"Why not?" I said. "Ethel does."

The phone remained dirty until Angelina solved the problem.

While Ethel tried to read her mail at the kitchen table, including a letter that was opened "by mistake," my mother insisted on reading her own mail out loud to show how people loved her. "See how much they miss me?" she said, continuing to talk of the world's devotion to her while Ethel loaded the dishwasher and then unloaded the washing machine in the connecting laundry room, transferring the wash to the dryer. "It's just like a factory in this house with all the machines," my mother said. One time she said she would be glad to help but she was afraid she would break something.

Once she caught Ethel using paper napkins that were hers. When my mother's boxes came from Arizona to be stored in our attic, I brought down napkins, toilet tissue, and paper towels, of which she had enough to stock a supermarket and which were not the safest items to keep in an attic. That night I took it all back up to join her stacks of aluminum foil, Nestlé's Quik, coffee, and the innumerable packages of sheets that she was saving for guests who would never appear.

"Who needs guests?" she often said. "I should wait on them, clean up their mess? Let them stay in a hotel."

What did she think we were doing for her?

Finished loading machines, Ethel counted the pills into a saucer.

"What kind of pills are those?" my mother asked.

Ethel looked at her. "The ones you take every day."

"Are you sure?" my mother asked, her mouth twisting in a thin, tight smile.

"It tells you on the labels," Ethel said. "See? Prednisone. Alkeran."

"Who can read such small print?" my mother said.

Ethel placed a glass of water on the counter next to the pills and opened the Mylanta.

"Why are you so anxious for me to take them?"—my mother's voice tightened.

Ethel glanced anxiously at the kitchen clock. A client was due in ten minutes. My mother's eyes narrowed, her fists clenched. "Are you sure these are Dr. Gordon's pills?" she screamed.

Ethel backed away.

"How do I know what pills you put in the bottle?" she cried.

"They're your regular pills," Ethel insisted.

"Why did you bring me here?" my mother screamed.

"To save your life," Ethel cried.

"I don't need you to save my life!" my mother howled. "God will save my life. I know people. Don't put up such a show. I know why you brought me here." Ethel backed away, my mother following her, fists shaking. "You think I don't know what you want from me? You think I don't know what's going on here?"

"Nothing's going on here," Ethel cried.

"Don't think you can fool me," my mother laughed. "My mind is still good. Better than you want it to be."

"Nobody's trying to fool you."

"I know plenty!" my mother cried. "Oh, do I know plenty. Where are my pills?"

Ethel slipped out of the kitchen.

"I want the real pills!" she cried after her, sweeping the saucer and pills off the counter, crashing to the floor. "I want the pills from Dr. Gordon!"

How long, how long, Ethel cried out loud, speeding away in the car as my mother stood in the doorway in her nightgown, shaking her fists and screaming.

18

ONE DAY MY MOTHER, beaming and full of energy, drew herself up to her full five feet and astounded us with the announcement that she wished to make her famous barley soup for us. No ordinary soup would this be, but her very special barley soup. A soup for which kings would give up empires. Lucky for Wally Simpson, my mother declared, that she got to Edward before my mother with her soup. "Except *I* would never let him give up the throne," she grinned. "England would have to take us both, like it or not."

I remembered my mother's barley soup from childhood. It was good soup, as I recalled, but it had not brought emissaries from Campbell's waving contracts. I remembered sitting at the kitchen table, doing my homework, while my mother hovered over an enormous kettle, stirring and sipping with a giant wooden spoon. Sometimes, when it was the slow season in the store and my mother's presence was not vital, she would immerse herself in the old-fashioned kitchen and wondrous creations would emerge from the stove on the spindly legs. There was her potato pudding and her apple cake, light-years ahead of mere apple pie. Sometimes an enormous sponge cake would arrive at the table. Or a chewy nut cake. Or a rich brown honey cake. And, of course, barley and pea soups whose aroma, alone, would bring the neighbors running if she were not so careful about locking the door.

It was no easy matter, making famous barley soup. It required an array of ingredients that were, naturally, not in the house. Someone had to get them. Ethel. A task that Ethel took on eagerly, thrilled at any hint that my mother was trying to help, ready to join the family rather than play the honored guest.

For days my mother devoted herself to creating her masterpiece. She could be found at all hours stationed in the kitchen—dicing, peeling, paring, soaking, simmering, sipping, presiding over a host of mysterious processes. She interrupted her work for teaser announcements. "Wait till you taste it," she predicted. "You'll collapse." She recited lists of guests who had not been able to contain their enthusiasm after one taste. "But don't like it too much," she warned, "because you'll want me to make it all the time."

She was making enough, she said, to feed the Russian army. It would last us for weeks. We could substitute it for all our meals, it was so nourishing.

Sometimes Steven or Paul sat in the kitchen and watched her, as I once did. We gathered secretly in other rooms to whisper our amazement and delight. Where had this new woman come from? It was as if a spell had been broken, the frog turning into a prince again. She hummed as she worked, sending joy through the house. Too bad my father had not been able to run the store without her. I might have had a lot more barley soup.

"He's a prince, your father," she used to say. "He isn't the type to weigh nails." But my mother weighed them—as well as cut linoleum and mixed paint. She was a man's equal long before it was the thing to be. And she was a natural salesperson, charming customers with compliments, joking with them, playing with their children, making up facts as needed, often lowering her voice and cutting the price, "because you're a regular customer, but don't tell anybody. If we gave it to everybody at that price we couldn't stay in business."

"Your mother knows how to twist people around her little finger," my father was fond of saying.

Although my mother was rarely at home like the mothers of other children, I never felt deprived. It was the other children who were missing out. They did not have a store to go to after school. I was needed. I ran errands, I watched for thievery, and, if there were no customers in sight, I played catch with my father out in front. What other boy in elementary school learned to assemble bicycles and wagons or cut and thread pipe? At Christmas I was put in charge of the Christmas tree light counter, testing and selling bulbs to the lines that sometimes stretched out to the street—we undersold the nearby dime store. I might have been ten years old. Nights, the shade with the "Closed" sign drawn over the door, I often watched my mother and father hovering over the big brass cash register, tallying the day's receipts, swelling with pride when they came upon a big sale I had made.

Christmas was the time of the year for which the rest of the year was a prelude. In the middle of the summer my parents took me to the wholesaler on a Sunday to order the toys they would stock for Christmas. A few months later they put up the Christmas shelves— floor-to-ceiling shelves designed to display the toys and games. And then the crowds came. My parents hired extra help in addition to the one or two steady clerks. Sometimes I was pressed into service from the Christmas tree light counter to advise baffled parents on what a child my age would like to find under the tree. I was the authority. It was not until the slow winter months after Christmas, when people bought only snow shovels, that my mother could get to her barley soup.

And now it was finished.

Out came the soup dishes, the spoons. We lined up with great ceremony at the huge kettle, dipping ladles and babbling about the tantalizing aroma. We carried our portions reverently into the dining room where my mother watched anxiously while we sipped.

"Didn't I tell you?" she cried before we had a chance to comment. "Isn't it delicious?"

"It's all right," Paul said.

Her face dropped. "What do you mean, all right?" she said, glaring at him.

We all rushed in to assure her that it was delicious, that Paul was teasing.

"You really like it?" she asked, still eyeing Paul with something less than pleasure.

"Love it," we insisted.

"Not bad," Paul grinned.

"In the best restaurants," she proclaimed, "you wouldn't find soup like this. Not for all the money in the world."

We unanimously agreed that never in all our culinary adventures had we encountered anything that came close.

"You see, Ethel," my mother beamed, "you aren't the only good cook in the house."

"I like your mother," Ethel said that night. "I think she's beginning to like me."

"She can be a charmer when she wants to," I said.

"No, I think she means it," Ethel said. "I think that deep down she really likes me. It might kill her to admit it, but I think she really does."

It was the last time my mother made her famous barley soup.

19

I AWAKENED at the sound of the crash.

Dreading the worst, I jumped out of bed, threw on a robe, and raced down the stairs. "The thing you have to worry about is her falling," the doctor said. "She could end up with a dozen broken bones."

I found her standing in her nightgown in the center of the room, looking like a ghost in the flickering light of the TV. It was three o'clock in the morning. At her feet lay the New Guinea mask, shattered.

"It isn't my fault," she cried. "It fell."

"By itself?" I asked. The hook was firmly in place in the wall, the wire still attached to the mask. "It fell off the wall by itself?"

"It slipped out of my hands," she said.

"What were you doing with it?"

"I was only trying to move it," she said. "Who can stand to look at such a scary thing in the middle of the night?"

Her world was populated by scary things. People, animals, shadows, darkness, silence. "Why didn't you ask?" I cried at her.

"Who should I ask?" she cried back.

"Who do you think?"

"You were sleeping," she shouted.

"We weren't sleeping all day. You had all day to ask. Weeks!"

"Ask who?" she cried. "Who do I have to do anything for me?"

Her eyes flashed past me to Ethel standing behind me in her robe.

Several nights before it had been the television blaring. Other nights she slammed doors or dropped the toilet seat, claiming it was not her fault that everything in our house was so hard. The doors, the windows, the faucets, the casement windows—like a jail, she said.

"Don't worry," she screamed, "I'll buy you another one."

"We brought it from Australia," I said.

"So I'll go to Australia. I'll go everywhere."

On the television screen Greta Garbo lay coughing on her chaise, smiling bravely at Robert Taylor on his knees beside her. The television was on day and night. She never slept.

Ethel brought in a dustpan and swept up the pieces.

"It's not such a big deal," my mother said. "Who can stand such an ugly thing?"

I told her that we happened to like it.

"I'm surprised that college-educated people should have such taste," she said. "I like beautiful things. I like natural beauty." She looked at me, her eyes narrowing, her throat tightening. "Oh, I can't wait to get out of here!" she cried.

"Any time!" I cried back.

"I can't wait to have my own place!" she went on. "I always hated favors. I always liked privacy; now everybody knows my business! Once people had to call before they could see me. Now everyone just opens the door. Oh, I'll kiss the bare floors, as long as they're my own. And don't think you'll be able to see me so easy. You'll have to call and get an invitation!"

I understood her plight, but that did not make her outbursts any easier to bear. I knew that I should be rational and patient and understanding, but when she screamed I screamed back. It was not easy being awakened regularly in the middle of the night, to be chronically tense from fatigue, to come home every day to a house filled with screaming. It was no pleasure having someone in your house smoldering because you did not change your way of living to please her.

She stopped screaming when she saw Steven standing in the doorway in his pajamas. He was the one person who was able to calm her. We looked at him, embarrassed. Three adults. He had an exam tomorrow, he said, apologetically. How many nights, I wondered, had he lain in bed, listening to the angry voices, wishing he were somewhere else?

Suddenly my mother looked pathetically tiny, small, shrunken, barely five feet tall, a wounded animal encircled by giants, fighting for its life. The chemotherapy alters the mind, the doctor said. It can drive you crazy, a friend put it more succinctly. It seemed to intensify my mother's feelings. Always emotional, she had become highly emotional. It turned her fears into terror, her suspicions into paranoia, her anger into hysteria.

"I'm going to sleep," I said. "Go to sleep."

"It's easy to say, go to sleep," she said. "Who can sleep with pain?"

"Where?" I was alarmed. She had been getting better. The pain had almost disappeared, she reported. But that was several days ago.

"My arm," she said. "I pulled too hard on the railing."

The disease was spreading.

"I'll get you a pain pill," Ethel said.

My mother glared at her. "She's always ready to get me pills."

"If you're in pain . . ."

"I'll manage," she snarled.

"Dr. Gordon said . . ."

"I know what Dr. Gordon said," she cried, tears streaming down her cheeks. "Who can live on pills? I want the pain should go away by itself. Steven, would you please get me a glass of water?" She would take the pill later, alone. She did not need an audience for her misery.

"Maybe," Ethel said, "if you did more during the day you'd be more tired at night."

"What do you want me to do—mop your floors?" she stormed at Ethel. "I sent thousands of dollars into this house." Clutching the bedrail, she eased herself back into the bed, lowering herself onto the pile of pillows. "Maybe I will have a pain pill," she said, her voice suddenly thin and frail as she lay limp. "Steven?"

"Steven has an exam tomorrow," Ethel interrupted.

Glaring, my mother took her pill from Ethel.

I shut off the TV as we left, leaving her door half-open behind us, the light on in the hall. As we reached the top of the stairs the TV went on.

"She isn't the only one who needs a pill," Ethel said as she opened the Valium bottle next to her bed.

"How many have you had?" I accused.

"You brought her to me," Ethel said.

The second half of the horror show was starting.

"Why do you have to keep giving in to her?" I said. "Where is it written that my mother must be given whatever she wants?"

"All I want is a night's sleep," Ethel said, downing the pill. "And maybe a day to myself. Some day."

It was our nightly torture. Ethel—angry, trapped, not knowing how to break out of it; and I—guilty, not knowing what to do, postponing decisions I was afraid of making. At some time each night we had the same discussion, going around the same circle, ending up where we started. Ethel, free of babies and the need to be home, tasting the thrill of liberation and achievement, had been captured and returned to her cell.

"If she only cared for me," Ethel said. "If she could only bring herself to say thank you."

How long could it go on?

She could live for ten years, she could die tomorrow. People told us the end came fast. People told us that cancer moved slowly in old people. Everyone had a sick-mother story. A mother was clinging to her apartment in Florida, refusing to give up her independence, taken care of by neighbors who had formed a mutual aid society. A mother had been tricked into a nursing home. A mother was attached to a hospital machine for three months. My mother looked remarkably well. She was gaining weight, her complexion was pink, she walked without her cane in the house. She had a fifty percent chance, said Dr. Gordon in one of his midnight phone calls, of being in her new apartment in a few months.

But how would we survive those few months?

The patient was improving, the family was collapsing.

"Maybe she can get her own apartment now," I said, as I said every night.

"She can't take care of it," Ethel said, as she said nightly.

"Let her get someone," I said. "Like other people do. She has money." There was Mrs. Barry down the block who managed for years with a series of housekeepers and a lung machine.

"Mrs. Barry was part of the community," Ethel said, as if I did not know what she was going to say. "She had her home, her friends nearby. Children. The priest used to visit her. Your mother doesn't know anyone. She needs us for everything. She belongs in a home."

"Did you see on television, they showed how old people are treated in nursing homes?" my mother asked when I was packing in her apartment. "Would you believe children should do such a thing to their parents?"

"I'll check into homes," I told Ethel.

"We can't drag her screaming into one," Ethel said.

Stalemate again.

"I'll call Dr. Gordon tomorrow," I said.

It always ended with my declaration of calling Dr. Gordon. As if he would have the answer.

Hearing something outside our door, I jumped up and flung it open. I stared at the empty hallway. Stepping into the darkness, I looked down the stairwell. Up came the glow of the hall light and the sound of the television.

We had discovered her hovering outside doorways. We had heard clicks on the telephone, and there were the letters opened "by mistake."

"What was it?" Ethel looked at me from bed.

"Nothing," I said.

"She can't climb the stairs," Ethel said.

But there was nothing to stop her from standing at the bottom of the stairwell. Our upper hallway was built around the stairwell. Her room opened to the hallway below. She had an uncanny sense of hearing, although she could play deaf. Once Ethel and I discussed the possibility of driving Steven to his debate workshop at Harvard and spending the weekend in Boston. Our problem was what to do with my mother. Two evenings later she mentioned that she could ask her cousin from the Bronx to spend the weekend with her if we wanted to go to Boston with Steven. No one had mentioned it to her. When we asked how she knew, she smiled and said that God told her.

As I turned off the light and tried to fall asleep I could feel her presence. Just as she once hovered outside my door after I went to bed, listening for a cough or a cry, I could feel her presence now—

hovering, listening—but now anger and suspicion had replaced love.

"It was in pieces," Ethel whispered in the dark.

"What?" I asked.

"The mask. It was in a hundred pieces. It didn't slip. She threw it."

20

AS WE DROVE UP to the portico of the Naomi Lawson Home, I understood for the first time why some of the old people who are neither infirm nor senile end up in institutions. Contrary to what television specials would have us believe, it is not always their heartless children who put them there. Sometimes they put themselves there.

These are the selfish, demanding elderly who were probably no delight to have around when they were younger and who grow impossible with age. After trying desperately to do "the right thing," their families, unable to take it any longer, begin their search for a suitable home, a search filled with pain and guilt. Yet it is the families who are judged guilty, the elderly the helpless innocents.

While most of the residents of homes undoubtedly have no choice—they have no families or they actually are the victims of callous children—I also suspect that many of the old, like people of all ages, have a hand in writing their own destinies. Those who have given love can expect to get it in return. After all, warm, loving, sharing people are a joy to live with whatever their age.

An awareness that did nothing to lessen the guilt and the pain I felt as I led my mother through the glass doors.

Every night my mother announced that she might be better off someplace else. "Maybe I should go to California," she said.

"If you'd like," I said.

"I have such devoted friends in Santa Monica. There's nothing they wouldn't do for me."

"You're very lucky," I said, determined not to give her the satisfaction of knowing that she was succeeding in her efforts to make
me feel that we were failing her.

Another night it was Florida. Hartford. Detroit. Anywhere was
apparently better than with us. A letter from anyone professing
concern with her condition meant more to her than what we were
actually doing.

"You have left the Jewish faith," she proclaimed one evening,
following me into the living room, clutching a letter. "I heard from
Israel," she announced. "They're begging me to come to them.
They say they have such beautiful places in Israel for old people. I
would be among my own."

Ethel's close friend, Jewish, had married a Catholic man, neither
of them adhering to any religion. After making the obligatory pro-
tests, her mother accepted her son-in-law, loved her grandchildren, and was a part of their lives. Her love for her daughter meant
more to her than her prejudices. But my mother, the fighter, made
no concessions.

"Why go to Israel and give up Dr. Gordon?" I asked my mother.
If she was looking for a place for older people, I was sure they had
them in New York. I thought she wanted to be near her grandchildren.

"Jewish places?" she asked.

"There have to be," I said. "After all, New York."

"Nice places? I must have something nice."

"Why not? All it takes is money."

"Find out for me."

I started making phone calls again.

I was not sure what I was looking for. She was not bedridden;
she did not need nursing attention. She required no bedpans, no
meals in bed. Yet she was sick. She needed assistance. Her pills.
Bath. She might need help if she reacted to the chemotherapy. And
would it be too much to ask for someone to take her to the doctor,
see that she received and took her pills? If not, she had to be close
enough so that Ethel could take her. She had to be close for us to
visit her. Wasn't that the point of bringing her to us?

A renowned home for the aged turned out to require its
"guests" to sign over all their assets, as well as present a doctor's

certificate affirming that they were not sick. What happened, I asked, if a "guest" became ill after entering—not an unlikely possibility considering the age of their guests. The answer—find a nursing home. But who would pay for it, I queried, since the guest had no more assets? Medicaid, they answered. An answer I was to hear often.

I quickly learned about Medicare and Medicaid. They were not, as I had thought, two names for the same thing. Medicare was the federal medical program for people age sixty-five and older. It was paid for by Social Security and covered most, but not all, medical costs. People on Medicare continued to pay a monthly fee for part of the coverage.

Medicaid was run by the states, although much of the money came from the federal government, and was another name for welfare. It paid the medical bills of people of any age who had no money. In addition to its other features, it offered the owners of old-age and nursing homes an ingenious way of confiscating a person's life savings. Once they took everything a patient had, they knew that Medicaid would assume the payments. So they took everything as soon as possible, assured that the money would keep coming.

Neither Medicare nor Medicaid covered homes for the aged, only nursing homes. If you needed what they called "custodial care" you were on your own. That was the category into which my mother and millions of others fell. With a thud.

One of my free-lance clients mentioned a home in which his mother lived in Rockland County. "She hates it," he said. "For $1,600 a month the food's almost edible. But the rooms aren't bad and the staff is civilized."

The staff was important, he said. Sometimes you came across some pretty kinky people working in those homes.

Another friend had an aunt and uncle lucky enough to be Norwegian. They loved their Norwegian Society Home in Brooklyn at $1,800 a month for the two of them after a two-year wait. We also heard of a snappy place in Connecticut for $1,000 a week.

While I searched, the newspapers shrieked of the nursing home owned by a rabbi where the patients lay in their excrement, while the rabbi covered his walls with Picassos.

The Naomi Lawson Home offered hope.

A nearly new building a mile from us, it was reputed to be a well-run institution untouched by scandal. Set back from the road on pleasant grounds, it looked almost inviting. At least it did not look repellent. No walls, no gates. A smiling telephone voice had informed me that "our home" consisted of two facilities—a nursing facility for patients requiring professional nursing care ($100.00 a day) and a health-related facility for ambulatory residents ($50.00 a day for a private room, $42.50 semiprivate). Since the health-related facility maintained one nurse for a hundred residents (not patients), she could hardly be relied upon for anything but occasional attention or the most dire emergency. Ambulatory residents were expected to function on their own, their chief obligation being to make it to the dining room and back unassisted. "They can use crutches, canes, walkers, wheelchairs, pogo sticks," chuckled the voice, "as long as they can do it without aid."

It was not, alas, Jewish, but it might offer my mother enough Jews to make her happy.

"Look, the Jewish Center"—I pointed eagerly to the building on the opposite corner, hoping the towering Star of David might shed some of its luster on Naomi Lawson.

"I see," said my mother.

"You can always run over and dance the hora," I tried a joke as we inched up the path to the double glass doors.

"And the hustle," she said.

"It's only a mile from us," I said.

"How convenient," she replied.

Sitting in front of the entrance, like so many clay figures left to dry in the sun, were a collection of shriveled, white-haired old people in wheelchairs. Skeletal heads rose and watery eyes stared at us as we passed. My mother at seventy was a kid compared to them. As I felt her fingers tighten around my arm I could have cried for her. "The reception committee," she said.

"He could be a millionaire," I grinned toward a gaunt, white-haired man slumped in a wheelchair.

"Maybe I'll catch him," she smiled.

Her fingers kept a tight grip on my arm as we stepped into the lobby, where piped-in music played, "Heaven, I'm in Heaven."

Floral carpeting. Paneled walls. Cheap reproductions of land-scapes. And more old people, dressed up for Sunday, arranged in chairs like potted plants. They looked up, hopefully, searching our faces for signs of recognition. Outside on this bright, warm Sun-day, the tennis courts and golf courses were filled, sailboats glided across the Sound, people were working in their gardens, playing with their children. A bulletin board headed NAOMI LAWSON FUN TIME announced church and temple services, bridge games, a knit-ting class, choir rehearsal.

Why was my mother forcing us to do this to her?

"Well, it's certainly cheerful,"   I commented on the pink-flow-ered carpet, the framed prints on the walls.

"Delightful," my mother said.

The social worker who was expecting us squeezed my mother's hands and flooded us in the beam of her professional smile. Speak-ing in the distinct, even-tempered voice of a Disneyworld manne-quin, never dropping her smile, she enunciated the attributes of Naomi Lawson. Balanced meals. Choice of two entrees. Always a meat alternate if a pork product was served. Over half the resi-dents were Jewish. Services for everyone. All holidays celebrated. Loads of activities. Residents not confined to the home. They sang in local church choirs, volunteered in the schools, went to the the-ater in New York. Many kept cars in the lot.

"Who needs a car?" my mother said. "I wouldn't know where to go."

Sorry, they did not have anyone to take my mother for regular doctor's appointments. Emergency ambulance service, of course. A doctor was called in if a patient took sick. As for taking her to a spe-cialist, they had no one. What about my wife? She looked at me suspiciously through her smile. My mother wasn't being treated for anything serious, was she? Anything that might make her, God for-bid, nonambulatory?

As for assisting her with medication, the nurse would certainly do her best, but . . .

Of course, only one nurse for a hundred guests.

We began our tour with the dining room, a large, floral-carpeted room filled with tables for four.

"You can't eat in your room?" my mother asked.

Miss Nice shook her head, never losing her smile. This was a *health-related facility*, she underlined the words, not a nursing home.

"What if you can't make it?" my mother asked.

She assured my mother they would not let her starve. But they did not like to make a habit out of bringing meals to rooms. They encouraged their guests to leave their rooms, to mingle and be independent.

"I imagine it costs too much," my mother smiled knowingly, her eyes darting suspiciously to the counter at one end of the dining room. "It's a cafeteria? You wait on yourself?"

Miss Nice explained that the residents selected their food at the counter and a staff member put it on a tray and carried it to their tables. That way people could see exactly what they were getting. It avoided confusion.

"You mean nobody takes your order?" my mother said.

Holding onto her smile, Miss Nice led us into a quilted pink elevator, like the inside of a candy shop, through a bright pink corridor with more of the same pink and green floral carpeting, and into a fiercely cheerful room, which for all its flowers and pink stripes could not hide the fact that it was depressingly small and sterile. It had the bare minimum of furniture, a tiny pink bathroom, and a tiny closet.

"Just like the Hilton," my mother said.

When my mother observed that there was no room for a television, hardly room for a phone, Miss Nice replied that those things weren't necessary; the guests watched television in community rooms and there were phones at the end of the corridors. Guests could have their own phones installed if they wished, she said. Even television, if she could find a place to put it. The miniature closet, she assured my mother, was far more spacious than it looked. Besides, they would store her out-of-season clothes for her, so how much space did one person need?

I wanted to grab my mother and run. I could feel her desperation. One moment independent—a "somebody" in a luxurious apartment, space everywhere, surrounded by the possessions she loved, anything she wanted at her fingertips, no need to ask someone if she could have her winter coat or an extra bowl of soup, free to watch any television program she wished to without consulting others in a community room. One moment a free and independent person, the next the inmate of an institution. Was this what happened to people? Was it for this that she wrenched herself away from her family to come to America? Was it for this that she struggled to prove to the world that she could become whatever she wanted? All her investments, her contributions to Jewish causes, her travels, her marriages, her son—was it all to end up in a cubicle at Naomi Lawson?

If we tried harder, I told myself, maybe it could work. If we turned the other cheek, and turned it again, if we made allowances for her plight, her pain. Maybe she had a right to be angry, maybe she had a right to expect special attention, maybe we owed her understanding.

Miss Nice led us through community rooms. Weaving, knitting, painting, carpentry. Book group, poetry group, choral group, drama group. "What do you like to do, Mrs. Sloan?" she asked.

My mother pretended not to hear.

She repeated the question.

"Me?" my mother asked.

"What do you like to do?"

"Oh, lots of things," my mother groped.

"Like what?"

"I play the guitar," my mother said.

"Wonderful!" beamed Miss Nice. "Classical or folk?"

My mother looked at her.

"Do you play classical or folk?" she repeated, speaking louder, enunciating carefully.

"I play everything," my mother said.

I suddenly realized the magnitude of the disaster that had befallen her. Other than buying or selling stocks, real estate, or napkins on sale, she had no deep interests. Or deep relationships. She knew a vast assortment of semistrangers she had impressed with her importance or put-on personality, but no one really knew the Dora Sloan behind the façade, and she did not know them. Or care to. She was concerned only with how she came across and with the number of people she could get to like her. The deaths of Betty Grable and Bing Crosby upset her as much as the deaths of people she knew; it was as if she knew them equally well, and perhaps she did. She had no use for women. "They're like a roomful of geese," she said. "I'm a businesswoman. I always go with the men. And it looks like they like me. They find my conversation interesting."

"You'll have to bring your guitar and play for us," said Miss Nice.

"I was always going to be a somebody," my mother told me often. She told Steven, she told Paul. "Don't think they weren't jealous."

Who was jealous?

"Everybody," she said.

But whom would she impress at the Naomi Lawson Home? Living in an identical room as everyone else, sharing the same table, eating the same food. How could she impress people with children who worshipped her, friends devoted to her?

Dora Sloan, one of two hundred residents of a health-related facility?

Just another old lady who couldn't get along with her family.

We had to find a way to live together. I had to find someone, a companion, someone to take the burden off Ethel. Maybe all we needed was someone to ease my mother's loneliness. Weren't there organizations? Community services? The temple? There had to be.

Handing me a form, Miss Nice said to be sure and call if we had any further questions. And be sure to apply as soon as possible, if interested. They had a waiting list.

"Who can stand to look at all the cripples?" my mother said, as we shuffled hurriedly past the aged figures baking in the sun, her fingers clutching my arm like a vise.

21

OLD AGE, if you could believe the media, was all the rage. Care of the dying was replacing Frisbees, skateboarding, and pet rocks in America's priorities. Gerontology and thanatology were right up there with jogging and soccer, courses springing up in institutions of higher learning across the country. Teams of Dying Psychiatrists were herding terminal patients into group therapy sessions, categorizing their stages, so we would all know the proper steps to take to die. Dying books were hot sellers, networks vied for dying docudramas.

Terminal illness was S.R.O. on Broadway.

Help, concern, love, attention for the family with a dying member was flourishing everywhere.

Except where we were.

When it came to finding this abundance of aid it was always someplace else or for somebody else. My mother either lived in the wrong county, town, or state, or she was too rich or too poor. Help, like the fox and the grapes, was always tantalizingly out of reach.

The telephone became a permanent extension of my cramped hand as I sought aid from local and county governments, public, private, and religious agencies, friends who had been through it, anyone. I called every organization in the telephone book with the word "senior" or "aged" in the title. I went to bed at night with my head buzzing—phones, tape machines, recorded voices, recorded music.

If my mother had the foresight to be a pauper, any number of government departments were poised to rush to her rescue. If she had only dissipated her money in the pursuit of pleasure instead of husbanding it for an independent future, an army of government specialists was ready to reward her with a flood of services. Homemakers, meals, taxi services would be at her disposal. But she had erred. She had amassed far more than the two- or three-thousand-dollar maximum (no one ever divulged the exact figure) that cut off all public concern. I was dismissed as a crackpot for even suggesting that the aim of government might be to serve all the people, not just the indigent. County phones clicked in my ear.

"Jewish!" people cried. "How lucky!"

The Jews, as everyone knew, offered a cornucopia of services. They had agencies, programs, battalions of The Concerned carrying on the tradition of help begun in the years of the great migrations.

"Call your rabbi immediately," I was urged by the Unchosen.

I did. He was on vacation for the summer.

Although I was not a member of any of the local Jewish religious institutions, my mother's credentials were unimpeachable. For thirty years both a temple and a synagogue member in Arizona, she had contributed handsomely to all things Jewish.

The woman who answered the phone chirped that she was sympathetic to my mother's plight—sick, a stranger in the community, no friends her age, aching to reach other Jews—but hadn't a clue what to do about it. Sorry.

I was fed up with sorrys.

Was there no one who might come and talk with her, offer her a little Jewish companionship? Wasn't there a sisterhood, a group that visited the sick, something?

They had groups for jazz, skiing, drama, Hebrew studies, tap dancing, and yoga, but no one to visit my mother.

Sorry.

If only my mother were not so lonely, so isolated, she might not need to pick fights to prove she was somebody. If the tribe she claimed to embrace so passionately were to take a little interest in her, her life might have meaning once more, her anger might subside, we might be able to live together in peace.

I left a message for the rabbi, but he did not call back.

When I called again after he returned from his vacation he did not return the call.

I considered writing a letter to our local newspaper, entitled, "The Rabbi Never Called Back," but I heard that the JDL had long tentacles.

It was not until I mentioned my experience to a devout member

I met on the train that the rabbi telephoned my mother, thrilling her by conversing in Hebrew and offering to have someone drive her to services the moment she felt up to it. She needed caring and he offered a taxi service.

"If we don't find someone for your mother soon," Ethel said, "I'll need someone."

Maybe I could get the rabbi to call Ethel.

The cheery codger at the Senior Citizens Center assured me they would love to have my mother join. Maybe she would like to join the bowling team. Her ability was unimportant; it was loads of fun.

No, they had no one to visit her.

Cancer Care, an organization recommended frequently, offered to send a specialist to help my mother prepare for death. Which was not the kind of companionship she had in mind. They also offered a homemaker service—for people on Medicaid. That word again. Too bad she was not eligible, they said, giving me a list of homemaker–health-aide agencies and the opportunity to track down help on my own.

I discovered a world of homemakers and health aides I never knew existed—legions of Jamaican women who journeyed each day through Westchester to care for the helpless. They did their shopping, cooked their meals, cleaned their dwelling places, and walked them. There were no longer any sweet little old lady companions. They were off on trips run by the American Association of Retired People, spared from the need to work by the largesse of Social Security and Medicare. The old and the sick were left to the care of Caribbean women who at $4.50 per hour, twelve-hour weekly minimums, were forbidden by their agencies from driving their patients or giving medication. State or insurance regulations. Anything to make things just a little more difficult.

One friendly agency owner confided to me that I was not legally responsible for my parents or anyone over eighteen. "No matter how much money you have," she lowered her voice, "Medicaid will pay for her."

And if my mother had savings?

"Have her sign them over to you right away," she cried, stunned at my innocence. "Everyone does it." If a nursing home might be in her future, she urged me to have my mother sign over her assets at once; it had to be done two years before admission. "Some of the richest people in Westchester are living in nursing homes," she said, "and Medicaid's footing the bill."

But a homemaker was not what we needed. Cooking and cleaning were not our problem. My mother needed someone, as the psychologists say, on whom to ventilate her feelings and not tell her, as the Cancer Care people insisted, that she had cancer. She needed someone, other than us, at whom to be angry. An uninvolved someone who could be dispassionately kind when my mother was cruel, patient when she was enraged. And someone, hopefully, who could drive.

"If I could just get out of driving her to the doctor," was Ethel's fervent wish. "All she talks about is how wonderful everyone else is to her and how nothing I do is right." And it was always a whole day out of the agency.

A taxi was impossible, Ethel said. My mother needed someone with her. She had to be taken downstairs for blood tests, upstairs for x-rays. She needed help with Medicare forms. "She never leaves without fighting with the receptionist about who's going to send out the Medicare forms. She wants them to do it; they want her to do it. It kills her that they don't treat her as someone special."

"In Arizona," my mother said, "the doctors did everything for me. They filled out the forms, they mailed them—I didn't have to do a thing."

New York, I said, had doctors who saved her life.

She shocked me by admitting that I was right. She told people who called how her son had come to rescue her; how he had found the world's most brilliant doctor for her. "I came here half dead," she said. "He brought me back to life, like Frank Buck."

The Red Cross, I learned, once had volunteers who drove people to doctors—until the woman's movement made volunteering bad form.

We were rescued by a German Mary Poppins. Shatzi Spiegelstrauss came to us from a volunteer agency whose object was to find employment for senior citizens—a category they defined as commencing at age fifty-five, giving one pause. Its existence was kept a closely guarded secret until I discovered it in an article one Sunday in the Westchester section of the *New York Times*, an article that disclosed everything about the group except its phone number. Taking off on another flight of phone calls (the rule: tell Sloan nothing until he makes at least six calls), I finally made contact with an elderly gentleman who promised immediate attention and, a week later, produced Shatzi Spiegelstrauss.

"Mr. Sloan?" her thickly accented voice hollered through my office phone. "Spiegelstrauss here, Doctor."

Who?

"Spiegelstrauss," she repeated. "From the Senior Committee, yah?"

Ah, yah!

"You are looking for your mother somebody?"

I was, somebody.

"Tell me, the position, its nature is what?"

I described it.

"I see," she mused. "A companion is what you are looking for. A good companion am I."

I could have kissed the telephone when she said that she drove. She would not only drive my mother, but—and this sent her into whoops of laughter—having once attended a lecture at Teller, she knew it well. A doctor she was. Research. Dr. Spiegelstrauss. A recent budget cut where she had worked freed her for other activities.

"You would never believe this," she lowered her voice, "but I am from America not."

"Seriously?"

"Ha?" her voice trumpeted.

"I never would have guessed it," I shouted.

"From Germany I am," she said. "Frankfurt. Like hot dog." She shrieked with laughter at her levity. "Do you get that?" she howled. "Like hot dog. That is my husband's joke."

"He is very funny, your husband," I said.

"Yah," she said. "But he is sick."

Oh. I said I was sorry.

It took ten tortuous minutes to explain how to reach our house from hers, which was no more than ten minutes away. Each word required repetition, synonyms, and an expanded explanation, but I would gladly have learned Swahili if that were required. Her rate, like all the seniors from the committee, was three dollars an hour. Seniors were evidently not in fierce demand.

22

WHO WOULD ambush her today?

Ethel tensed as she turned into our crumbling driveway, bags of groceries clunking in the trunk, something else clunking ominously in the engine, which she hoped would survive long enough to receive care.

She was not sure which was worse—coming home to a solitary screaming mother-in-law or to a swarm of attendants overrunning the house. Nurses, aides, companions rooting through her kitchen for tea bags, putting things in the wrong drawers, breaking dishes, scouring the finish off Teflon pans, sending her scurrying for soap, towels, shampoo, and her hair dryer, which had a habit of remaining in my mother's bathroom until Ethel, naked in a towel, discovered she did not have it.

Three days a week the tall, stooped figure of Dr. Spiegelstrauss emerged from my mother's room to follow Ethel around the house and converse without stop. The first time the visiting nurse encountered the white-haired old woman shuffling in her space shoes, she thought she was the patient.

One day a week the visiting nurse appeared to give my mother her injection and an examination, giving Ethel a detailed report of pulse, blood, temperature, and constipation, and frequent reminders to provide my mother with prune juice, which she complained was always in short supply.

Two days a week Annabel Washington, the big nurse's aide, lumbered in to bathe, oil, powder my mother, shampoo and set her hair, and flood the bathroom.

Occasionally the Visiting Nurses supervisor appeared to check up on things, insisting on giving Ethel a detailed analysis.

The discovery of the Association of Visiting Nurses was a miracle that occurred only because Dr. Gordon prescribed a weekly injection of Delatestryl, a male hormone, and suggested that Ethel spare herself the trek to his office by finding a local doctor to do it.

When local doctors wanted fifty dollars to perform the two-minute injection, and the nearest hematologist, who was connected with another famous cancer center, refused to do anything for the patient of a Teller doctor, a kindly receptionist suggested the Visiting Nurses, whom I found after making the obligatory six phone calls. Finding them was like coming upon a staff of angels.

Not only would a nurse appear weekly to do the injecting, said a sweet, understanding voice, but she would also give my mother a weekly checkup. In addition—too good to be true—they would send an aide twice a week to bathe my mother, shampoo her hair, and provide other personal services. Best of all—it was not only covered by Medicare, but they handled all forms. My mother need do nothing more than sign her name.

The two months of improvising with Angelina turned out to have been money wasted. The team of nurses and their aides did far more than Angelina could do and at no cost. But who was to know? "Even doctors don't know all the things we do," an angel giggled.

No matter how carefully Ethel tried to time her arrival, someone was invariably there, promptly enlisting her help, reporting more than she wanted to know, dispatching her for supplies. Once Ethel tried sneaking up to the bedroom to eat lunch but was discovered by Annabel Washington seeking towels, my mother refusing to vacate the steamy bathroom unless swaddled. The toilet had been stopped up (twenty dollars), fuses blown, Dansk spoons thrown out in the garbage, forks bent out of shape from being wedged in the dishwasher whose interior was now scarred with nasty scratches. Nothing was where it used to be; everything was a search.

"It's like Grand Central Station," my mother glowed, reveling in the attention, especially satisfying because it was all covered by Medicare with the exception of Dr. Spiegelstrauss, who was considered custodial.

I could never understand how Annabel Washington slipped into
the Medicare category. Medicare not only paid her for bathing my
mother and washing her hair, it insisted she spend a minimum of
an hour-and-a-half doing it each time she came, twice a week.

"Strong like a bull," was my mother's description of Annabel,
who dunked her in and out of the tub like a rubber doll. "And
twice as big," she added. "I don't know how she fits into your bathroom."

Juggling two bags of groceries, Ethel shouldered her way
through the screen door and slipped through the dining-room
route to the kitchen, avoiding the hall that passed my mother's
room, from which emerged the shouting voices of my mother and
Dr. Spiegelstrauss. Their initial love affair had hit a rocky period.
My mother's delight at having a genuine doctor to tend to her
wants cooled as she discovered that her doctor companion had no
qualms about eating pork and no intention of speaking Jewish to
keep their conversations secret. Even worse, Dr. Spiegelstrauss
continued to accept her three dollars an hour plus mileage long
after having had the opportunity to know and fall in love with my
mother.

Ethel winced at the paint flaking from the dining-room wall, the
laundry she had washed that morning folded over a chair. The
house on which she once lavished such love was in chaos. Chairs
needed cleaning, curtains washing. But there was time for nothing
but my mother. In spite of all the attention she was getting, my
mother still found things for Ethel to do for her. And the attendants found more things for Ethel to do.

". . . the gentiles," my mother's voice boomed from the room.

Ethel tried not to hear as she put away the groceries that would
disappear quickly. Once she was able to shop once a week; now
once a day was not enough.

". . . the junk they eat."

For a woman who was supposed to be sick, her appetite was ravenous. But only when Ethel was not home. It was a marvel of planning, devouring everything between attendants. She must race out
of her room like a little bug, dart around the kitchen and devour
food, and slip back into her room just in time to greet the next attendant, to whom she would complain of being starved.

"Mrs. Sloan, hoo hah!"

She would never have a moment to herself again.

The tall bent figure of Dr. Spiegelstrauss stood in the doorway, her mouth parted in a crooked smile under a crooked nose as she squinted at Ethel. She shuffled into the kitchen on spindly legs, her feet shaky in her space shoes. No matter what time Ethel arrived, that would be the time Dr. Spiegelstrauss made her kitchen entrance to make for my mother a cup tea. An operation that would take forever, like everything else she undertook. It took her the better part of an afternoon to park her car in exactly the right position in front of our house, although there was rarely another car in sight. Getting out and up the walk to our door took the remaining part of the afternoon. "Why should she rush?" my mother said. "She's getting paid anyhow."

"Not too much salt you shouldn't have," Dr. Spiegelstrauss warned as she grunted her way to the cupboard where she withdrew a clanking cup and saucer in her shaking hand. She thumped them on the table where Ethel was eating. Banging open a succession of drawers and banging them shut again, she finally located a spoon, which she dropped on the floor and threw in the sink. She blasted water into the teakettle, which she thumped on the stove, lighting three burners until she found the right one. She assured Ethel that the gas odor would vanish before she finished the mail she was trying to read.

"A tea bag," Ethel said.

"Hahhhhh?"

"You forgot to put in a tea bag."

"Hah hoo!" Dr. Spiegelstrauss whooped with laughter.

Making her way across the kitchen with great effort, she pried open a canister labeled sugar and found—sugar. She had better luck with the canister labeled tea, somehow making the tea bag clunk as she dropped it into the cup. Standing over Ethel, she read the mail over her shoulder. "Such a good daughter-in-law you are," she said. "What I wouldn't give for a daughter like you."

"Too bad she doesn't agree with you," Ethel said.

"Don't pay her no attention," Dr. Spiegelstrauss said as she scraped a chair out from the table and sat across from Ethel. "The chemotherapy, it affects something terrible the mind. You think I

like it when she screams at me? You think maybe I don't want to
scream back? But I stop myself. I know she is sick. Pain she has. So
I take it, like you say. Don't think it is because I need so much the
three dollars an hour. I try to do some good."

Dr. Spiegelstrauss could walk out anytime, Ethel thought. She
could be patient. She knew she did not have to face her every
morning and night, seven days a week, no days off, no holidays.
Once she walked out she was free. My mother occupied a small
part of her life; she was the center of ours. Our world revolved
around her. Paul might be developing into a great guitarist, Steven
an Einstein, but what mattered most in our home was my mother's
supply of milk of magnesia.

Ethel was never free, not even at the travel agency. The nurse
called her there to report on my mother's condition. The aide
called her there when she could not find hair rollers. They called
her there to make and break appointments since my mother either
did not answer the phone or, if she did, referred them to Ethel.

If Spiegelstrauss were not hovering over her she would pour
herself a Scotch.

"What you need," said Dr. Spiegelstrauss, "is a little whiskey."

Ethel could have thrown her arms around the wonderful woman
and kissed her crooked mouth. A smile creased the old woman's
wrinkled face. "But she does not like drinking. I know."

Ethel sliced a Sara Lee chocolate cake, topped it with ice cream,
and to hell with the calories. She offered a piece to Dr. Spiegelstrauss who, with a furtive glance toward my mother's room, glee-
fully took it and savored it. Thank God for Dr. Spiegelstrauss. If
she did nothing more than take my mother to the doctor, she was
worth her weight in chocolate cakes. "She gets lost maybe fifty
times," my mother returned from each trip with another tale of the
woman's incompetence. "It takes a whole day to get there."

Dr. Spiegelstrauss was afraid of thruways. She felt secure only on
local streets that turned into long involved routes.

"She takes as long as possible," my mother said. "The longer it
takes her the more I have to pay her."

"Communist!" my mother screamed when Dr. Spiegelstrauss
said she might consider returning to Germany where they took

care of old people. Ineligible for Social Security, she lived on a combination of earnings, savings, and money from her married children. She spoke of a sick husband no longer able to work. "You should go to Israel!" my mother roared at her.

But Germany, she protested, was her home. She had close friends there.

"Gentiles?" my mother cried.

"They helped us escape," she replied.

"You should go to Israel," my mother repeated as if she had not heard. It has her directive to everyone. It was turning me pro-Arab.

Swallowing the last crumb of her chocolate cake and clearing her throat vigorously, Dr. Spiegelstrauss leaned across the table and lowered her voice. "She tells me," she whispered, "that she is planning to take her own apartment. Listen, you must not let her do this. To say the truth, she cannot manage." She glanced nervously at the teakettle beginning to simmer. "Do you know her disease? Multiple myeloma? It cannot be cured. The doctors, they tell you one thing and another, but they know nothing. The most the chemotherapy can do is prolong life a little maybe, hold it back from spreading the cancer so fast. But completely stop it, no. It moves through the body until when it reaches the vital organs, it is finished."

She had to be wrong. The pain had dulled. Most of the time now my mother was almost free of pain. She walked with a bounce, her eyes were bright, her cheeks glowed. She talked about buying a wig. "Maybe a honey blonde." We drove to visit Ethel's parents, an hour away. She spent an afternoon flattering them, telling them she would not trade their lives for kings in their palaces. She was going to join organizations and meet the important people in Larchmont, maybe even catch a rich husband.

What did the giraffe know? That was my mother's name for tall Dr. Spiegelstrauss.

Although every now and then, unexpectedly, a pain surfaced somewhere. It popped up in her leg, her chest, her neck. She always had an explanation. She slept on the wrong side, used too many pillows, walked too much, too fast, twisted something when she sat down.

After finding a nice apartment, she said, she was going to make a big donation and make a name for herself. One thing she had no problem about, and that was making friends. People liked her.

The teakettle shrieked.

"Keep her with you," Dr. Spiegelstrauss hissed, "until it is time for a nursing home. But do not a nursing home call it. You understand what it is I am telling you?" She uttered the words as if God were speaking through her. "Believe me, I am telling you what it is so."

We had mentioned an apartment to friends, one of whom had a mother in a building that would be perfect for my mother. We drove my mother around the area, pointing out buildings.

"You are living in a dream world," Dr. Spiegelstrauss said. "All of you."

Shuffling to the stove, Dr. Spiegelstrauss turned off the gas and heaved the teakettle to the table, which she splattered with boiling water even though she was very careful to fill the cup no more than halfway. Clutching the cup and saucer with quivering fingers, she carried them from the kitchen as though stepping through landmines. "I thought you went to England for it," my mother said in the next room.

As Ethel hurried back through the dining room, my mother, seeing through walls again, called out to ask if she would mind bringing back some buttermilk, it would be soothing for her stomach. And check the date, make sure it's the latest.

"Why didn't you ask me?" Dr. Spiegelstrauss said. "I could have got some on the way."

"Ethel doesn't mind," my mother said. "She isn't so busy anymore."

23

LIKE BONNIE AND CLYDE we sped into Manhattan, tensed for the shriek of sirens, flashing lights. Calling all cars, the Sloans have escaped; victim accuses pair of failing to carry out duties—capture and return to maximum security.

Deep in my heart, no matter how well I knew she could manage,

I could not free myself of the guilt at leaving the shrunken figure alone in the room that would give off the sounds of Merv and Mike till the house crumbled.

"It's all right, kids, go," she said, propped up against her pile of pillows in a sea of mangled sheets, tissues, torn envelopes, and sunflower seeds. "Why should you worry about me? I'll have Steven."

But she would not have Steven. He would be baby-sitting for a neighbor.

"A boy?" she cried. "Whoever heard of a boy baby-sitting?"

"Boys sit all the time," I said quickly, hoping her voice had not reached Steven somewhere in the house. "A lot of children would rather have boys sit for them."

"So let him sit for me," she said.

He had been doing too much sitting for her. A woman talking of getting her own apartment could certainly manage being alone for a few hours.

"So I'll have Paul," she said.

But Paul was going to a concert, which meant Chick Corea, not Leonard Bernstein. Paul had no intention, he announced, of giving up his life to satisfy Nana's whims. He would help when she really needed help, and that was it. He caught on to her quickly, and she knew it. He put her on immediate notice that he was not about to feel guilty for putting his life first.

"Only Steven understands my problem," she often said. "He's like a prince. I always liked refined types."

"Why don't you call Dr. Spiegelstrauss?" I asked.

"What do I want with Spiegelstrauss?" my mother glared.

"If you're afraid to be alone . . ."

"Don't give me any suggestions," she snapped. "Besides, Spiegelstrauss doesn't come out at night. Like Cinderella. She's afraid somebody will grab her."

"It'll be good practice for your own apartment," I said.

"Don't be so anxious," she cried, her fists trembling. "I'll move when Dr. Gordon says I'm ready to move."

We had not seen a movie or gone out to dinner in months. As for anything that required tickets in advance, forget it. If we accepted an invitation it was always tentative—in case something came up with my mother, and it invariably did. A sudden onslaught of pain, depression, hysteria, or simply that Ethel was too weary to face getting dressed and making conversation about things that were no longer relevant. We stopped having people over, and people, understandably, stopped having us over. Life went on around us, and we were left out. There was no time or energy to cope with entertaining, and the house seemed in perpetual chaos. Even if we did venture out, Ethel was still obliged to cook dinner for my mother, a sentence that was never lifted day in and day out. The boys could survive on an occasional MacDonalds or pizza, but my mother demanded a real dinner at which to grimace every day.

"Go ahead, kids, escape," my mother said. "Who wants to stay with a sick woman?"

"We can get you a sitter," I said.

She glared at me. "What do I want with a sitter?"

It was not a sitter she wanted, but a family who would prove their devotion by forsaking any pleasure in order to make her happy. My mother seemed to be playing a game with us. She knew that we believed she was dying, but she knew that she was not. She was going to milk the deception for everything she could get and walk out one day in perfect health, delighted with her joke. Sorry to disappoint you, kids, she would tell us, and exit laughing.

Leaving the Hunters' number next to the telephone that had once been "a disease," we took off. "She'll make me pay for it next week," Ethel said. "The minute you leave for work."

I felt so elated I took the Triboro instead of the Willis Avenue Bridge—and screw the seventy-five cents.

Pete and Kitty Hunter lived in a Chelsea brownstone they had bought and renovated after the city promised to transform the area into a harmonious balance of rich, poor, and middle class. Instead, a block of towers went up across the street which the city filled with welfare tenants, among them a group of youths who terrorized the brownstone owners.

"Let's face it," confided a city official to Pete after yet another meeting with the brownstone owners' association to protest the broken promise, "they have more votes than you."

Built at tremendous cost, the towers were now defaced with graf-

fiti, doors off hinges, windows broken, clusters of teenagers blocking the sidewalk day and night, the air sweet with pot.

Wouldn't it be far more sensible, and humane, if the same money that went into housing destined to be vandalized went to provide housing for the old—housing designed to meet their physical
needs and enable them to remain independent? Why not housing
for people who had contributed to society, who had done their
share, rather than bases for marauders to prey upon the innocent?
Didn't my mother have a right *not* to get along with us? Didn't we
have a right not to get along with her? Didn't she have a right to
expect some attention from the government, too? And she would
be no threat to her neighbors; she would pay rent.

If you were poor, I discovered, social workers visited you in your
apartment provided by the government. Homemakers brought you
meals. Cabs took you to your doctor. You did not have to trouble
yourself with such details as filling out medical forms. The nice social workers did it for you—paid by the people forced to do it for
themselves. No distinctions appeared to be made between the unfortunate victims of circumstances and the calculating abusers of
the system. Plead poverty, and you had government staffs at your
disposal. My mother had only us.

As the gleaming varnished door opened, we stepped into a
shower of screams, hugs, kisses, dim lights, dim Middle Eastern
music from the stereo. Posed in the shadows were the usual bearded men in jeans and turtlenecks, women in peasant skirts, and
a great many undifferentiated sexes in caftans. Kitty wore harem
pants, Pete a caftan. The Arab look was coming up strong among
New York Jews that year.

"Is it safe to leave my camel outside?" I made a little joke in my
slacks and sportcoat. Ethel wore a pants suit that also screamed
suburban.

Kitty burst into hysterical laughter, squeezing my arm and pressing her tits against me. No beauty, Kitty was tall and shapeless,
with reddish hair that never looked combed, but she managed to
go a long way on her tits. After automatically asking for Scotch, I
realized I was hopelessly out of it, the group being into white wine,
Amaretto, and Sambuca.

Armed with our drinks, introduced to some faces we might have met before, we were sent into the arena to talk. Ethel froze. She found herself with absolutely nothing to say. With so much that was going on in our lives, she marveled at my ability to plunge into an instant discussion comparing the merits of suburban and city living. "I'll scream," Ethel whispered, "if I hear one more person defend their decision to send little Debby to a private school." Everyone seemed to be from nearby blocks—brownstone owners' association members—experts on window bars, burglar alarms, and cops sleeping in their cars. They went wild over Kitty's hors d'oeuvres, a new etching Pete had discovered buried in a junk shop, and Gretchen in her pajamas as the maid presented her, like a lobster being selected for boiling. Pete had two daughters from his first marriage, Kitty bad memories from hers. Two months after Gretchen was born, Kitty raced back to forecasting trends for IBM. "Maybe I don't want children, after all," she giggled, as if she had selected the wrong wallpaper pattern.

While Pete sailed back and forth to the kitchen, replenishing drinks, Ethel sipped and smiled, pretending to listen to whoever talked to her. Didn't any of these people have mothers and fathers, I wondered. Didn't they get sick? What did they do with them? Or didn't anyone care? Were they too busy finding old fireplaces?

"Advertising?" a caftan-clad woman cried at me. "So am I." She named a string of creative shops, all of which were desperate to have her back, and moaned when I named the agency where I had worked for twelve years. "I'd die at a place like that," she gasped. "I interviewed there and all they talked about was insurance and profit-sharing. *I* want to do great advertising."

"Thank God for profit-sharing," I said, recalling the day the ax fell. "You can't pay the mortgage with creativity."

She looked at me as if I had suggested giving head on the spot.

"You're damn right," said another caftanned woman. "I worked at a place for twenty-one years. I thought I had a pension; the company folded and I had zip."

"I'm incapable of doing pedestrian advertising," said the first caftan.

"I'll do any kind of advertising that sends my kids to college," I said.

She drew back uneasily, not sure what to make of a partygoer not playing his part. Which gave me a deep sense of satisfaction. It was pure pleasure telling the truth, not caring if she liked it or not—or if she liked me or not. No more role-playing, no more party games, no more pretending. A year earlier and I would have played the isn't-it-awful-so-much-advertising-isn't-creative game. Now my mother was dying.

"Relax and enjoy it," Kitty said, her face grinning up at me, her tits pushing against my arm.

"Delicious"—I swallowed a minced papaya on a Zaire cracker.

"Thank Lorna, she's a real find. Can't clean, but a great cook. How's your mother doing?"

I almost said delicious.

"Ethel's had some real crying sessions with me," Kitty said, smiling.

Did Ethel have to go running to everyone in the world with her problems? I who grew up instructed to keep everything, especially misfortune, a closely guarded secret, had married a woman who told everybody everything.

"It's rough," Kitty said. "We went through it with Pete's father."

"He lived with you?" I asked.

"Are you kidding?" She withdrew her tits. "I'd leave Pete first."

"So what did you go through?"

"The search," she said. "You should see the nursing homes they put people in. I've seen better kennels. Thank God we finally found one that's halfway civilized. In Long Beach."

She called that going through something.

"We talked about having him live here, but it would have driven me crazy. I told Pete it was his father or me."

"Is he sick?"

"Oh, the usual," Kitty said. "*Old* mainly. Forgetful. Shakes a little. Has trouble walking. He stayed here one weekend; slept over there." She pointed to a sofa bed under caftans. "Sunday morning we heard this thumping over our heads. He was walking around in his shoes. Pete got up and asked him if he had to walk, to do it in his socks. But a few minutes later he was at it again. Who can live that way?"

"What if he gets sick?"

"Oh, they have nurses and a doctor on call."

"I mean serious," I said. "Heart. Cancer. Is there anybody to take him to a specialist?"

"Oh . . ." Kitty glanced away—"there's something I have to ask Margo. We'll have to get together soon and really talk."

She melted into the dimness, her ass shifting like a sack of oranges in her harem pants. I looked around, stranded. Ethel had vanished. The bathroom, no doubt. Pete and Kitty had sensational bathrooms thanks to their anal fag decorator. Suddenly I felt as if I were on one side of a chasm, looking over at the shrieking people on the other. From the other side came the Arabic music whining from concealed speakers, floating trays of hors d'oeuvres, glasses clinking, people howling with laughter.

"My mother is dying," I wanted to shout at them. "We are all dying and we don't even know each other. Cut out the shit! Life is too important to fill with shit!"

"I hear you have your hands full." It was Pete, grinning.

"Very full," I said.

"If I know you"—Pete seemed to find it all hilarious—"Ethel's been taking care of your mother while you've been out playing tennis."

"But the guilt has played hell with my serve," I said, as if it really were a joke.

"We have the same problem," Pete said, as if it really were the same problem.

"I know, your father."

"Found this terrific home for him."

"He loves it."

"As much as he can love anything," Pete said. "A pain in the ass. Always was, still is."

"What about Kitty's parents?" I asked.

"She's lucky," Pete said, breaking into giggles as he realized the significance of what he said. "In a manner of speaking," he corrected himself. "Her father died when she was in college; her mother died about two, three years ago. In Florida."

"Lived alone?"

"Sick for a year. It was hell on Kitty. She flew down every time her mother had an attack, which got to be like every other day. The cost. It was while we were fixing up this place."

How thoughtless of Kitty's mother.

"My father lived with us," interjected the woman robbed of her pension. "Cancer. Prostate. They gave him six months. Do you know how long it lasted? Seven years. Seven years of chemotherapy, radiation, cobalt. Seven years of pure torture. I don't think he spent one day free of pain."

I told her my mother was on chemotherapy.

"Oh, God," she said. "You throw up, you lose your hair, you go crazy."

I told her that so far my mother did not have all the reactions people warned about. Except for the emotional. But she was always emotional.

"She's lucky," she said. "That means she's getting the benefits of the drugs without the side effects."

Or they were not working at all, I thought.

"We tried every nursing home in New York," she said. "They were either hellholes for people on Medicaid or palaces he couldn't afford. There's a fabulous place in Connecticut if you can spare a thousand dollars a week. They won't even take you if you need special treatments or have to be taken to a specialist. They want you to lie there and not make waves while they collect. We ended up with a series of what they call 'homemakers.' My God! Half were on drugs and the other half drank, and they all stole. There were times I came home from work and found dad crying with pain, the woman zonked out. Near the end we were paying almost three hundred dollars a week."

"What do you expect?" said a bearded man in a turtleneck with a moodstone ring dangling from a chain. "A nursing home's a business like anything else. They aren't in business to serve humanity any more than doctors or lawyers or financial analysts are. The next big thing is going to be hospices."

Moodstone was a financial analyst with a big brokerage firm.

"I tell you, they're all looking into it—Holiday Inn, Hyatt, Hilton. With the goddamn population getting older it's a sure thing. For the long term it's going to be bigger than home computers."

"I suppose they'll use testimonial advertising," giggled a man in safari shorts. "From satisfied customers."

"Eats!" Kitty sailed through the crowd, ringing a bell, sending us all to a table laden with viands, in the center of which was a suckling pig that Pete was carving. Their grins matched.

"Now that deserves applause," said the man in safari shorts. We all clapped while Kitty curtsied in her ballooning pants.

"Pete," cried a blonde woman with bulky jewelry, "I've always wondered what men have under caftans."

"More than you dreamed possible," he leered.

"I can attest to that," Kitty squealed.

"Nobody'd better second that," a voice roared.

I looked anxiously for Ethel, who was taking a long time wherever she was. "I have a friend who looks like that," a woman said, as she speared a slice of pig with her fork.

"If he tastes anything like this," said another woman, "he's delicious."

"Seven years we took care of him," said the woman as we balanced plates on our laps, ottomans, or little tray-tables, while Pete and Kitty distributed glasses of wine. "Near the end I didn't think I could cope. But he was my father."

"Everyone's our father," I found myself saying. "We have responsibilities. We weren't hatched out of test tubes."

She looked curiously at me. So did Moodstone.

"I believe we have an obligation to our parents and to our wives' and husbands' parents."

"You haven't met Gloria's folks," said a voice.

"Yours aren't any bargain," retorted Gloria.

"Marriage has enough problems," said the creative advertising woman. "All we need is each other's parents."

Everybody laughed.

"When you marry you take all of a person, not just the part you want"—the words rushed out of me. "And parents are part of a person."

"It cost me twenty-five thousand dollars to dump mine," laughed a voice, provoking howls of laughter and a series of shrink jokes.

"What's the big sacrifice?" I asked. "So you miss a few parties, so you don't get the Tiffany lamp at the auction."

I managed, without even trying, to offend everyone in the room. Above me hung a Tiffany lamp surrounded by other auction finds.

"Delicious, Kitty," said a voice, "I'll do anything for the recipe."

"He wouldn't be happy here," Kitty said. "He would never adjust to our life-style."

I like the way people make decisions for others, as if the happiness of Pete's father were Kitty's chief concern. I was jealous of Pete and Kitty. They had avoided the problem that was tearing our house apart—they simply put the old man on a shelf and looked away. Were they being selfish or smart? Were we being noble or weak?

"You know," said a man in a caftan, a psychologist, "some people's character defects can put a strain on any family situation. There are people who are incapable of fitting into any but the most limited family group. And the older they are, the harder it is for them to adapt. In many cases old people expect the world to bend to their needs. Like it owes it to them for growing old. If they don't get the respect they think they deserve, they get furious."

"The Eskimos have the answer," a voice said. "They set old people adrift on ice floes."

"The Indians," said another, "put them up on mountaintops."

"In the Orient they revere them."

"I have a gut feeling," said the psychologist, "old people are a pain wherever they are."

"Maybe the world *should* bend a little to their needs," I heard myself saying. "Maybe we're so involved with our own pleasure we're missing out on the greatest pleasure of all—giving love to another human being."

"Wait till your mother starts shitting in her bed," said the woman who cared for her father.

"I have an aunt in a nursing home," someone said, "and she's so busy with these marvelous activities she doesn't even want visitors."

"If you can't get along with someone, I say make a clean break," said Pete. "Hell, I couldn't stand my first wife, so . . ." He slapped

Kitty on the fanny, which she wriggled wildly. "If you can divorce your spouse, why can't you get a divorce from your parents?"

"Damn, if not for modern medicine most of them wouldn't be alive today. They're only technically alive."

"I'm taking a pill at the first sign of senility," said a voice.

"Better hurry," said another voice.

"There's a woman throwing up downstairs," someone informed the room.

I knew who it was.

"I'm sorry," Ethel said, emerging from the red, white, and blue bathroom, her face the color of the white tiles. "You go back up. I'll lie down."

"Did you have to?" I asked her.

"I didn't know what to say to anybody," she said.

I lashed out at her all the way home, past the towering government projects that lined every inch of the Bruckner Expressway. Why couldn't she be strong? Why couldn't she be firm with my mother and not run to people and moan of her plight? Why couldn't she handle her the way I was sure other wives would? "Be a person," I raged at her. "It's your home."

"Not anymore," she said.

It was irrational, but I often blamed Ethel for the tension in our house. If she were only stronger—if she were firm with my mother instead of scurrying to answer her every demand and then resenting it afterward when she was rewarded with abuse. That was when the arguments flared. The tears. The Valium. But how could you be mean to a dying woman, Ethel argued, incapable of fighting my mother, who had all the cards and knew it.

The lights were blazing, the TV blaring when we walked in the house at half-past two in the morning. My mother was lying in her usual position, flat on top of the sheets, arms thrown back, nightgown pulled up over her knees. She looked at me as I lowered the volume of the TV. Didn't she ever sleep?

"You know who called?" she said. "My friends from Hartford."

I waited for the knife.

" 'Dora,' they said, 'you aren't alone, are you?' 'Of course not,' I told them. 'My children only stepped out for a minute. They would never leave me alone.' "

Thanks.

As we closed the bedroom door the TV volume went up downstairs, the sound drifting up like a mushroom cloud through her half-open door.

24

I STARED OUT MY WINDOW at the people moving eagerly on Madison Avenue, fifteen floors below. From the corridor outside my office came the animated chatter of the newly liberated. I had to be the first employee in the history of Monty Bliss Advertising, Inc., who was reluctant to leave at the end of the day.

Run by quick-moving Monty Bliss, who was rumored to set the reception-room clock ahead in the morning and back at night, the Bliss company cleverly welcomed the two categories of people unwanted by the big agencies—the very young and the no longer young. A policy that provided Bliss with some of the ablest people in New York at marked-down prices. At fifty (or forty-five as I claimed on the forms), my category was all too clear.

I might once have written the line that sold millions of cigarettes, I might once have been a titled executive with a corner office, I might once have been indispensable to the fortunes of a $150-million advertising agency, but now I was copy chief of Bliss, a somewhat honorary title since Monty passed on everything and often wrote, I had to admit, excellent ads. My desk was a slab of formica-covered plywood bridging two file cabinets. My office had flaking gray walls, a rattling window that let in more cold air than it kept out, a radiator that gave off nostril-drying heat on whim, and erratic air conditioning that could keep orange-juice concentrate solid.

I did all the wrong things in my life as an adman.

At my previous firm I was the one who wrote those solid campaigns that sold millions of dollars' worth of detergents and air fresheners but made no splash in the creative advertising world. I even helped save an occasional account, quietly. I never grew a beard or wore jeans. The day I wore a sportcoat was an act of bravery; letting my sideburns grow was a revolution. I believed what I

was taught—that dedication and talent would be properly rewarded.

So it was only logical that when a new creative director arrived, I
was among those to be dumped. At the age of forty-eight I learned
for the first time what it was like to be fired, canned, sacked, termi-
nated, let go, or, as they say now, outplaced. It was hell. It was
something that happened to other people, not dedicated me.

"Sorry," smirked the new CD, "we need fresh blood."

Who, I wondered, gave him the authority to fire me? I who had
been a loyal employee for twelve years; entrenched, a pillar.

After a shattering year of interviews by children seated behind
enormous desks, reality penetrated and I staggered into the hos-
pice of Bliss, victim of Over Forty, for which there was not even the
hope of chemotherapy.

It was not exactly a state that made a middle-aged man loving
and giving and capable of absorbing still more stress with equa-
nimity. I was wounded. I carried anger around with me like a time
bomb, ready to burst. Matches were now being lit under me daily.
Instead of coming home to serenity, to a refuge from a hostile
world, I stepped into new arguments, new problems, new decisions
to be made. Every day.

Every day I dreaded going home to another round of combat at
the dining-room table, my mother screwing up her face at the food,
Ethel defending herself, the boys anxious to escape.

Ethel would burn another pot, break another dish. My mother
would smirk. I would hate them both.

"Nothing would make her happier than if I died," Ethel said.
"Except she wouldn't have anyone to wait on her."

I dreaded meeting my mother emerging from her room in the
same robe she wore over the same nightgown every day, odors em-
anating from a body untouched by soap and water until the arrival
of another nurse's aide. She used them up like toilet tissue, screaming at them for not bathing her properly, for using too much soap,
too much shampoo, for stealing her hand lotion.

I dreaded hearing my mother answer every question with a cutting edge. "Oh, just wonderful. Sunday I'm playing tennis with
you."

I did not need another night of watching her conspicuously wipe her silverware and run a napkin inside her glass.

"They're clean," Ethel glowered. "We have a dishwasher."

"It depends how you put them in the dishwasher," my mother smiled—she who left urine and fecal stains on the bathroom floor. "In my apartment I cleaned them first."

"You can do that here too," Ethel said.

"I should wash your dishes?" My mother laughed at Ethel as if she had gone mad.

"I cook your meals," Ethel said.

"You don't cook anyhow? For your own family?" My mother had no intention of admitting that Ethel was doing anything out of the ordinary for her. "Fat"—she grimaced at whatever meat Ethel placed in front of her. Expensive butcher, lean cut, it made no difference. "Steven, would you please cut off the fat for me, I don't have the strength."

Steven, whose pimples were multiplying, was caught in the war.

My mother's aversion to Ethel's food was not preventing her from gaining weight at a remarkable pace. Her cheeks were ballooning, her arms and legs thickening. She looked as if she had been on a cruise.

"Why doesn't she appreciate anything I do for her?" Ethel cried. "I keep trying."

"Maybe if you stopped trying . . ."

But Ethel was a born giver. Ask her to do something, she did it. As the children grew up she was always doing things for them, rarely insisting they do things for themselves, eager to give while she still had them, convinced they would be grown up and out the next day. Good or bad, right or wrong, that was the way she was.

"She makes me hate her and I don't want to," Ethel said. "She's sick, she needs help, and I want to help her. If she'd only say thank you."

Thank you for what? For being healthy while she had cancer? For living free of pain while she could not survive without pills? For being the only person in the world willing to care for her? For seeing the truth—that with all her talk of devoted friends desperate to do anything for her, she ended up with Ethel?

She was dependent on Ethel, and she was going to make her pay for it.

I slipped through the thick glass agency door just as Bernadette was about to lock it. Each Bliss employee was furnished a key and instructions to keep the doors locked after five-thirty. (A receptionist was once fired, so the story went, when a messenger surprised Bea Bliss in the reception room and showed her far more than his manila envelope.)

Bernadette was one of those young women classified as perky. Long brown hair, owl glasses, impish smile. She wore jeans, Indian blouses, and clunky handcrafted crosses—because she was "into Christianity." She sprinkled soy nuts on homemade yogurt for lunch, wove baskets, wrote poetry, meditated, and recently won a snowcat by persistently phoning Frank and Stein, the monstrous disc jockey show, tying up the agency switchboard for an hour.

Occasionally I lingered in the reception room and discussed life with Bernadette over my own yogurt or raisins and nuts. She had been a first-grade teacher, a hippie in a commune, and mugged by three giggling boys in front of her apartment building. She was "getting her head together" at Monty Bliss's reception desk.

"What a shitty day," she said as we waited for an elevator that might or might not come. (I hoped she did not notice the shock I continued to feel at today's language.) "I must have been dumped on a dozen times by one Bliss or another. I thought they hired me as an assistant. I'm trapped in an IBM."

Monty Bliss cleverly staffed his agency with some of the brightest young people in New York at bargain prices by calling them trainees or assistants and promising them a foot in the door and quick moves up. Promises he eventually fulfilled to those with patience.

"I think you've turned into a great typist," I said.

"Thanks," she said. "I can't wait to tell my therapist."

Now there was a word out of my past when everyone I knew spoke of their therapists instead of their children's teachers.

"What a session we had the day I spilled the white-out all over the mechanicals," she laughed.

Bernadette's obliteration of five hundred dollars' worth of artwork had produced a closed-door meeting in which Monty Bliss, according to Monty's "assistant," warned that he would "white out" Bernadette if she did not display significantly more conscientiousness.

Bernadette asked about my mother. I looked at her, surprised, wondering what my mother had to do with the carnal thoughts I was entertaining about Bernadette.

"One day she's better, another day worse"—I shrugged, not really wanting to discuss my mother. Why did everything have to be my mother? Was there nothing else going on in the world? "She's talking about getting her own apartment," I said, hoping that ended the subject.

"Wonderful," said Bernadette. It really seemed to make her happy. More wonderful would be winding up in bed with Bernadette.

I had always been, like the geyser, faithful. No matinees, no out-of-town interludes. One of the benefits of marriage was being freed from the chase. I could not understand the men in the after-tennis sauna with their tales of massage parlors and obliging secretaries.

"Big plans tonight?" I asked Bernadette as we stepped into the lobby, a gem of shiny brass elevator doors, marble floors, chandeliers, left over from the golden age of New York. Fred Allen, Walter Winchell, Evelyn and her Magic Violin.

"Very heavy," she said. "The A & P."

"How about a drink?" I heard myself asking.

"Now that's the best offer I've had all week," she said.

"And it's only Monday," I said.

On the Third Avenue sidewalk where we sipped white wine I tried not to feel like the good little boy playing hooky. And I tried to convince myself I looked a young forty. After all, all that tennis . . .

Never before in nineteen years of marriage had I deviated from the route to Grand Central. And never before had I been so aware, and terrified, of time passing. I was twenty years younger than my mother, and what was twenty years?

The tables around us were filled with young men and women with lots of hair. Tight buttocks. Flat stomachs. Smooth faces. Did they have any idea how free they were?

Bernadette said she lived in a walkup in the east eighties, giving me an instant picture as clear as if she had handed me a photograph. Fire escape clutching red-brick walls, tall stoop, garbage cans, surly cat, single men and women in an endless parade along the sidewalk carrying little bags of provisions and walking little dogs.

Up three flights of odorous stairs sagging under the weight of a half-century of hope, her apartment would have white walls, big posters, big cushions, foam-rubber couch, Salvation Army chairs, tables, and chests. I would be warned not to trip on the frayed rug, salvaged from a garbage pile or other interesting source.

"You're a terrific writer," she said. "I love your ads, they're really good. They aren't heavy, you know?"

I steeled myself for the question.

"What are you doing at Monty Bliss?" She asked it.

We would step out of our clothes, wrestle our way down to that foam-rubber couch.

"Getting my act together," I said, trying not to sound self-conscious mouthing the phrase of another generation. I explained I had a few free-lance accounts. A few more, I lied, and I would be able to open my own shop.

"If you need a great typist," she said, "I'm available."

I divulged my past to her. Big agency. Senior vice-president. Reorganization. Never played the game. Out. No more big agency for me. Too much tension for a man of my . . .

When something was on your mind there was no suppressing it. Your mind sprang a million leaks.

I would slip my hand between her leg, and she . . .

They were all doing it. A young woman in media lived with her boyfriend, another in traffic made no secret of dispensing it to a succession of applicants. The bosomy production lady appeared in slinky pants and no bra when her accountant-husband was out of town on someone's books.

Down on the foam rubber.

"Dynamite!" she would cry.

They were supercool nowadays. Take pleasure as it comes and no hangups. Boys and girls lived together in college dorms now and earned credit for it. What was the big deal?

"You're a great fuck," she would say while I dressed, glancing furtively at the Conrail schedule. "Let's not louse it up with a guilt trip." She would tuck it in with a final pat and a personal zip.

"Hey, Bern . . ."

We both looked up. It was for her, not me. A lean, tight-jeaned young man in his twenties loomed over our tiny table. I felt his puzzled look. He bent down and kissed her. Former lover? Future lover? Present lover? Happily, she introduced me by both names. If she said "Mr. Sloan" I would have crawled under the table. Grabbing a chair from a nearby table, he joined us without being asked, and I felt like a senior citizen.

They talked about a world I left a lifetime ago. Cheap rents, cheap wine, boring parents, breaking away. My wedding ring felt as if it weighed a ton. I mumbled something about a train.

"See you tomorrow," Bernadette perked. "Thanks."

The boy smiled slightly.

On the way to Grand Central I passed three buses loaded with old people lined up in front of the Summit Hotel, pennants on the sides heralding the arrival of the senior citizens of various New Jersey communities. As I watched them climb down through the doors, struggling over steps and rails as laboriously as if they were descending Everest—round-faced women girdled into doubleknit pants suits, bandy-legged men in tight plaid sportcoats, their cackling voices shrieking out commands to watch the luggage—I hated them.

The old were taking over—tomorrow's majority. We were hobbling into an old gray world filled with wizened faces shrieking through dentures for special attention, special privileges, special everything, as if growing old were to be rewarded, as if it were an achievement like inventing the laser beam or writing *Hamlet*. As if piling on years like emptying cereal boxes took brilliance.

I hated the old people playing gin, cha-chaing in Miami, swarming like ants in the sun, bitter at the young for their years still ahead, being coy with their doctors, filling the benches with their uselessness, assuming a right to demand and get because they had made it past sixty, seventy, eighty. Big deal.

I threaded my way angrily through them as they blocked the narrow sidewalk. Two fat ladies with dyed hair were flirting with the big-haunched uniformed driver.

On the train I was caught by Maury Lipshitz, the Shoe King; or was I catching him? He asked—what else—about my mother.

"Great," I said. "Her hair's falling out, hair's growing on her face, and she goes into tantrums. She has become the center of our lives and we are on the verge of divorce."

Peggy, he said, would never put up with his mother in the house. "I call her every day," Maury said. "The first thing she asks is why didn't I call sooner. It can drive a man to drink."

"Rotten luck, Maury," I said. He and his brother inherited a chain of shoe-repair shops (The Shoe King) from an uncle, saving Maury from driving a bus.

Opening his Wings briefcase, Maury asked me to offer an opinion on some ads his agency had just given him.

"Are you offering me your account?" I asked.

"There's not enough money in it for you," he laughed nasally as he covered my lap with ads, a lap that was almost covered with Bernadette.

"Sorry, Maury," I said, exhibiting a side of my personality I had never unearthed to strangers, "I don't give it away on trains."

Fumbling his briefcase closed with a nervous nasal giggle, he said if he or Peggy could do anything to be sure and call; but not in the mornings—Peggy had her tennis game.

The television blared from my mother's room—surprise—as I stepped through the front door. Steven was up in his room, the door closed. Paul was out. He was out a good deal lately.

"I keep telling you, don't work so hard," my mother scolded from her bed as I lowered the volume. "So late."

"Thanks for telling me," I said.

"You know I've provided for you," she said.

"I have to live now," I said.

"You want me to die sooner?" she cried. "I'm not ready yet."

What happened? What did I say?

"Go, run upstairs," she called after me. "Your dear wife ran up already."

In the bedroom Ethel lay in a deep sleep, the sleep of the

drugged, the television on. I was being pursued by the sound of television.

That boy and Bernadette were probably making it, I thought as I slipped into bed, trying to remember what sex was like.

25

ETHEL'S HEAD drooped over her plate. The boys looked at her curiously. I tensed. "What's the matter, Ethel?" my mother asked. "See, you shouldn't work so hard."

"Ethel," I said, "why don't you lie down?"

She mumbled that she was all right. But she was obviously not all right.

I wanted to scream at her. Did she have to broadcast the fact that she could not step through the door without fortifying herself with Valium? Or worse. We were turning into a statistic. Too many nights Ethel's speech was slurred, her eyes glazed. Like my mother, she always had a reason. She was tired, she had not slept, it was a headache, her period, she hadn't eaten all day.

Having a sick mother was bad enough; I hardly needed a sick wife.

It was a totally different Ethel from the woman who a few months earlier went loyally to exercise classes at the Y and even substituted for the teacher. She no longer exercised, she ate foods she once scorned, stuffing herself angrily with sweets and starches. She had grown indifferent to her appearance and seemed constantly on the verge of tears.

"Wait till I have my own apartment," my mother smiled. "I'll cook some real meals."

"Rye bread and farmer's cheese?" Paul asked.

She gave him a look. "Wait till you taste my potato pudding," she said. "It could win prizes. Remember how you used to love it, Bernie?"

When would it stop?

"You don't have baked potatoes?" My mother winced at the platter of boiled potatoes Steven offered her. "They taste like soap. I only eat Idaho baked potatoes."

"Why don't you bake some?" Ethel asked. "When I'm at work."

She looked at Ethel as if she had suggested she bake herself. "I can't even turn on your stove," she said. "You need an engineer."

"I'll show you," said Paul. "It's easy."

"When you're healthy"—she gave her customary retort—"everything's easy."

After dinner we all did our disappearing act. Steven to his room to study. Paul to the phone. My mother to the television. Ethel to the kitchen to finish her daily servitude. I hid in my den where I could always find a free-lance ad to write, bills to pay, stock market advice to consider.

Be understanding, said the books on dying. Make allowances. Love. Easy to be an expert from the outside. Interviews. Discussions with colleagues over lunch. Weekends on the golf course. Try living the scene, you experts who want us to keep the dying at home. Day after day, night after night, no break, constant responsibility. Not a move could we make without first thinking of my mother. She the sick one, she the weak one, was controlling our lives. And I had the awful feeling that she loved it. Even if she had to die to do it.

I read book after book on "the dying," as if they were some newly discovered species. I looked to experts for the answers. Just as we once poured over Dr. Spock. Just as others read sex manuals. How do we Americans manage to grow to adulthood removed from so much direct experience that we need books to tell us how to perform the most fundamental activities of life?

All the books make the same mistake. They all speak of the dying as if they are different from the living. And as if they are identical. I have news for the "experts." The dying are the living and the living are the dying. We are all the same people. Dying is a part of living, the final step. And everyone walks a little differently.

It may not make for neat index cards and well-organized research papers, but all the categories make no difference when you are dealing with your own parent, who is different from somebody else's parent. Nobody is qualified to give instructions. Because they just don't know. You blunder through it as best you can. There are no experts.

My mother had no intention of letting go of the self that was seventy-odd years in the making and turning into some expert's conception of what a dying person should be. Even if she thought she were dying.

As the crevices widened in our family, I questioned what I had done so automatically. For love, guilt, fear, who knows? Why was I subjecting my family to this unbelievable strain? Wasn't our living just as important as her dying? We were all dying. She hardly had a monopoly on it. And each day lost in argument and anger was a day lost forever. Dead. Just as dead as if it came at the end of life.

That evening's after-dinner explosion came when I picked up the phone in my den and heard Paul's voice. I stormed down the stairs, shouting that the phone was not for his exclusive use. There were other people in the house. What if Dr. Gordon called?

"He's getting help with his homework," Ethel intercepted.

Paul insisted that he had only been on the phone for five minutes.

We looked at each other in silence. I said I was sorry, but I would appreciate some consideration. In case the doctor called, I said lamely, all of us knowing the doctor never called before eleven when he returned from his hospital rounds at the end of his fifteen-hour day, evidently unaware that doctors no longer toiled with such dedication.

Paul told me that I was always angry about something. He was right. I walked in the door angry, I walked out the door angry. I found fault with everything. Too many lights on, the door to the attic open or closed, the toilet paper hung the wrong way, the dishwasher improperly loaded. I lived at war.

The next explosion came when the telephone rang again. This time a voice asked for Ethel. A travel client. But when I called her there was no answer. I roared her name from the top of the stairs. Neither Steven nor Paul had a clue to her whereabouts. I looked out the window. The car was gone.

"Where is Ethel?" my mother called over the sound of the television. She was smiling.

"A travel meeting," I said.

"I thought someone kidnapped her," my mother said.

I told the caller that Ethel was at a travel presentation, I had forgotten.

When I heard the car pulling into the driveway an hour later, I pounced.

"Where the hell were you?"

"I went to get some milk," she said unconvincingly.

"Two hours?"

"I was near the Lianettis, so I stopped in to see Sally."

"Do you think," I asked, "you might do the courteous thing and let someone know when you're going out, and where?"

"I thought it would be a few minutes."

"All right, but . . . ."

"Do you know what it's like telling someone who calls that my wife is out, and I don't know where, and I have no idea when, if ever, she'll be back?"

"I didn't expect . . ."

"It doesn't matter what you expected . . ."

She was meeting men at the travel agency. Airline representatives took her out for lunch, drinks. Men came in to book trips; divorced men, widowers, men who did not bring her a mother.

"How would you feel if I disappeared in the evenings?" I asked. "Wouldn't you wonder?"

"I'm not having an affair," she said. "I don't even remember what sex is like."

"Thanks."

One night she said she drove over to the water, walked through Manor Park.

"Alone? At night?"

"I had to think."

"You don't have to live in the city to get murdered, you know."

"I had to get away."

"Can't you talk to me?" I asked.

"You're the problem," she said.

"Maybe I can help solve it."

"You'll just get angry and scream."

"I won't scream."

"I'm so tired of everyone screaming. Your mother screams at me downstairs, you scream at me upstairs."

"I won't scream," I said, raising my voice.

"I wish I could cope better," she said. "I wish I were stronger. But when someone is sick I try to help them. I don't know what to do when she attacks me. I keep trying to make her happy, but the more I try the worse she is. I don't understand her. Doesn't she know all I'm doing for her? She doesn't have anyone else. She's all alone. And still she screams at me. I want to help her. She's dying. I don't know how to scream and fight. I never learned how. I never had to. Does that make me so awful?"

I took her in my arms.

It was time to live for ourselves again.

If we could only figure out how.

26

THE WEXLERS WERE COMING, the Wexlers were coming.

It was the biggest social event in our house in months. We were seeing people. Not visiting nurses, nurses aides, companions, social workers, but friends. Our friends in our house. We were going to spend one day not focused on my mother.

"We can't keep on living like recluses," I stormed at Ethel. "We have to see people. We have to live a normal life."

"She'll make it impossible," Ethel warned. "She'll come out in her housecoat and talk about Israel and how everybody loves her."

The Wexlers were coming for tennis at the town courts, followed by dinner.

From the moment Ethel set foot in the kitchen that Sunday my mother pursued her with comments. The meat was too fat, the spices not good for people, the pot not as good as her pot in storage. Who could eat asparagus? How could Ethel even consider entertaining without a cake? "Bernie," she said, "always loved double chocolate layer cake."

Nelda Wexler arrived, alas, with a bandaged ankle, twisted in yoga class, dashing Ethel's escape plan. Dick and I played tennis, leaving "the three girls," he joked, in the house.

The moment my mother heard that the Wexlers had been to Israel, she captured Nelda to inform her that the high government officials had virtually declared a national holiday to celebrate her arrival. Her friends were, without exception, among the most influential in the country, showing her sights kept secret from lesser mortals. "Do you think my friends would let me miss a thing?" she asked.

When Nelda attempted to talk to Ethel, who was working like Cinderella in the kitchen, my mother followed Nelda with stories of her nieces whose cooking could win medals. "Wait till I have my own apartment," she promised Nelda, "you'll come for real Jewish cooking."

Nelda did not bother to tell her that she was Protestant.

It was a red-eyed, tight-lipped Ethel who greeted Dick and me on our return from tennis. "I'm glad you had fun," she said, her words slurred.

We changed and had drinks, my mother watching me disapprovingly at the bar. All through dinner my mother offered a running commentary on the shortcomings of the meal. "You must be a wonderful cook," she smiled at Nelda. "I can tell."

The last time we had dinner at the Wexlers the casserole was burned and everything that was supposed to rise fell.

In the middle of my mother's comments on the lack of rye bread, Ethel jumped up and fled to the kitchen, Nelda following.

"It's the heat," my mother said to Dick and me. "What can you expect from old air conditioners?"

Dick said it felt cool to him.

"Not like I had in Arizona," she said. "I had it so cold you could freeze to death."

"You want to freeze to death?" Dick asked.

"I will in the winter here, if I want to or not," she said.

"They don't have heat?" Dick asked.

"Who knows what they have?" she said.

I told Dick my mother was thinking about looking for an apartment and she was terrified that it would not be warm enough for her.

She glared at me.

"See anything you like?" Dick asked.

"All they have around here are old buildings," she said, making a face. "I'm not going to take just anything—no matter what anyone wants me to do."

"My mother has very high standards," I said.

"Of course," she said. "Look at you."

"I hope you find what you like," Dick said.

"Don't worry," she said. "I always get what I want. Maybe people don't want me to, but I do."

"You're very lucky," Dick said.

"The luckiest girl in the world," she said.

As Nelda emerged with Ethel from the kitchen, hands linked, Nelda said it was time to leave, tomorrow was work. Nelda, one of the legions of women returning to work, did proofreading for a technical magazine on the Island, and Dick was an advertising writer. We once worked on a peanut-butter account together. Dick came to work each day expecting to be fired, a thought that never crossed my mind. So, naturally, I was the first to go. It took another six months for him.

"Next time our house," Nelda said at the car. My mother's silhouette was outlined in the darkness against the screen door.

"I'm sorry," Ethel whimpered. "I knew it would happen."

"I'll call you tomorrow," Nelda said as they sped off.

"I've never known a grown woman to cry so much," I tore into Ethel as we stood on the curb. "You're always crying."

"I'm not always crying," she said.

"When Angelina left you cried."

"It was one thing on top of another."

"And today . . ."

"You expect me to be happy about today? It was one of the worst days of my life."

"Is it my fault that Nelda twisted her ankle?"

"Is it my fault that your mother is here?"

"Ignore her for one day."

"From the minute I got up this morning she kept after me. She followed me around the kitchen to tell me what was wrong with everything I was doing."

"So you cry?"

"What's my choice?"

"A grownup woman doesn't go around crying all the time."

"Maybe I'm having a breakdown," Ethel sniffled. "People do."

"Go ahead and have it," I cried. "But don't have it here."

"Thanks for the sympathy."

"That's what you want, isn't it? Sympathy. Poor Ethel. Her mother-in-law bugs her in the kitchen. Her mother-in-law doesn't say the right thing to her; she looks at her the wrong way and poor Ethel is upset. Damn it, do something. Being upset isn't doing anything. Be a person, for God's sake, be a person."

"I'm trying," she sniffled, "but I'm cracking up. Don't you understand? It can happen."

"That's crazy," I said.

"Of course it's crazy, that's the idea. I tell myself I won't let her affect me. I tell myself I'll ignore her, turn the other cheek. I keep hoping she'll change, but it gets worse. You wouldn't believe the thoughts that go through my mind."

"Choose not to crack up," I said.

"People can't always choose how they're going to react."

"They sure can," I said. "You can decide to be a person, or you can crumble and cry 'pity me.' "

"You try spending a week in the house with her," Ethel said.

"My God, she's an old woman dying of cancer. Surely you're strong enough to cope with her. You think Nelda would go around crying?"

"Nelda once tried to slash her wrists," Ethel reminded me.

"Before therapy," I said.

"You know what Nelda told me to do?" Ethel said. "Take the boys and leave you with your mother."

"Great solution," I said.

Ethel never demanded. She never became the mainstay at Saks and the local hairdresser. No beach clubs, no live-in help. She cut out coupons, bought clothes on sale. Ironically, if she was the Jewish princess my mother wished I had married, my mother would have been slammed into any home but ours. Those "nice Jewish girls" did not give up their tennis games, club meetings, and hairdresser's appointments to take care of sick mothers-in-law.

"I'm going to bed," Ethel said. "I'll do the dishes in the morning."

"It's only nine o'clock."

"It's my privilege. You stay and keep your mother company for a change."

"I'll be up soon."

"I'll be asleep."

"I'll wake you."

"I'm taking a pill."

"You used to condemn people who relied on drugs."

"I used to do a lot of things," she said as she went inside, passing my mother in the foyer without saying a word.

"She isn't feeling well, Ethel?" my mother asked.

"She'll manage," I said.

"I'm sure," my mother said. "Strong like a bull. Germans."

A few weeks later when I bumped into Dick on the street in New York, he said they could not wait to get out of our house. "The tension was palpable," he said.

That was the last time we got together with the Wexlers.

Nothing like having good friends.

27

ONCE AGAIN I STIRRED UNEASILY in what passed for sleep—an on-and-off semiconsciousness in which the world was never totally extinguished, dreams and reality mingling. Through the open window came the wheeze of trucks on the thruway a mile away, a sound that had escaped my notice for fourteen years.

Sensing something wrong, I climbed out of bed, put on a robe, and stepped out to the hallway. From downstairs came the glow of the hall light and the perpetual sound of television. Light seeped under Steven's closed door. Paul's door was partly open, as always. Paul sleeping soundly in a room filled with guitar, amplifier, microphone—all the essential equipment of a jazz guitarist. From his radio came the sounds of progressive jazz. Brubeck born again.

I rapped gently on Steven's door.

As he stood in the doorway in his striped pajamas I was shocked at how gaunt he looked, like a concentration-camp inmate.

"You're still up?" I asked, wincing at the crack of his knuckles. "Are you all right?"

"Why?" he smiled.

"It's two o'clock," I said, as if that were enough to make him sick. "Studying?"

He hesitated.

"I'm thinking of dropping one of my courses," he said.

Not Steven. The boy who always took more courses than were required, the boy who devoured learning.

Feeling like an intruder, I stepped into his room and closed the door. The room looked like the proverbial tornado. Papers, books, clothing piled everywhere. Exactly like my room when I was his age. "English history," he said. "It's an elective. I don't need it for credit."

"You don't like it?" I asked. For which I would not blame him. I majored in English in college and regretted every wasted year.

"I like it," he said.

"Then how come?"

He hesitated.

"Too big a load?"

His knuckles cracked. After a long, painful pause he squeezed out his feelings. "It's hard to study," he said, "with all the screaming in the house."

It was a slap in the face.

"You're either screaming at Nana or Mom, or Nana's screaming or Mom's crying." He paused. "The AP courses aren't easy."

AP meant advanced placement. They were college-level courses offered by our high school, which the top colleges accepted.

"Sometimes," Steven's eyes watered, "I wish . . ."

Why was this happening to us?

"It won't make any difference for college," he said. "I'll have all my credits."

The hell with college. It was his life.

"What if the screaming stops?" I asked. It had to stop. I had to make it stop.

"I don't know," he said.

"Let me try," I said. "Don't do anything yet. Can you give it another week?"

"I guess so," he said.

"You don't have to if you don't want to," I said quickly. I had never pressured either of our boys. I felt it was up to them to fulfill their potential, whatever it might be. All I could do was provide them with the opportunity for a good education and exposure to life's possibilities. I had learned that neither college, money, nor a home in the right suburb had anything to do with self-fulfillment or happiness.

"I'll try," he said.

"So will I," I said.

As I started to leave, I took another look at him. "You think you might try eating?" I asked. "I understand food is required for survival."

He smiled nervously, shifting what little there was of his weight. "I don't get hungry," he said.

I understood.

Two weeks later he dropped the course. It followed an explosive night in which my mother burst into the kitchen crying that it was not true she hated gentiles and that Ethel was trying to poison the boys' minds against her. I cried back that it was logical for Paul to think that, considering all she talked about was Jews, Jews, Jews and how much smarter they were than gentiles. "I can't wait to get out of here!" she screamed. "And I can't wait to see you go!" I raged.

A month later Steven was in the hospital. None of the tests explained why he had stopped eating. As the needle fed nourishment into his veins, the doctor announced that it was a bad case of nerves—common among high-school seniors with so many pressures, especially sensitive ones like Steven who had been accepted by M.I.T. and might be worried about living up to it.

Teenagers had it rough, the doctor said. The chief cause of teenage deaths was suicide.

"But I wouldn't worry about Steven," he said. "He's a level-headed boy. And smart. He'll do fine."

He was out of the hospital in a week.

28

A SMILE LIT UP my mother's face. "I went a whole day without a pain pill," she announced. "I felt so good I could have gone to a dance."

I tingled with her.

Maybe the chemotherapy was working. Maybe the doomsayers were wrong. She had a fifty-fifty chance, said Dr. Gordon. Maybe the fighter who had outsmarted the Cossacks and the Germans and the inspectors at Ellis Island and the doctor who said she would never walk—the fighter who had shown everyone that she was a somebody—could beat the damn myeloma cells. "It's a diabolical disease," said Dr. Gordon. "It tortures you, then it lets up, then it tortures you again. But if we catch it in time, if we find the right combination of chemicals . . ."

"I would confidently put my life in the hands of Jerry Gordon," said Dan Green.

"I think soon I can start looking for an apartment," my mother said. "Your problems will be over."

It was unbelievable that everything might work out the way it was supposed to. Yet every day there were stories of new cures in the newspapers. A discovery here, a breakthrough there. We were not living in a dream world as Dr. Spiegelstrauss suggested.

"I'm going to give a big donation and be a somebody in Larchmont," she said again. She had donated to a Hebrew home for the aged in Arizona—and to a hospital and school in Israel. Plaques bearing the names of my mother and father announced them all. "Everybody sees them," my mother said proudly. "They can't wait for me to come back to Israel. They all know me. All the high government officials."

"I'm sure with your personality they would want you even if you didn't give a penny," I said.

"I'm sure too," she said. "Still, it doesn't hurt. No one refuses a gift." She looked at us meaningfully. "You have to make a name for yourself. Why do you think Raskin wanted me? Because I was young and beautiful? Believe me, he could have had a spring chicken. I had a big name in the city. People couldn't say I married him for his money. Don't think they weren't jealous. Even Pearl, your sweetheart. 'Don't marry him, Dora,' she told me, like I needed her opinion. 'He isn't right for you.' You think I didn't know what she wanted? A hundred women were ready to grab him. I wish they did."

She groaned at the grim memories.

"I was a regular bird in a gilded cage," she said. "On the outside everything looked beautiful. But I was a prisoner. He expected me to have a big lunch ready for him every day. Like I married him to be his cook. Every place I went he had to come. He stopped me from living."

"So you've had four years of freedom," I said.

"Do you know what it's like being alone?" she asked. "You can go crazy talking to the walls."

You couldn't win.

Only my father succeeded in pleasing her; and that required surrendering his life. He decreed her to be the most beautiful, intelligent, desirable woman attainable. Balding, graying, paunchy, he looked much older than she and professed to be delighted at being taken for her father. Nine years older, they told me. But my birth certificate, which I needed years later for a passport, said it was nineteen.

"Don't aggravate your mother!" I can hear him roar to this day. He lived in dread that if one of us upset her she would vanish.

They toiled from eight in the morning until nine at night in the hardware store, saving for the day when they could live. While Cousin Florence played Mah-Jongg and Aunt Sarah danced at charity balls, my mother hovered over customers and worried about losing a sale. It was ten o'clock by the time they tallied the day's receipts and climbed to our flat upstairs. The next day they repeated the process.

They installed a buzzer in the flat to summon my mother when there were more customers than my father and the clerk could handle. "It always buzzes when I'm on the toilet," she used to say.

Convinced that her family wished to see her fail, too embarrassed to invite them to our flat over the store, she had a falling-out with nearly every relation, so that I grew up without knowing aunts, uncles, cousins. The war that wiped out their families left in Europe brought my parents enough money at last to pay up their properties, sell the store, and retire to Arizona for my father's asthma.

"I had eight beautiful years," said my father from his hospital bed.

Cancer of the pancreas.

"Saul, don't do this to me," my mother wailed as the breathing mask dangled over the edge of the bed.

"Tell them distinguished," she screamed as I wrote the announcement for the newspaper. "Tell them he comes from a distinguished family."

My mother eyed the crowd at the funeral home angrily. "Now they can feel sorry for me," she said.

Three years later she married Cy Raskin, widower, owner of Tecumseh's Indian souvenir shops. She sold her elegant home ("How would it look for him to move into my house?") and they moved into the apartment, selling everything but her bedroom set. Although they summered in Santa Monica, traveled to Europe and Israel, she complained that he came home for lunch. "Let him eat out," she said, befitting a woman with a Marie Antoinette bedroom set.

"Would you believe?" she glowed. "Not a second of pain. All day."

Suddenly we were all free of pain. We were jubilant. Her happiness was contagious. It affected all of us.

"Come," she said, "Let's go out to dinner. My treat, kids."

The boys looked at me as if they were witnessing a miracle.

We went to a Chinese restaurant where she astounded us all by eating the wonton soup without questioning the slices of meat, undeniably pork, and devouring an egg roll with its forbidden shrimp. She loved the fake waterfall and the murals of Hawaii, where she had been with Raskin.

"I can't wait to get my own place," she said. "I'll fix it up like a doll's house. If you're lucky I'll invite you for dinner. It's nice living near children, but you don't have to live exactly in the same house with them. I'll be able to have what I want when I want it; I won't have to ask for favors."

We were swept up in her happiness. We felt a joy at being together that briefly erased the months of tension. She could be fun and delightful. Why not all the time? Was it only the pain? The chemotherapy? She pronounced every dish delicious. She had been transformed, and so were we.

Ethel said she had a friend whose mother lived in a perfect apartment building. Paul knew a teacher in another building. And Steven had a friend in a building with a pool.

That did it.

Her face darkened. Her voice tightened. "I'll look when Dr. Gordon says I'm ready to look," she said. Her moods changed unpredictably. Say the wrong thing, lightning flashed.

"I've never known such a suspicious person," said Dr. Spiegelstrauss. This was a month after telling me "what a remarkable person was my mother," so different from other old people who were dull and had nothing to say.

As my mother was getting into the car outside the restaurant, her legs gave way and she fell to the curb, sitting helplessly, her legs sprawled out like a rag doll's. She did not trip or slip on anything. She just fell.

"I'm fine," she insisted. "It's the excitement of being out."

But that night she asked me to open her bottle of pain pills. "A curse on these caps," she cried.

"It hurts?" I asked.

"A little," she admitted, which meant it was excruciating and she was afraid of hospitals. "In my chest," she said. "From when I fell. You had to park so far from the curb."

If she hurt anything when she fell it would not be her chest. On the shelves a few feet from her bed were medical books. She had only to open one to find the definition of multiple myeloma.

Multiple Myeloma
A progressive and ultimately fatal neoplastic disease characterized by marrow plasma cell tumors and overproduction of intact monoclonal immunoglobulins ... and often associated with ... anemia, renal damage, and increased susceptibility to bacterial infections. Persons over the age of 40 are most commonly affected.

Persistent unexplained skeletal pain (especially in the back or thorax), renal failure, or recurrent bacterial infections, especially pneumococcal pneumonias, are the commonest presenting symptoms. Anemia with weakness and fatigue may predominate in some patients. ... Pathologic fractures and vertebral collapse are common. ...

The disease is progressive, but optimal management improves the quality and duration of life. Life expectancy is related to the time of diagnosis, adequacy of supportive measures, and response to chemotherapy.*

Even if she refused to look in a book or hear what a doctor said, the doctor bills and Medicare forms clearly stated "chemotherapy." And if by some remote chance the significance of the word had eluded her all these years, the television and newspapers were filled with reports of Hubert Humphrey undergoing chemotherapy treatments for his cancer.

As she eased herself behind the bedrail and lay back on the mountain of pillows, she took a deep breath and looked at me. "Maybe we *should* see about an apartment this weekend," she said. "I might as well enjoy it now."

*Reproduced from *The Merck Manual*, thirteenth edition, copyright under the Universal Copyright Convention and the International Copyright Convention 1977 by Merck & Co., Inc., Rahway, New Jersey.

29

"HER ULCERS have cleared up," said Dr. Gordon in one of our near-midnight phone conversations, "but . . .

"But" is the word I could most easily do without in the English language. "But"—a flashing yellow signal. Trouble ahead.

". . . but I'm afraid . . . not much success . . . the myeloma . . . chemotherapy not working as well as . . . blood count poor . . . no sign . . . remission."

Then why, I protested, did she seem to be getting better? The pain in her shoulder, gone. She raised her arm over her head without a wince. She had gained weight, walked with a bounce, long ago abandoned her cane, even drove her car with me beside her for two blocks.

There was no explanation, he said. It was the nature of the disease. It was enough to encourage belief in the devil.

I asked why the area devoured by the myeloma cells did not continue to hurt. If bones had been ravaged, how could they feel perfectly normal?

"We don't know the answer," he said wearily. "We don't know why, but the patient appears to get better while the myeloma continues to advance. We don't know why."

He was going to start her on a more aggressive cycle of chemotherapy, one that might cause stronger reactions.

"Is there hope?"

"There's always hope," he said.

If he had started earlier?

"Any treatment should be started as soon as possible," he said.

"She's been looking at apartments," I told him.

A pause. "Your mother is a very independent woman," he said. "She says she'll invite me for a kosher meal as soon as she has her apartment"—he burst out laughing.

"Can she manage it?"

A longer pause. "If she has someone with her, I suppose."

"We'll find someone," I said. "It would be nearby."

"Why not?" he said. "If she really wants it, give it a try."

I wanted him to assure me that it was the right thing to do, and he was telling me to give it a try, like a new shaving cream.

"She's very lucky to have you people to give her so much support," he said.

"What do people do who don't have a family?" I asked. "Who helps them?"

"They die sooner," he said.

Ethel looked up at me from the bed, turning off the TV news with the screams of yet another angry mob demanding theirs. "The chemotherapy isn't working," I said, slumping into the big vinyl club chair left us by a psychiatrist friend. Its bottom was, appropriately, falling out.

She visibly whitened.

"We have to do something," she said.

For nearly six months we had to do "something." All our conversations began with the hope of reaching what that "something" was and ended in exhaustion and frustration.

We heard of a couple brought to the brink of divorce by a dying father. Please, I thought, not us, not now. The logistics, the legalities, the moving. I could handle sickness, unemployment, and losing my wife, but I could not cope with putting the house on the market.

"Dr. Gordon said she could try an apartment," I said quickly.

"Impossible," Ethel said yet again. "She can't do anything for herself *here*; how is she going to manage on her own?"

"If she has to, she will," I said. "If she doesn't have you to do everything for her . . ."

We had the same discussion night after night. We were using up our lives discussing my mother. What did other people do? There was Mrs. Barry with her oxygen tank. The police were always rushing over to save her life. She made do with a series of companions. Women, high-school girls. But she also had children and grandchildren nearby. The priest came to see her every week. Perhaps he could give a course for rabbis.

"Sally Lianetti says there's an apartment coming up in her mother's building," Ethel said.

It was my mother's kind of building. The kind where you had to know someone to get in. They never put up a sign, and everyone knew why.

"Even if she's only in it for a few months," I said. "At least she'll enjoy it before she dies. And . . . she won't be here."

"Why does it have to be this way?" Ethel asked. "In our family the young took care of the old."

Because in her family the old cared for the young. They gave love, they received love. But my mother, I had come to learn, cared for no one. Not for Ethel, not for her grandchildren, not for me.

I actually envied people whose parents had died.

"Ask Sally about the apartment," I said.

"SHE HAD TO COME with a cold!" my mother screamed, the cough wrenching her chest apart, the spasms exploding pain through every bone in her body. "She brought me a gift!"

The nurse's aide had come in sniffling. The next day my mother had a runny nose, the next a slight cough, a few days later a deep cough that rumbled in her chest and strangled her as she fought to hold back the spasms that felt as if they were cracking her ribs.

"I who was always so careful," she cried. "I have to have a shampoo? The world would stop if one week I didn't have a bath?"

It struck just when she was euphoric. After weeks of searching she found an apartment that met all her specifications; no easy accomplishment. A spacious four rooms in a building she could describe with her favorite word—impressive. The lobby with its beamed ceilings, paneled walls, fireplace, and doorman looked like a castle, lacking only ropes and tour groups. She would have large rooms, big closets, a modern kitchen, and—status of status—a bathroom with both a tub and a stall shower. Her windows opened on hills and trees, yet the building was a few steps from a supermarket and the center of town. Even the incinerator and elevator were just where she liked them—near her door.

It had been no easy find. If Ethel liked an apartment, my mother accused her of wanting to be rid of her. If Ethel did not like it, it was because she did not want my mother to live in a nice place. All the while, Dr. Spiegelstrauss continued to hiss that "a mistake we were making." Nursing homes were what she should be investigating, not apartments. "Wait and see," she warned, "I am talking not just through my cap."

"But she seems better," I insisted.

"Do not judge by what it seems"—she called me at work where she knew my mother could not listen. "I know this disease. We have for it a cure not found. We can only prolong life; do you understand? Maybe a few months. But stop it we cannot. It keeps on advancing until when the internal organs it hits that is the end, finished; do you know what I am saying?"

I knew what she was saying.

But Dr. Gordon said she had a fifty-fifty chance.

Somewhere there was a combination of chemicals.

"There is no combination that can stop the disease," whispered Dr. Spiegelstrauss. "Slow it down it could happen maybe, but stop not. And even then . . ." she paused, "who knows if it is worth the pain? She will have to take all the time stronger pills. The worst is cobalt treatments. Don't let them give to her the cobalt treatments. It is torture, and they don't do no good finally."

Even if she were in the apartment one month, one week, one day, I thought, it was worth it. Let her have some pleasure before she dies. Let her have her bedroom set and her crazy lamps.

She arranged for phones after much discussion with the phone company; she arranged for utilities after fighting Con Ed over their demand for a deposit; she came to terms with the local moving company for moving her possessions from our attic. She also decided to take the piano she once announced was for Paul. "I'm only borrowing it," she insisted to Paul, "you can come and play anytime." She needed it, she said. It was good therapy for her fingers.

Ignoring warnings that her cough could turn into pneumonia if she did not move, she clung to her bed like a barnacle, the congestion thickening. "It hurts when I move," she cried.

It was Catch-Cancer: to prevent pneumonia she should move,

yet the myeloma pain stopped her from moving. Each day as the rumble deepened she protested that she was getting better, it was nothing, until at two o'clock on a Saturday morning we heard her screams and ran down to find her sitting up in bed, gasping for breath, tears streaming down her puffed face, eyes bulging with terror.

While Ethel massaged her chest and pounded her back, I called Dr. Gordon, reaching his answering service, which answered almost immediately. And within five minutes Dr. Gordon called. He said he would meet us at Teller at seven in the morning when all the facilities would be in operation.

It was pneumonia, he told me in the corridor. Both the myeloma and the chemotherapy weakened the body, he explained, leaving it vulnerable to the slightest infection. "More cancer patients die from secondary infections than from their cancer," he said—information that might have been more valuable if offered earlier.

"If not the aide," people said, "it would be something else. You can't keep someone sealed up in a jar."

Still . . .

"He has no idea she lies in bed all day," Ethel defended Dr. Gordon. "She tells him how active she is. He thinks she's doing all the shopping and cooking while I'm having fun at the travel agency. When she's with him she's peppy and charming and bouncy. He would never dream she would take to her bed with a little cough."

My mother was succeeding in impressing people right into her grave.

"I shouldn't say this," Ethel said, "but when I saw you come back from the hospital alone I was glad."

So was I.

On Monday morning I canceled the telephone, Con Ed, and the local moving company until further notice. There was no stopping the furniture on the way from Arizona to my mother's new apartment.

31

"IF YOU AREN'T DEAD when they bring you here, it won't be long before they finish you off," was my mother's verdict of the famous medical center with its brilliant staff, responsible for some of the most important discoveries of the century.

Waves of gifted medical students surged around my mother's bed to poke, prod, scrutinize, interrogate. Delighted at first with the attention, eagerly describing the state of every inch of her body, she soon dreaded their arrival.

"They have doctors here from all over the world," she announced, impressed. Later, weary of their examinations, she said, "Who needs them?"

They plugged her in and wired her up so that she looked like an octopus connected by a maze of tubes to the nozzles, hoses, and couplings jutting from the wall behind her bed. Running out of wall space, they hooked her up to overhead bottles on stands. At her fingertips a plastic mask was ready to dispense instant oxygen, and a machine stood poised to shoot a snake down her throat to suck up phlegm. "A cup of hot water works better," she said.

She proudly announced that she was having a blood transfusion, which involved a plastic pouch (the world was turning into plastic pouches) suspended overhead sending a steady flow of blood through yet another plastic tube jabbed into another vein.

When I joked that she might be getting a black's blood, she surprised me by saying she hoped she did. "They're strong like iron," she said. "Nothing bothers them."

They stopped the chemotherapy. It canceled the effects of the antibiotics. It was a choice of fighting the pneumonia or the myeloma. Death was playing games with her again.

"The worst thing medical science did was find a cure for pneumonia," said Dan Green, trimming his hedge. "It used to be a way for people to die painlessly. Now we save them for years of agony."

"They give you enough food to feed a horse," was my mother's comment on the kosher meals she was getting at last, meals I thought she would love. "If you want you can order the whole menu," she said, hiding rolls and cartons of spoiling milk in her night-table drawer. "As soon as you finish one meal they come with the next," she said, "they don't give you a second to digest anything." Teller, like other hospitals, was run for the convenience of the staff. All meals were packed into an eight-hour shift.

My mother was one of three women in a room originally built for two. Televisions hung from the ceiling, aimed like death rays at the beds. Curtains, attached to ceiling rails, could be drawn around each bed for privacy.

"All night long there's a regular orchestra in the hall," she said. "You can't sleep for a second."

Which was nothing compared to her war with the nurses.

"They're so vicious," she shuddered. "Even the doctors are afraid of them. That's not my job, they say. Do you know what one of them told Dr. Gordon? He asked her to do something and she told him to do it himself, she only had two hands. Did you ever hear of such a thing? To a doctor?"

I dismissed her observations as exaggeration combined with a failure to wangle special attention until one afternoon I witnessed a sullen nurse enter the room without uttering a word, stick thermometers into the mouths of the three patients, note their temperatures, and leave. A nurse. Without uttering a word.

It was once a wonderful hospital, said a roommate, a cheery lady, and she unreeled the familiar story of the impossibility of firing the incompetent. "And they know it," she said. "All the hospitals are like that now."

"If you aren't finished eating when they come, they grab your tray anyhow," my mother said. "'You're all finished, aren't you?' they say. 'I am *not*,' I tell them. 'You'll take my tray when *I'm* ready, not when *you're* ready.'"

She might be plugged into the wall and connected to machines, but she had no intention of yielding to anyone's system. The nurses were there to serve her needs, and she had every intention of seeing that they did. "I expected an old lady," said a specialist sent by Dr. Gordon. "Instead I found a ball of fire."

She related that to me several times.

"A ball of fire," she repeated, tasting the words.

She alternated her fighting with her charm strategy. "You know what?" she said to a particularly strict nurse who was going about her duties with grim efficiency, "The more I see you the more I like you. You really run things beautifully."

There was no response.

"Would you believe it?" my mother said. "Nothing. Like talking to a wall."

One day a woman was brought in screaming on a stretcher, doctors swarming over her like locusts, my mother reported. She was placed in the corner bed, where she shrieked at the slightest touch. She screamed if anyone touched the bed, if a tray dropped, if a chair slid.

"She has the real McCoy," my mother said, looking without knowing at her own fate.

How, my mother asked, did they expect a person to get better in such an atmosphere? Just having a woman like that in the room could kill a healthy person. At other times she said that as bad as things were for her, there was always someone who had it worse.

"Such a devoted family," she said of the screaming woman. "She has somebody with her twenty-four hours a day. They love her so much."

"She must love them," I said.

"Why not?" my mother asked. "Look what they're doing for her."

She missed my point.

I called her daily but visited her only on weekends with either Paul or Steven. It was, I was quick to admit, a relief having her out of the house. The arguments subsided, the tension eased. Ethel spent a day cleaning the TV room—throwing out crumpled tissues and stale bread in napkins, discovering missing pens, photographs, and dish towels. I scraped and painted the flaking dining-room wall. We cleaned upholstery and washed curtains. It was clear we were hoping she would not return. She was already paying rent on her apartment, which was now officially hers. We were determined to move her directly to it from the hospital if her furniture would only arrive. It was somewhere between Arizona and her apartment. Not even the moving company knew for sure.

Much of our visiting time was spent watching my mother frown over the mail I brought her, mostly dividend checks and bank statements. Ethel had given her a red totebag with a kangaroo on it—one of our Australian acquisitions—into which she stuffed checkbooks and ledgers before leaving for the hospital, adding when reminded a robe, slippers, and toothbrush. She soon asked us for additional bags to accommodate the rubbing alcohol, tissues, baby powder, lotions, and hard rolls.

As I watched her claw with pained fingers at envelopes and ledgers, I refused to make a move to help. I was angry and hurt. She had only to give me power of attorney and I would have kept her books, handled her banking, eased her expiring life. Nearly everyone we knew had that authority for their parents, as well as keys to their safe-deposit boxes. We were giving her far more than money could ever buy, and she did not trust us.

"You're dying without having lived," I wanted to cry to her but never could. "Open up, discover the world. Let go of the pennies and discover the gold."

Discover your daughter-in-law, who is doing more for you than all your beautiful nieces with their handsome husbands in their impressive homes. Discover your grandchildren and enjoy them for what they are, not for the "types" you want them to be. Experience the thrill of seeing them develop into themselves. Be surprised. Don't hate us for not being what you think we should be, but enjoy us for what we are; and let us enjoy you for what you are.

But she knew—and no one was going to tell her anything.

I said nothing. I was weary. Like Ethel I wanted no more screaming.

ONE NIGHT DR. SPIEGELSTRAUSS phoned to ask if I would pay the fifty-four dollars my mother owed her. Impressed by my celebrity status as the author of a "My Turn" page in *Newsweek,* she pro-

posed that we collaborate on her autobiography, which she had entitled, *How I Always Wanted to Become a Doctor Ever Since a Little Girl I
Was.*

"Not once did she visit me," my mother cried, tentacled like a
medieval prisoner to the wall. "Because she couldn't charge."

She dug furiously into the kangaroo totebag until she came up
with the proper ledger. With a mind whose sharpness would have
done credit to an M.I.T. professor, let alone a desperately sick
woman, she calculated that she owed Spiegelstrauss exactly fifty-
one dollars and fifty cents, including transportation. The giraffe,
she said, was late plenty times, every minute of which was recorded
in ink.

"What's another two fifty?" I asked. "She has no Social Security."

"Let her children give her the money," she cried, stuffing everything back into her totebag. "And what's the matter with her husband? I'm sure he isn't so sick."

"Aren't you going to write her a check?"

"When I'm ready," she said.

Why shouldn't others suffer a little too?

Thinking she might slip the telephone bill through Medicare,
she called people from the past. Countrymen from Europe, relatives, distant cousins of whose existence I was dimly aware. Some
had died, others had moved to Miami or old-age homes. The survivors expressed amazement at hearing from her ("What? You aren't
dead?"), and distress at her condition. They promised to make every attempt to visit her when they could get a ride.

The nurses may have been "murderers," but the doctors were
"angels." They neglected other patients, she reported proudly, to
be with her, so taken were they with her charms. And she was
speaking the truth. One of the doctors told me that my mother was
a terrific gal. "She's with it," he said. "You should see some of my
other elderly patients. I get a kick out of her."

"Everybody likes me," she told me, "except you."

"Maybe you're different with them," I said.

"Maybe," she said, after a pause. It was the closest we ever came
to reaching each other.

In her third week in the hospital Dr. Gordon told me that they had licked the pneumonia. Now they would be able to resume the more complex chemotherapy cycle. Hopefully, it would show better results.

I dreaded hearing what he was going to say. "She's ready to come home," he announced. "There's nothing more we can do for her in the hospital."

The moving company said it would be at least two weeks before her furniture arrived. It had been on the way for more than a month.

"Well, kids," she grinned as we helped her into the house, "like it or not, I'm back."

She was still coughing, her chest rumbled, and she could walk only with the aid of her walker.

It was the Sunday before Thanksgiving.

"Once they start going into the hospital, it's usually over in about six weeks," said a social worker friend.

Deep down I hoped she was right.

We could not continue this way.

If she was not going to get better . . .

33

ALTHOUGH PRONOUNCED FIT by the medical profession to leave the hospital, upon coming home my mother burrowed into her bed and would not leave it except for bodily needs.

Ignoring our pleas that movement was critical, the congestion could deepen once more, history repeat itself, she wailed that every bone in her body ached. Her only relief came from lying absolutely still. "Let me get better first," she cried, "then I'll do somersaults."

"How can a doctor let her out in her condition?" Ethel said. "She can't walk."

"He's sending her a physical therapist," I said.

"She's still congested," Ethel protested. "She sounds as bad as before."

"He said to use a vaporizer."

"If only you'd taken her to Harborneck Hospital," lamented our next-door neighbor, "she'd be in this marvelous extended-care pavilion." She described a heaven on earth where patients who no longer needed hospital treatment convalesced. No worries about companions, visiting nurses, therapists, meals.

But like most of the services that might have made life easier for us, it was out of reach. We had evidently made the mistake of seeking a hospital to save her life rather than ease her dying. Teller offered no such frivolities as an extended-care pavilion. And to be admitted to Harborneck you first had to be a patient in the basic hospital. It was a prerequisite, like English 101.

While clinging to her bed she asked continually about her furniture, as if she were about to move if it arrived tomorrow. "I won't be able to fix it up right away," she said, "but with God's help, soon."

She invoked the name of God frequently. God had brought her to our house, God had brought her to Dr. Gordon, God would restore her health.

Once again they poured in—the visiting nurse, a new aide, Dr. Spiegelstrauss, and, a new addition, a physical therapist Dr. Gordon had ordered from somewhere, paid for by Medicare. Before her pneumonia she ventured out to the living room to sit with Dr. Spiegelstrauss. Or she walked with Steven, proudly clutching his arm. But now she needed both hands to pilot her walker. And both hands had developed pain. From squeezing the walker too tight, she said.

Pain was also gnawing at the base of her spine and licking once again at her shoulder. She could not get out of bed now without taking a pain pill an hour ahead of time, pills that were now stronger.

"It's so good to be home," she said. "To sit and eat with people."

She was actually praising Ethel's cooking, rating her meals above hospital kosher.

Two days after coming back from the hospital she began to eat at the table standing up. Hovering over us from her walker, she bent to get the food from her plate—like a flamingo. She finally confessed to Ethel, but not to me, that the pain had intensified at the base of her spine, making sitting agony. Ethel found an inner tube left over from postpregnancy hemorrhoids, and my mother sat.

"It's from being in bed so much," my mother said.

The night before Thanksgiving she wet her bed. "Don't tell Bernie," she begged Ethel. "It's from the excitement of being out of the hospital."

On Thanksgiving Day we brought her to Ethel's parents, where she sat on the inner tube at the table. "I'm like a car," she joked. "I can't go anywhere without my tire."

For all her suffering she still managed to perform, complimenting Ethel's parents on a new painting on their wall. "You have very good taste," she announced to the gathering. "Everything you pick is simply beautiful." She joked with them about who really chose the furniture. Both Ethel's father and mother hovered over her, filling her plate, making sure that she lacked nothing. "Your mother is a wonderful cook," she proclaimed to Ethel. "Now I see where you learned." Ethel's mother beamed, Ethel said nothing. Her parents liked my mother; they felt that any problem was due to Ethel's lack of patience.

She looked like a shrunken doll once more—her face oddly youthful, framed by the ash-blonde wig she bought during the summer when Dr. Gordon appeared to be fulfilling his promise to make a new woman out of her.

Sitting next to Ethel's Aunt Barbara, a retired bookkeeper, my mother promised that they would take trips together in her Cadillac as soon as she had recovered. "I wanted to cry," Barbara told me later. I did.

That night she wet her bed again.

"It was an accident," she cried to Ethel. "The trip to your parents was too much for me. It shook me up."

The next night she defecated in her bed.

She hid it under mounds of sheets and blankets until the visiting nurse discovered it.

"I took too much milk of magnesia," she cried.

The visiting nurse cleaned it up, bathed my mother, put her

soiled linens, nightgown, and robe in the washing machine, made her bed with fresh sheets, and gave her the Delatestryl injection that caused hair to grow on her once-smooth face.

"Don't put me in an institution!" she cried.

"We're getting you a practical nurse," I said.

"I don't need a nurse," she protested.

"Ethel does," I said.

I spent hours calling for help. And being rebuked. "Don't you know," scolded stern agency women, "it's the middle of a long weekend?" How could anyone be so stupid as not to know that health aides either had weekend assignments or were away?

Should I be so lucky as to obtain the services of a leftover aide (did they admit to not being busy or did they feel like co-eds once felt about Saturday night?) I was warned of their rights. They were qualified to handle bedpans, prepare meals *only* for the patient, clean *only* the patient's area. They were absolutely forbidden, even in the direst emergency, to give medication, even aspirin.

The twenty-four-hour rate for a sleep-in aide was $45, the eight-hour rate $35. One agency owner offered three eight-hour aides.

"You mean $105?" I said.

"It's short notice, Mr. Sloan," she said.

An agency lady suggested Pampers to get us through the long weekend. Although my mother objected when Steven returned from the supermarket with them, Ethel later found the box opened.

After the visiting nurse informed Dr. Gordon's office of my mother's condition, an associate called to tell us that Dr. Gordon was away for the long holiday weekend, but since the symptoms in her spine sounded ominous to be sure to call first thing Monday morning. And be ready to rush my mother to Teller for cobalt treatments.

What an obliging disease, I thought, to wait until Monday.

I wondered what a person did who had no family. Who communicated with doctors, rushed him in for radiation, fought to save his life? A health aide? A health-related facility? They took only ambulatory patients. Old-age homes evicted you when you were sick. And nursing homes sedated you so that you lay in bed and made no waves.

Miraculously, the Never-Fail Agency called to report the unearthing of a wonderful, reliable Jamaican lady in Brooklyn, who would arrive without fail the next morning. If I encountered anything remotely resembling a problem, chirped Ms. Never-Fail, I was to call her at once. Her beeper kept her in constant touch with her twenty-four-hour answering service. Dedication.

Both the aide and my mother's furniture were due at the same time. Only my mother's furniture showed up.

As boxes, crates, paper, cardboard piled up in my mother's apartment, I tried desperately to reach the Never-Fail lady who had apparently gone beepless. Once again my mother defecated in her bed. Ethel cleaned it up. It was the lamb chops, my mother cried, that Ethel served the night before. Who could stand so much fat?

In came the long white sofa with legs missing, Marie Antoinette's bedroom set with chipped carved heads and scratched drawers. Her possessions looked as if they had been through a bombing. Deep gouges, veneer stripped off, broken figurines, torn lampshades. The movers, angered at our refusal to accept Thanksgiving Day delivery, dumped and banged cartons without mercy. I shuddered at the fate of the fragile objects trapped inside. A list was thrust at me. Note damages, anything missing, sign please. I signed. I would have signed a confession to heresy, anything to avoid counting and inspecting. I could only hope for business honor, a commodity in short supply with that famous moving company. When I discovered later that items were missing, they disclaimed all responsibility. You signed, they said, so there. They sent a letter thanking us for letting them be of service and looking forward to handling our next move.

Hurrying home, I met a young couple turning up our walk. "Hi!" sang out the young lady, offering me her cheek. "Diana Crane; my husband, Mel. You must be Bernie?"

It was one of my unknown Detroit cousins, the daughter of Uncle Zach with whom my mother was reunited after forty years of not being on "speaking terms," an expression I grew up hearing. Diana and Mel lived in Boston where Mel was in practice with his father, a dermatologist. Coming to New York for a wedding, Diana had called to say they would love to squeeze in a visit to dear Aunt Dora. When would it be most convenient for us? We agreed on

Sunday. This was Saturday.

"Sorry to pop in a day early," chirped Diana, "but it was so much easier for us. You don't mind?"

Her husband followed her through the door carrying a wilted plant. "They said it would pick up with a little drinkie," Diana laughed.

"The sinkie's over there," I pointed to the kitchen and disappeared upstairs. When you are involved with life, death, and feces, you don't worry about being a good host.

When they left, my mother said that it wasn't nice of me not to stay and talk with them.

"It wasn't nice to unpack furniture all morning," I said.

All day Monday, which finally came, Ethel and I made frantic phone calls—she from the house, I from the office. The doctor, the hospital, and agencies, to arrange for an aide in case my mother did not get admitted. When I finally broke through the receptionist barrier to Dr. Gordon, he expressed surprise at my mother's incontinence ("the nurses never said anything"), as well as the pain in her spine. No one had reported that, either. He promptly ordered a bed for my mother at Teller, which they, of course, could not confirm.

While we were on standby for a bed, we had a health aide on standby in case there was no bed.

"Those nurses should be fired, every single one," Ethel said. "They knew she was incontinent. She said the reason for the pain in her spine is that the nurses left her in a wet bed."

Only by calling the doctor did I learn there was a bed awaiting my mother. On the same floor from which she had just escaped. "The nurses are murderers!" she screamed. She cried that she would die before returning to their clutches.

The voice of Dr. Spiegelstrauss appeared on the phone to beg me to "try another floor to get for my mother who was very upset." The doctor's receptionist told me (her voice juicy with pleasure) that my mother was lucky to get any floor, and there was nothing anybody could do about it.

Only if *anybody* did not try.

I called the hospital directly. The admissions office could not possibly deviate from hospital policy, which assigned rooms as they came up. "Maybe you could bend your policy a little," I said. "My mother is dying of cancer."

They found a bed on another floor.

A triumph that so pleased my mother she forgot to be fearful of returning to the hospital.

A saintly nurse with a glowing face bent over her in the wheel-chair and squeezed her hands. "We want to do everything to make you better," she spoke softly, bringing a smile to my mother's tortured face.

"See?" she whispered to me. "I always fight for what I want, and I get it."

It was like being in a different hospital. I had no idea a floor could make so much difference. I was told that one bad nurse could demoralize an entire floor, so they took all the bad nurses and concentrated them on one floor. The fifth floor from which my mother escaped was notorious to those who knew.

There was a time, of course, when they could fire the incompetents and troublemakers. "The [government] won't let us," said a nurse in confidence.

"You'll love your roommate," smiled the saint. "Daphne. She's adorable. But she isn't feeling too good right now. Operation."

From the bed across the room a big black woman raised her head with great effort, opened big white eyes, and flashed a dazzling smile at my mother, who turned on an even more dazzling smile as she waved and called out an exuberant, "Hi, neighbor!" My mother would have launched a deeper conversation, asking her about her condition, her family, and her life story if the nurse had not stopped her with questions of her own. "We'll talk later," my mother promised her roommate, as if they were old friends.

After questioning my mother at length, the nurse took me into the hall. "She doesn't know what she has, does she?" she said.

"I don't think so," I said.

She smiled sympathetically and promised to note it on my mother's chart so no one would mention it to her.

"What did she ask you?" My mother eyed me suspiciously.

"Nothing," I said, giving her the answer she taught me to give. Nobody has to know your troubles, I was told as a child. Why give them the satisfaction?

Her lips turned up in a slight smile. A specialist in the art of concealing, nothing could be hidden from her. Nothing.

"It's uncanny how she can read your mind," said her brother in San Francisco. "It's ESP."

Once again I left her in a hospital bed, this time with her walker and inner tube nearby. Each time she required more equipment to function. A month earlier she had walked with a bounce.

"What happened to me?" she asked. "I thought my troubles were over."

34

"NOW I KNOW what hell is like," my mother said.

In a voice drained of strength, but remarkably full of humor, she described the tests they were putting her through, each more punishing than the last.

"They put me in a freezer," she said. "Six doctors stood outside working on me. Six doctors. It must have cost thousands of dollars. 'Are you all right,' they kept asking. 'Are you all right?'

"'I'm just fine,' I told them. 'I couldn't be better.'

"It took four hours," she said. "Doctors were looking through windows at me, like a fish. 'Do this, do that,' they said. 'If I could do this and do that,' I told them, 'I wouldn't be in your freezer.' Oh, I can't describe the things that happened to me. You should write about it. I would make a much more interesting book than Australia."

I was trying to write a book about the two years we lived in Australia, an adventure to which she never related.

"They put me on a drum and strapped me down, like I was going to run away," she said. "Then they pounded me like a butcher pounding veal. With regular hammers. Each time they pound, the drum booms. Sometimes loud, sometimes soft. Like a symphony orchestra. How anyone could invent such a thing; it's unbelievable."

She endured a spinal tap without protest.

"Your mother is a terrific gal," said Dr. Gordon. "She never complains. If she says something hurts, I know it really hurts."

"It was torture," she said, barely able to squeeze out the words. "But you know what the doctors said? If they didn't do it I could become paralyzed. I tell you, the doctors here are wonderful. They take such an interest in you. They are so delighted when they have a success."

The hospital staff was something else.

Once, after a particularly agonizing test, the doctors ordered her to return to her room for complete rest. Instead she was wheeled on a stretcher into a basement room filled with blaring music and dancing hospital workers. They were jumping like wild, she said. One of them ordered her off the stretcher for her exercises.

"What do you mean, exercises?" she screamed. "I'm supposed to have complete rest. Dr. Gordon said."

After a series of phone calls, voices hollering over the music that no one considered lowering, it was determined that someone had erred, and they shoved my mother into a corner where she lay in agony amidst the blaring music for an hour until someone appeared to retrieve her.

"Mama," she said, "I thought I would never get out alive."

Each time I saw her she looked worse. Smaller, thinner, shrinking like a doll in a horror movie. Her face turned ash-gray, the life draining out. Her hair was white.

I called the doctor angrily. Why the tests? Didn't we all know what she had? Why put her through needless torture? What were they trying to find out? And if they learned anything, how long did she have to live? For whose benefit were the tests taking place—for her or the medical students?

The fact that she had multiple myeloma, said the neurological specialist in the lofty tone reserved for specialists, did not exclude the possibility of neural complications. How would I feel if they assumed it was the myeloma, ignored other possibilities, and my mother spent the rest of her life—no matter how little time was left—paralyzed?

How do you challenge that?

I was as helpless against the doctors' arguments as she was

against their tests. Yet deep in my heart I knew that they were avoiding the obvious because it was the obvious. Anybody could say it was the myeloma advancing. Only a specialist could come up with other possibilities, all of which had to be proven false to set minds at rest. I suspected they had to justify their years of medical training and millions of dollars' worth of equipment on every patient passing through. "Hell, why not try the Spectoray X–12 on her, we might learn something."

I was no longer so sure about the superiority of teaching hospitals. The time had come when my mother needed a little kindness and common sense more than brilliant medical minds and millions of dollars' worth of apparatus. But who was to know? How did you decide? When did you give up and opt for a peaceful death? More important, why did you have to decide whether it was better to be a lesson or a person?

They injected colored fluids into her veins, they clamped her to a counter and scanned her brain, they pumped her organs with dye, they starved her, they bloated her, they plugged her in and wired her up, they sent currents through her, they froze her and heated her, they drugged her, they had her perform for them, and they listened to her screams. They studied dials and followed needles, they nodded and shook their heads and pondered; and when they were finally finished in nearly a month, exhausting every test in the hospital, they came to the conclusion that it was the myeloma advancing into her spine.

Her backbone was turning into sawdust.

"I passed all their tests," my mother announced. "They can't find anything wrong. I'm in perfect condition. My only problem is I can't walk and I can't sit. They're sending me for therapy treatments."

One night when I came to visit her she was missing. They needed her room for dialysis, the nurse explained, and rushed her into a private room, which I thought would delight her since she was getting it at no extra cost.

"How do you like what happened to me?" she moaned. "They came like the Gestapo in the middle of the night and wheeled me away. 'Where are you taking me,' I screamed. They could take me anywhere; what could I do? I can't walk." She choked back tears. "I'm alone again."

I thought she did not really want to be with a black woman, that her friendliness had been artificial.

"You know what she did?" my mother said. "In the middle of the night, as sick as she was, she came over with a blanket and covered me." Then, remembering her prejudices, she said, "Still, it's scary seeing a face like shoe polish looking down at you in the dark."

On leaving the hospital, Daphne came to say goodbye to my mother, leaving her a partly eaten box of chocolates as they exchanged telephone numbers. "You'll have to visit me in my new apartment," my mother said. "I'll fix a nice dinner."

"I see you've made a friend," I said.

"Right away," she answered.

She refused to buy a newspaper or pay for a TV, claiming she could not tolerate the earphones. Not even Sadat's journey to Jerusalem would get her to order a television. "He'll get there without me," said she who never stopped talking about Israel when she was in our house.

I brought her a radio, which remained silent beside her while she lay staring at the ceiling.

"Don't you want to hear the news?" I asked.

"I have plenty of my own news," she said.

"Like what?"

"Do you think I should put the breakfront against the living-room wall, or would it look better in the dining room?"

35

ONCE AGAIN SHE WAS RELEASED from the hospital and once again in no better condition than when she entered. The pain still crunched at her spine. She still required the inner tube to sit, the walker to walk. We had no idea whether she was incontinent, but it no longer mattered. She was going to her own apartment with her own homemaker.

She won again.

Rising from her tests like a phoenix, determined to outfox the agencies and their outrageous prices, she asked everyone in the hospital if they knew someone to share her beautiful Larchmont apartment and, incidentally, take care of it and her. She found Hattie, a stolid woman from a Caribbean island, who asked for $230 a week but melted when my mother pleaded poverty and widowhood.

"Can you pay half?" Hattie asked.

My mother seized her.

Like the wise men following the star, we inched our way through the tinsel and holly of the Teller lobby, my mother in her walker, Ethel carrying totebags, and Hattie carrying a frayed suitcase bound with rope.

"Meet Hattie," my mother beamed, while Bing Crosby sang about the kind of Christmas he was dreaming of. "Like Hattie Lamarr."

Hattie, after making certain that my mother was comfortable, sat in the back and spoke of her island home in a lilting voice with impeccable diction.

"Don't you think I found a good one?" my mother whispered to me in Yiddish, as if she had found a fresh chicken at the butcher.

Like Proust, my mother in her bed accomplished far more than I with my calls to agencies, two nursing schools, and a Jewish newspaper. Nursing students expected thirty-five dollars a day, homemakers ten dollars more, and older Jewish women were doing the mambo in Miami. If my mother were on Medicaid, said the hospital social services director, it would be no problem. The government would send her a homemaker. Medicaid is a word I would be happy never hearing again.

With Hattie hovering over my mother, guiding her with her walker, carrying her pocketbook, rushing to open doors, we made it into the apartment she had wanted so desperately—and had made us want so desperately. While she was in the hospital, the boys and I had arranged furniture, unwrapped and plugged in lamps, stocked the kitchen with food, as well as dishes, pots, cutlery—tried to make it livable. But cartons still huddled in corners holding her fragile treasures. Flat cartons containing her pictures leaned against walls. Artificial flowers shot up through opened flaps of still more cartons. A mirror, rising from a sea of wrapping paper, leaned against another wall.

"It's beautiful," my mother smiled, gazing at the sun streaming through the uncurtained windows, shining on the bare floor. Making her way to the bedroom with her walker, Hattie hovering over her, she stood in the door and smiled at her bedroom set. "Beautiful," she sighed. "Look how it all fits. This is the perfect apartment for it."

The heat gushed from the radiators, dispelling her fear of freezing in the New York winter.

"It's so nice and warm," she sighed.

She touched her dining-room table, she gazed at her shepherd and shepherdess lamps, she looked lovingly at the sofa the boys and I had propped up on books until the moving company returned with legs.

"I'm so happy," she said. "God is good to me."

CHRISTMAS HAD THE KINDNESS to fall on a Sunday that year.

God saved her from being alone for an extra day, or paying Hattie for a holiday.

"So what are you doing Sunday?" she probed, refusing to invoke the name of the holiday, as if that would be selling out.

I did not tell her that Ethel's parents were coming over.

Or that we had our usual tree.

"We really should invite her," I said to Ethel, although I was not exactly eager to have her see the tree and expose my defection. "She's all alone."

For the first time Ethel was firm. "I don't want her here," she said decisively. "And she doesn't want to be here. She'll just sit here glaring."

"But she's alone," I said.

"Haven't I done enough for her?" Ethel asked. "She's had six months of my life. Why does she have to spoil my Christmas?"

Ethel's mother expressed her disapproval. She blamed Ethel for my mother leaving our house. The old were sticking together, their fears crossing religious and economic lines. Everybody's turn was coming. "She's even turned my parents against me," Ethel said. "She tells my mother that I never visit her, that I'm a terrible daughter-in-law. All the time I took care of her doesn't count. It isn't that she really wants to see me. She wants me to play her game of the devoted daughter. Well, I'm not going to do it anymore. I'm not doing any more than I absolutely have to."

"I imagine you're having company for Sunday," my mother said.

"I'll come over in the afternoon," I replied.

She conducted an investigation that the C.I.A. might envy. When neither the boys nor I would confirm her darkest suspicions, she called Angelina.

"I called Angelina," she said, "to see if she could help me unpack on Saturday. She said she was busy cleaning your house; you're expecting company Sunday."

"Don't you have Hattie?" I asked.

"Not Saturday," she said.

I did not dare ask why her unpacking had to be done on Saturday.

"My holiday is Chanukah," she said through tight lips. This was the woman who told me as a child that Chanukah was nothing more than an excuse by worthless Jews to celebrate Christmas.

The articles on dying I was reading so avidly said that the dying yearned to come to terms with life, to make peace with the people around them, to free themselves of hate. Approaching death, they had new insights as they yearned to be at one with the world.

Any relation to our experience was purely coincidental.

The closer my mother came to death, the more determinedly she clutched her separateness, as if relinquishing one inch of distance was an admission that she was weakening. The weaker she grew, the more fiercely she fought to prove she was strong. She was prepared to stay in her apartment on Christmas Day, alone and helpless, before yielding an inch.

And what was she proving?

When she asked the superintendent to hang her mirror for her, he burst into rage. "After what you gave me for getting you the apartment?" he shouted. She had given him ten dollars. "It's going to cost you," he said.

"Twelve dollars he charged me," she wailed. "He spent maybe ten minutes."

While hanging her mirror he eyed the emerald-green lamp on her dresser. "We could use a lamp like that in our apartment," he said.

"I thought he was going to murder me for it," my mother said.

Her apartment was costing her more than the Naomi Lawson Home. Rent, utilities, Hattie, food. "As alone as I am," she said on Christmas Day, "it's my own place. You didn't put me in an institution!"

As she spoke church bells rang.

Joy to the World.

37

THE ENTIRE EAST disappeared under snow that winter, like a buried civilization. From December through March the snow fell in a variety of forms—huge heavy flakes, blasts of ice balls, showers of fine powder—alternately melting and freezing so that under each new deluge the streets and sidewalks were sheets of ice. Legs broke. Cars collided. Children turned into tycoons shoveling and reshoveling at five dollars a minute. Blizzards stopped trains, closed schools, created panic at hospitals, trapped the old and the sick.

My mother sat in her apartment, staring out at the white woods, the bent tree limbs encased in sleeves of ice, cars burrowed like rabbits in the snow mounds in the parking area below her window. The wheezing of spinning tires drifted up to her all day long.

"It had to happen just when I'm here," she said.

"You're part of history," I said.

"Some history," she said.

How, she cried, could people endure such a climate? Why didn't I get a job in California? Greenstone, she screamed, destroyed her life. "May he rot in hell!" she cried, as the snow poured down without stop. She lashed out at everything like a wounded animal. "Not once," she said, "did your dear wife come to see me in the hospital."

"She drove you to the doctor a hundred times," I said. "She took care of you . . ."

"The visiting nurses took care of me," she cried.

"They didn't drive you . . ."

"Spiegelstrauss," she said. "If not for her I would never get there."

She remembered what you did not do for her, never what you did. One C canceled out all the A's.

She was taking masses of pills. Enormous quantities of prednisone, Alkeran, new chemicals, the Delatestryl injections—all boiling up inside her. Lines surfaced again on her face, deepening into hard gray crevices of pain. More hair dropped from her scalp, leaving bare patches. Hair sprouted in tufts from her face. When she was at our house she had had an aide remove the facial hair with Nair. She no longer bothered.

"I wish you'd left me to die in my beloved Arizona," she screamed one night on the phone. "If I knew the reception I was going to get!"

Hattie, like so many of my mother's finds, soon fell victim to her distrust.

"No matter how much money I give her to go shopping," my mother cried, "she doesn't bring back a penny change. I can give her a thousand dollars, she'll come back with nothing. And the refrigerator is always empty. Go look, see if you can find anything."

I never knew how much truth was in my mother's accusations. I did know that she was unlikely to dole out more than a few dollars at a time for Hattie's shopping expeditions. Which would give the woman little opportunity to amass an illicit fortune.

The big event was the twelve-dollar mop. "I sent Hattie for a mop," she said. "'Without carpeting you need a mop. You don't have one for me.' Twelve dollars she spent. Before, I used to be able to put something away. Not here."

As for Hattie's cooking, "she puts in enough seasoning to burn iron. I beg her not so much pepper. You think she listens to me?"

Hattie would not eat with my mother. After serving her she ate by herself in the kitchen, like the palace help. At last, my mother was being treated like a queen. And she hated it.

"All day she sits in the kitchen and eats. Like a cow. I'm surprised she isn't as big as one."

It was like living with a corpse, my mother said. "She never speaks. Only if you ask her a question. But go have a conversation with her."

Supposedly docile Hattie rejected my mother's check, claiming they had agreed on $150, which she said was still a bargain. "What could I do?" my mother said. "She knows I need her."

Hattie's six-day week turned into five as she left earlier each Saturday morning and returned later each Sunday night. At first she left cooked meals for my mother to warm, but soon she left only scraps. Once Steven rushed over with milk, Hattie having left her without a drop. Another time my mother claimed that she caught Hattie slipping a salami into her suitcase. "I thought you didn't want it," she quoted Hattie as saying, since my mother had rejected the salami for containing pork. We heard only my mother's version of their confrontations; Hattie had no chance to defend herself.

Snow once meant sleighing, skiing, and a canceled-train vacation from work. Now it meant that Ethel drove my mother to the doctor once again, Dr. Spiegelstrauss refusing to venture out.

"Who can blame her?" my mother said. "She can't drive when it's nice; how do you expect her to drive on ice?"

I told Ethel to let my mother take a taxi, she and Hattie. She could afford it.

"She needs someone who cares," Ethel said, missing work again, listening to my mother tell her about her devoted friends again.

"I didn't know you were that devoted," I said.

"She's suffering enough," Ethel said.

My mother was never ready when Ethel came, always expressing surprise at the hour. There seemed to be a law that prevented her from starting to dress until Ethel arrived. Which was usually after chopping through ice and snow to get the car moving.

I called her daily from work but visited her only on weekends. I was too drained to give her any more of myself. My steps quickened as I passed her building between our house and the station, grateful she was no longer in our house.

On Saturdays and Sundays I came to face her anguish. She was invariably in bed, the TV on. She had an outdoor antenna installed, her remote control fixed. Without her remote control she did not know how to operate the TV. Hattie had covered the living-room furniture with chenille spreads. Nothing else was touched. Boxes remained as I had left them, stacked in corners. Pictures in their boxes were leaning against walls, plastic flowers were jutting from opened cartons.

The boys and I always arrived carrying something. Pillows, pots, dishes, robe, nightgowns. We brought over the file cabinet with her records. Even dying, taxes go on. The government does not accept a note: "Dear IRS—Sorry, but I'm dying right now and I can't file my return." We brought her our previous week's Sunday *Times*. She would not buy her own copy. "So I'll read it a week later," she said. "What difference does it make?"

She had a point.

She had the local paper delivered. For the television listing and supermarket specials.

I dreaded the weekend visits.

I dreaded encountering the doorman, who felt compelled to say clever things like, "Looks like more snow."

I dreaded passing through the opulent paneled lobby with its electric logs glowing in the fireplace.

I dreaded entering the elevator and meeting old people standing on their own legs, carrying their own bundles; their faces washed, hair combed, many no younger than she. The building was filled with elderly ladies. Larchmont Jews, Catholics, and Protestants, indistinguishable from one another.

I dreaded ringing her bell, opening the two locks with my extra keys, and calling out with false enthusiasm. The apartment was always stifling—heat blasting, windows sealed. It had a faint odor at all times. Nothing escaped. And always the television.

"If not for the television I would lose my mind," she said.

She refused to read books I brought her. "You want me to read the way I feel?" she cried.

Sometimes I found her with a towel wrapped around her neck, unable to turn her head. She slept with too many pillows, she said. Other times it was her arm or pains shooting through her legs. She leaned too hard on her walker or the therapist told her to walk incorrectly.

At first she eagerly snatched the mail that I brought her from our house. But as weeks passed she told me to leave it on the table next to her bed, where she let it pile up, too weak to face the problems it produced, yet unwilling to trust me to handle them. She fought to get Dr. Gordon's office to handle her Medicare and Blue Cross paperwork. "In Arizona they did everything for me," she cried at his receptionist ("who has more paint on her face than Sherwin Williams makes in a year"). "All I did was sign."

"This isn't Arizona, honey," said the receptionist, glancing at her pointed plum nails as she pushed the forms back into my mother's trembling hands.

"As if she has anything else to do," my mother said.

"They have other patients," I said.

"They're afraid it will cost them a stamp."

"And you're afraid it will cost you a stamp."

She smiled. Caught.

I took over the medical forms for her, learning more than I ever wanted to know about Medicare. To chart your way through its complexities required a clear mind unhazed by drugs. It was cleverly designed to foil the sick.

First you filled out your part of the Medicare form and paid the doctor, who then filled out his part and either sent the form to Medicare or gave it to you to send to Medicare. Your claim, I discovered, was handled not by the government, but by an insurance company, the government appointing a different insurance company in each state. In New York it was Blue Cross that handled the paperwork, while the government put up the money. So the insurance companies were getting a piece of the pie, after all.

Medicare, I discovered, did not pay the full amount of a doctor's bill, often not even coming close. It paid 80 percent of what the local insurance agent decided was the proper fee for the area. The patient made up the rest from either his own pocket or a supplementary health plan. Since it was a rare doctor who came close to charging the mythical proper fee, Medicare could leave a big gap.

My mother, like most elderly people, had a supplementary health plan—in her case, Arizona Blue Cross/Blue Shield. I nearly made the mistake of transferring her to New York Blue Cross/Blue Shield, but the doctor's nurse informed me, just in time, that nearly every state paid greater benefits for lower rates than New York. Arizona paid for office visits to doctors, for instance, not just hospital stays, a benefit unheard of in New York. Even when she moved into her own apartment and had a Larchmont, New York, address, Arizona Blue Cross continued to accept her payments and pay her benefits.

Medicare needed no change-of-address notice. They sent benefits to whatever address appeared on each claim form. But Social Security had to be notified, or her checks would continue to go to her last address.

One of my most brilliant moves was to photocopy all her cards the moment she came to us and keep copies in my wallet and desk. When she could not find her Medicare card the first time I took her to Teller, they accepted my photocopy without question and promptly copied it.

The hospital bills were simple, the hospital collecting directly from Medicare and from the Arizona "Blues," as they say in the trade. She had only her phone bill to pay. But other bills pursued her like the furies. Bills from the army of specialists dispatched by Dr. Gordon. For each specialist she had to fill out her part of another Medicare form and send it to him with her check. Not until he received her payment would he fill out his part of the form and send it to Medicare, who sent her a check for 80 percent of what they decided was the appropriate fee. At the same time, she was supposed to send a form and an itemized bill to Arizona Blue Cross, which paid either 20 percent of the total bill or the proper fee—I never understood which, since forms and checks were continually crisscrossing the country.

I suspect that my mother never did get all she was entitled to. But keeping a record of every claim required the services of a staff, and only Medicaid people had that. Occasionally I found a half-completed form under her bed or a Blue Cross or Medicare check stuffed into a box with advertising circulars and coupons. Many times she brought back a form from the doctor untouched. "Oi, I forgot," she would cry, "it was in my purse all the time."

I had a job, a family, a house, and my own investments and taxes to cope with. How many more forms could a mere mortal handle? Dealing with medical insurance was no job for the sick or the well.

Even hospital stays could be tricky. After a deductible for which the patient was responsible, Medicare paid in full for the first thirty days, less for the next thirty, and then dipped into a hundred-day lifetime reserve, for which it paid even less. If you could manage to stay out of the hospital for at least thirty days before reentering, you went back to home base and started fresh. But if you stayed in the hospital longer than sixty days and used up your lifetime reserve, God help you!

I did not push the boys to visit her. If she, with her knowledge of people, could not make them love her, how could I?

"She hates me," Paul said, refusing to visit her alone.

"Lovable you?"

"She said so," he said.

"She didn't mean it."

"She expects everyone to try to be what she wants them to be," he said.

I tried to reassure him that she loved him. That she had peculiar ways of trying to reach people. "She doesn't know how else to be," I explained.

"She's old enough," he said.

Paul, the realist, told it like it was. "She wants me to visit her so she can tell people how her grandchild visits her. She doesn't care if she sees me or not."

He had no intention of letting her get away with anything just because she was a few steps closer to death than other people, and he was right. I wish that, at fifty, I had had the strength of my fourteen-year-old.

He saw her on the occasional Saturday or Sunday he accompanied me to her apartment. He sat silently, responding to her questions with a mumble. Once when he returned from a ski trip, elated at winning a bronze star, she said, "Maybe next time you'll win a gold."

I told him of the times I brought home a report card filled with A's except for one B, and how she pounced on the B.

"She can't help it," I said.

"You were her child," Paul said. "You had to put up with it."

The little psychologist.

But she did not get Paul's message. If he did not come to see her, it was because he was not a good grandchild.

I was reliving the frustrations of my childhood. Nothing I did was ever good enough. And it still wasn't. After bringing her to our home, disrupting our lives, finding her a doctor, taking care of her, moving her into an apartment, shopping for her, unearthing nurses, aides, companions, it was still not enough. There was always that B to pounce on.

Yet the experts blithely went on grouping people as "the dying," as if they were different from "the living." As if the prospect of death caused them to shed their individual personalities, trade them in for a common "dying personality" that marched in neatly categorizable stages to the end.

How handy, if true. How much easier for "the family" if "the dying" could be counted on to die by the rules. Then we could treat them by rules. "Ten Ways to Deal with the Dying." Sorry, it doesn't work that way. Life—and death—is not that simple. A dying person is not a recognizable type but a person who is dying. His personality does not necessarily change, his relationships do not alter. Miracles do not happen. Don't look in the guidebook under "D."

One Sunday night I answered the phone to hear her screaming, "Never sign anything! Your father, who worshipped the ground I walked on, used to tell me, 'Dora, give gifts, give money, but don't give away your name.' "

Money was all she had left, and that was failing to buy her what she had spent a lifetime convinced it would.

"I've been abandoned," she cried one afternoon to Steven and me.

And she was.

Had she ever asked herself why? Did she really want to know, as she stood on the threshold of death, why it had all gone sour? Was that something anybody would let themselves know?

"You think Raskin's grandchildren were so devoted to him?" she laughed. "You think they were so delighted to see him if he didn't bring them something? He never set foot in their house without coming with a carload of presents. Just like Santa Claus came. That's the way children are. Not just children. Give grownups presents, there's nothing they won't do for you. But nothing gets nothing."

There was nothing that anyone could say or do to change her mind. She knew. She learned it as a little girl seventy years ago, and she knew.

"Don't you think I'm right?" she said to Ethel when she was still in our house. "Where would I be without money?"

"Exactly where you are now," Ethel said.

My mother looked at her with a knowing smile.

"YOU'LL NEVER GUESS what I did today," she announced proudly during one of my daily phone calls from the office. "I walked."

"On your own?" I cried.

"All on my own."

"How?" I asked, thrilled.

"I put one foot in front of the other and I walked," she said. "Like a child." She described how the therapist, walking behind her, holding her waist, suddenly told her to look to her right. He was standing on the other side of the room, smiling. "I was walking all by myself."

"Wonderful," I said.

"God is good to me," she said.

When she was alone the therapist told her not to take chances, to use the walker. "But when he comes, I walk alone. Like the song."

"What about Hattie? Walk with her," I said.

"That's all I need," she said. "We'll fall together and that will be the end."

"At least exercise during the week."

"Don't worry, I exercise plenty."

But she refused to walk for me. Like a child timid about playing the violin for his parents. Each day she assured me that she exercised. "I run, I jump," she said. "Don't think it's so easy. I can't just perform. When I know the therapist is coming I take a pain pill. An hour ahead of time. If not for the pills, I couldn't do a thing."

She knew what was happening to her. She had to know.

"Some patients make it so goddamn hard on their families," said a radiologist we met at a party. "And for what? For another week of life? Another month?"

So inconsiderate of the dying.

He would have been most disturbed by my mother, who had no intention of making her dying easy for anyone, not even herself. And why should she? Why should she live as if she were about to die? Why should she give up, mark time? Why shouldn't she plan on buying rugs for her floors, curtains for her windows? Why shouldn't she plan on attending a bar mitzvah in Detroit, a wedding in Santa Monica? Why shouldn't she be encouraged to fight until every ounce of strength was used up? There would be plenty of time to rest afterward. Death lasts a long time.

"You know," she said, "there are some very nice people in this building."

On her way to the doctor she met some ladies in the elevator. "Very refined," she said. "Very friendly." But she drew away, not wanting to be known as the sick old lady leaning on a walker, dependent on a companion.

"Ask them in," I said. "Make friends."

"The way I look?" she cried. "You want they should see the

apartment like this? Wait till I have it furnished properly. When I can entertain in a nice way."

"But you're alone now," I said. "You need friends now."

"I have plenty of friends," she said. "Oh, do I have friends."

"Where?"

"Everywhere. Arizona, California . . ."

"But you need people here."

"Here I have God," she said. "Here God is my friend."

In one of my countless searches through the phone book I came upon the Friendly Visitors. Volunteers, said a voice, who visited elderly people with similar interests. They had a woman who spoke French with an invalid, another volunteer played chess, several simply talked current events. I told her my mother was interested in all things Russian, Jewish, and financial. The woman promised to call back as soon as she found someone. She is still looking.

Once more I called the Senior Citizens Center and was told they did no visiting but would be happy to see my mother there. They were organizing a new square-dance group . . .

And Cancer Care, which insisted that my mother be ready to talk about her impending death if she wanted the companionship of one of their people.

A friend who edited a magazine for retired people advised me to call the county offices of aging. Feeling I might have missed something the first time around, I tried again. Once more I was put on hold by every department in the magnificent new county center. I had only to reveal that my mother did not qualify for Medicaid for everyone to lose interest. The only kind of aid they knew was money. Dying of cancer was not enough to merit government concern.

"Better to be alone in my apartment," she said, "than be with a bunch of corpses at your Naomi Lawson."

Alone, no one could embarrass her with questions about what she liked to do. Alone, she could dream of California, Arizona, admiring relatives, devoted friends. Alone she was Dora Sloan of Larchmont, where Joan Rivers's father was a member of the temple. "You never know," she laughed.

One day on the phone she announced, jubilantly, "I have a surprise for you."

My heart knotted.

"Hattie left," she said.

Oh, my God.

"Three days ago."

"You've been alone?"

"It's been a blessing."

A phone call from Jamaica from Hattie's family. "If they needed her, I feel sorry for them," my mother said. "I'm so happy. I was trying to think of a nice way to get rid of her so she wouldn't get angry and kill me. And it came. God heard me."

On her own she called a Jewish agency that was sending her someone exceptionally good—Darlene—someone who would not eat up her food. Darlene would come five afternoons a week. She would shop, cook, clean, take care of her. She needed no live-in, she insisted. She could not stand them.

She was no longer afraid to be alone at night. It was a safe building, she said. No one was going to grab her. "Who needs an earthquake in the next bed?" she asked. "The noises Hattie makes, she can wake the dead. And not just people who died lately. People who've been dead for a thousand years."

Only six weeks earlier she was terrified at the prospect of being alone. She was unable to take a step without clutching the walker. Although she had gained no weight, she began to look brighter, sound more alive. Or was it because it was her period of low-level chemotherapy?

"Don't worry about your mother," she said. "As long as I have bread I won't starve."

Maybe she would make it, after all.

39

I AWAKENED to the far-off ringing of the telephone in the hallway. As I reached for the silenced extension next to our bed, Ethel was already whispering into it. It was not quite six in the morning.

"Who the hell was it?" I asked as she hung up.

"Your mother. She can't open her pain pills. She wants you to stop by on your way to the train."

"She had to call now? She knows I don't leave until eight."

Ethel said she would go over while I went back to sleep; a lost cause.

It turned out that the cap was not the problem. The bottle was uncapped, but the pain in both my mother's arms was so intense she could not stretch to reach it. "Darlene had to put it a mile away," she cried to Ethel. "It's a good thing she didn't move the phone." My mother kept it nestled beside her on the bed.

Ethel stayed with her for two hours, giving her the pills, taking her to the bathroom, feeding her breakfast. Guiltily, she left for the agency, leaving her alone to wait for Darlene. "I'll manage," my mother assured her. The more helpless she was, the more independent she acted. And the more independent she was, the more helpless she acted. She clearly needed someone full time.

"It's the goddamn money," I said. "She's saving it for the future."

"She said it was from sleeping on her side. She thinks she'll be all right when the therapist comes. He'll give her treatments."

"What's he going to do? Walk with her?"

"When they go," Dick Wexler said months earlier, "they go fast."

Ethel found a dishpan next to my mother's bed. Darlene left it there for my mother to use at night.

She belonged in a nursing home. Or a hospital.

"How can a doctor look at her and not insist she go into a nursing home?" Ethel cried.

"He thinks she has someone with her all the time."

"I told her she woke you up this morning," Ethel said.

"What did she say?"

"She said what difference did it make if you woke up a half-hour early."

I suppose she was right. What was a little sleep when you were in so much agony you could not stretch your arm to take a pain pill?

She began to call every morning after I left for work. It was the pain pills again, or she could not get out of bed to use the dishpan, or she was desperate for prune juice. Each time Ethel rushed over.

"I'll talk to her," I said. "She'll have to go into a home."

"She keeps hoping the therapist will cure her. He's coming tomorrow."

But the next morning Ethel found my mother sprawled across the bed, clutching the phone, unable to move without screaming with pain. She roared at the slightest touch anywhere on her body, at the slightest jolt of the bed. Ethel put a pain pill in her mouth and held a glass of water with a bent straw to her lips.

"Why is God punishing me so?" she sobbed. "I who did so much good for people."

She said she felt something snap in her arm during the night when she pulled the blanket. "Darlene tucked it in too tight," she said. "I told her. Like she hammered it in." Now her arm was swollen and turning blue.

Ethel called Dr. Gordon, who was not in. When she told the receptionist that she thought my mother's arm was broken, the receptionist said to bring her in.

"But she can't move," Ethel said. "She screams if I sit on the edge of the bed."

"How do you expect doctor to treat her if he can't see her?" asked the receptionist.

"She belongs in the hospital," Ethel said, pleading for her to have the doctor call as soon as he arrived.

"He has a busy schedule," said the receptionist, helpfully.

"I can't wait until eleven tonight," Ethel cried. "We have to do something now."

My mother screamed with pain as Ethel tried to ease her back into a normal position on the bed, which, Ethel noticed, was soaking.

While Ethel was trying to decide whom to call for help, the physical therapist appeared. Together they got my mother back into bed, propping her against her mountain of pillows, Ethel tucking towels underneath her. "I'm so much better now," my mother gasped as the pill began to take effect. "I'm going to be fine. As long as I don't move."

But she could not stay in one position forever.

"I'll be fine," she cried. "Don't try to send me back to the hospital."

The physical therapist called the doctor's office to report that he did not think my mother's arm was broken, simply bruised. And he left.

"I couldn't believe it," Ethel said. "How could he look at an arm that's swollen and turning blue and say it's only a bruise? Especially when he knows what she has."

When Ethel called the doctor again (he did not bother to call her), the receptionist told her once more that the doctor wanted her to bring my mother into the office. "Every time she moves she screams with pain," Ethel cried at her. "I know her arm is broken."

"The physical therapist said a bruise," the receptionist countered. "But if you still think that doctor should see her . . ."

"I *know* he should see her and I know she belongs in a hospital," Ethel cried, hanging up and calling me in desperation at work.

"Your wife already spoke to me," said the receptionist, sharply, like a teacher scolding a second-grader. "I told her to bring your mother in . . ."

"But she can't move; she screams with pain."

"Doctor is very busy . . ."

"We are all busy," I said.

"How do you expect doctor to treat her if he doesn't know what's wrong?"

"If he doesn't know what's wrong with her by now," I said, "we've been seeing the wrong doctor. Her bones are breaking. She's in agony."

I was put on hold.

"Doctor will get back to you as soon as he can"—she clicked herself back. "He's very busy today."

He never did call me back.

The next call came from Ethel, who told me Dr. Gordon had actually phoned her to say he reserved a bed for my mother at Teller. Ethel was trying to arrange for the volunteer ambulance to take her. Since the hospital was out of the immediate area it might present an additional problem.

"I'm coming home," I said.

Steven met me at the station and we drove to my mother's apartment, where she lay propped in bed, tears streaming down her creviced face. Darlene, a bouncy, round Jamaican lady who exuded love, was at her side, my mother's kangaroo totebag packed. The volunteer ambulance, Steven reported, was on its way, sending their transport van.

"And Darlene just cooked a chicken," my mother cried, as if that were the real tragedy. "Take it home."

Her roars filled the apartment as the volunteer ambulance drivers, two high-school boys, transferred her to the stretcher. She screamed at each bump as they wheeled her through the corridor and over the sill into the elevator. After a few seconds' respite in the elevator, she screamed continuously as the boys jostled the stretcher out of the elevator and through the building to the waiting van. She shrieked as they hoisted her in the stretcher into the van, her cries finally subsiding when they set her down, a tiny package of crumbling bones covered by a coat and a blanket. She let out a cry with every bump in the road. The potholes were torture.

Once more I sat at a desk giving an indifferent woman my mother's name and address, her mother's name, her father's name, her Social Security number. Once more I handed her the photocopy of my mother's Medicare card. Once more up the elevator, through a corridor, past a nurses' station, and into a hospital room. This time she was put in the windowless half of a double room, the window territory occupied by a white-haired crone who babbled about the lack of attention while the ambulance drivers transferred my screaming mother into her bed.

"Sorry if I'm not very alert," smiled the red-haired nurse as she entered the room with a clipboard to record my mother's condition, "but I only had three hours' sleep last night."

"Work?" I asked.

"Are you kidding?" she laughed. "Now, doll," she asked my mother, "how do you think your arm broke?"

When my mother said that she did it by pulling up a blanket, the nurse laughed and said it must have been some blanket.

"Yes," my mother said quietly, "some blanket."

She knew, she had to know.

"I begged her not to make it so tight," she said.

The nurse asked if she wanted a Pap smear.

She had myeloma, I told her, no longer whispering the word.

The nurse looked at me blankly.

"She's getting chemotherapy," I said.

"Oh," said the nurse.

"What happened to me, Bernie?" she asked. "I was doing so well. I was even driving the car. Until the pneumonia. It was the pneumonia that set me back."

"Don't worry, honey," the nurse squeezed my shoulder, "we'll take good care of her."

ALL MORNING I PHONED her room without getting an answer. By afternoon I had tried all the Teller numbers the phone book could offer. After fighting my way through a Maginot line of busy signals, disconnections, and holds, I reached patient information, who reported, after putting me on hold while contacting the nurses' station, that my mother was out of her room for tests.

"All day?" I asked.

An explosion of static shattered my ear as the phone died.

It was not until five in the afternoon that she answered her phone. Speaking in a thin ghostly voice that sent shivers through me, she said that she had been in her bed listening to the phone ringing but could not reach it because her arm was in a sling. Luckily a nurse just arrived with the dinner tray and was holding the receiver so she could talk.

"You know what time they took me for x-rays?" she said. "Two in the morning. It was packed, like Grand Central Station. Even Dr. Gordon was there. Ethel was right; my arm was broken."

A voice interrupted her. I heard fragments of conversation and then my mother telling me that she would have to hang up because the nurse who was holding the phone for her had to give the other patients their dinner. When I asked why she could not hold the phone with her other hand, she answered, "They have such funny phones here. It slips out of my fingers."

Steven and I saw her that night. Although only one arm and hand was encased in a sling, she could not move the fingers of her free hand. Not only was she unable to grasp the telephone receiver, she could not hold a fork or spoon. They were taking away her meals untouched. If not for a male nurse who fed her milk through a straw, she would not have eaten a thing all day.

"They grab your tray," she said weakly, "before you have a chance to eat anything."

"Don't let them," I said, still picturing her as the fighter.

"Who has the strength to fight with them?" she sighed, her head limp on the pillow.

At the nurses' station I succeeded in gaining the attention of a giggling nurse teasing a resident. Registering amazement at my mother's lack of food, she promised to write "hand feed" on my mother's chart. Like a goose. A benign housekeeper hovering nearby beckoned me to a locked refrigerator and gave me yogurt and orange juice for my mother.

While I fed her, the voice of her roommate's visitors outshouted each other on the other side of the curtain. "She's so much older than I am, maybe a hundred," my mother said. "Still, she gets up by herself, she goes to the bathroom—and how does she go to the bathroom! It looks like she'll survive."

"You'll survive too," I said.

"Who said I wouldn't?" she said quickly. "I have to come to Steven and Paul's graduations—and their weddings. Even if you don't invite me."

Tomorrow, she said, they were giving her treatments. She would feel better.

The treatments never came.

After telling me that cobalt treatments would ease her suffering, Dr. Gordon reversed himself to say that the agony they caused would outweigh any future good they might do. She would probably not live long enough to reap any benefits. Why, I wondered, had he waited to think of cobalt treatments? If it was too late today, was it too late three months earlier? When was it not too late? You had to be a doctor to know if your doctor was doing the right thing.

Since his change of plans was not transmitted quickly enough through hospital channels, my mother was trundled to the radiation room, howling with pain (no one thought to provide her with pain relief more powerful than the Tylenol with codeine she had been taking). There she was strapped to a table and kept in an agonizing position while voices argued around her about which of the doctor's orders to follow.

"I don't understand what's going on here," she cried to me that night. "Nobody knows what they're doing. They take you here, they take you there, and they don't accomplish anything."

Another time she was at the door of a radiation room when someone discovered she lacked a relative's signed permission. After wheeling her back to her room, a resident called me at work to make sure I would visit her that night and sign the form permitting them to treat her the following day. The next day they decided not to give her the treatment. Everyone always had second thoughts. Which did not engender confidence in their first ones.

They continued to take away her meals untouched.

" 'You aren't hungry, are you?' they say and grab the tray."

They evidently felt there was no point in wasting time on a patient who was dying. They had a limited number of arms, legs, and hours; why use them up on the doomed? Her light went unanswered, her cries unheard, her needs ignored. She no longer counted.

One night Steven and I found her in agony. While being given a bath early in the day she felt a bone snap in her leg. "You should see how they threw me around," she cried. "I begged them to be gentle, but the nurse gave me a pull like I was going to fight with her. Right away I felt something break. She denied it, she pretended it was nothing."

They left my mother lying in bed all day with the pain flaming through her body. Only if she lay perfectly still was it bearable, but the slightest movement sent an explosion of excruciating pain through her bones. There had been no examination, no treatment.

At the nurses' station, where I was fast becoming a threat to the social life, I was told that they could do nothing about my mother's leg until they received instructions from the doctor. And the doctor did not make his rounds until evening. No one had thought her suffering important enough to contact the doctor. They call him, they said, only in an emergency. Exactly what qualified as an emergency I would hate to guess.

Nor did they make any attempt to give her suitable pain medication. They continued to provide her with her pain pills "on request." Since she was unable to move without agony, she made no requests. No one was concerned enough to propose a stronger painkiller that was now essential.

It was only after I called the doctor's office and raged at his receptionist that a nurse sauntered into my mother's room to give her a Demerol injection. Future injections were to be given—again—on request. Which meant that my mother, who could move neither hand, was expected to push the call button, which in any case, I discovered, was disconnected from the light outside her door. No one had noticed. According to her roommate, the only way to evoke a nurse was to cry "chocolates."

More harassment at the nurses' station. Finally, agreement to give her a Demerol injection automatically every four hours. Which did not prevent a nurse from skipping the scheduled injection when she found her asleep. Although she awakened later in pain, no one would give her an injection until the next four hours elapsed, making it eight hours between injections, the last few in agony.

I horrified a nurse by suggesting something stronger, such as morphine. "You want her to become an addict?" she cried, as if that were my mother's greatest danger.

Finally, at the suggestion of Dr. Gordon, who apologized for the nursing staff, I ordered a sitter. Sitters were people sent by an agency to sit by the patient's side and do what I thought nurses were supposed to do—feed her, handle her bedpan, moisten her forehead. A sitter cost forty-eight dollars for a twelve-hour shift—"leave a check in the drawer of the bedside table." At the nurses' station a nurse reluctantly gave me the number of the sitter agency, looking at me as if it were a comment on her conscientiousness. Which it was.

It did not take a genius to know from the pain in her leg, and the fact that she had myeloma, that it was most certainly broken; yet they insisted on x-raying not only her leg but her entire body. It was the straw that broke her back.

Ethel arrived to meet her being wheeled out of her room on a stretcher. "Stay with me," my mother cried out, clutching her hand. Ethel accompanied her through the corridors and down the elevator, my mother screaming at each bump, the attendant banging the stretcher carelessly against the elevator walls. At the end of a long basement corridor they reached the x-ray room, where they joined a line-up of patients on stretchers and in wheelchairs. As an attendant took her away, my mother let go of Ethel's hand and disappeared through the double doors of the x-ray room.

"Why did they have to do it to her?" Ethel cried. "You know how thick the doors are to an x-ray room? I could hear her screams inside. As if they don't know what's wrong with her. Just so some medical students can see what bones look like that are riddled with cancer? If I ever get sick, don't ever send me to a famous teaching hospital."

When they brought her out, Ethel said, you could not tell where the sheet ended and her face began.

That night I did not let Steven come with me to see her. I knew she wanted to see me alone.

41

IT WAS ENDING, it was ending, it was ending.

As I sped along the thruway in the night, my thoughts alternated between my dying mother in the hospital and the apartment with its furniture to dispose of once more, papers to sort through once again.

Her darkest suspicions were coming true, her most dreaded fears coming to pass, and she had made them happen. Instead of concentrating on her and her dying, instead of allowing myself to feel the grief I wanted to feel at the death of a mother, my mind

shifted to her safe-deposit box, for which she had never entrusted
me with a key, and her bank accounts, to which I had no access. My
thoughts were on the piles of money that would be needed for the
funeral expenses, the flights to Arizona. Although far from poor, I
did not have a few thousand dollars lying around. While she lay dying I was debating which stocks to sell, the advisability of going on
margin or borrowing—matters I did not want to think about,
would not have had to think about, if she had only trusted.

While speeding to her bedside I found myself hating her for
making everything I did for her harder than it had to be, even as
she lay dying. And I was angry with her for depriving me of the
pure grief it was every child's right to feel when a parent died.

She would leave rifts in our family that would never come together. Wounds that would never heal. She had made an impact,
the grandmother from the West. Her ghost would live with all of
us.

I knew her now. It took her disease and her dying for me to know
her. There went the pretenses; there went mother. Obligation fulfilled. Payment rendered. Debt canceled.

Perhaps we had failed her, but wasn't she responsible too?
Wasn't she obligated to be as kind to us as we were to her? We had
to be considered too, even if our turn to die had not yet arrived.

It was ending.

Day after day of focusing our lives on my mother's condition.
What did the doctor say? How is your shoulder? How did you like
the nurse's aide? Dr. Spiegelstrauss? Where is the Medicare form?
No, I will not call Con Ed to fight about the deposit for you. Yes, I
will check on your furniture. No, she is not Jewish.

I often wondered if she had not willed her illness in order to gain
the starring role that had eluded her since my father died. In the
last year of her life she controlled me with her dependence, just as
I had controlled her in the first year of mine.

After the usual tense search, I found a parking space several
blocks from the Teller entrance and walked past the Archie Bunker
houses with signs warning of dogs, burglar alarms, and penalties
for blocking driveways. Televisions flickered inside the windows,
playing to what seemed like empty rooms. A car slowed down
alongside me and picked up speed again, the red sticker of the

neighborhood volunteer patrol on its windshield. Although the area looked safe—no housing projects, no burned-out buildings—I felt comforted by the surveillance. At one time I would have been outraged.

It was the middle of March. The winter was retreating at last, making a last-ditch stand with dirty mounds of snow, inky puddles, jagged potholes. Winter would never be the same to me. No longer would it be skiing and snowmen and snowball fights among the kids on our street. Winter was a cancer-stricken woman, half crazed with pain and loneliness, trapped in a strange apartment.

I walked past the parking lots reserved for doctors (life was easy if only you had the right license plate) and threaded my way past emergency vehicles with flashing lights to the Teller entrance. The lobby was bustling with a mixture of races, colors, and languages. The armed guard was speaking into his walkie-talkie; TV monitors aimed down from the walls and from inside the elevators. Upstairs I hurried through the corridor—dimmed for the evening—past the beeping monitors, the voices of visitors and television programs. In all her stays at Teller we had been her only visitors, with the exception of that distant cousin from the Bronx who managed one visit with her husband, who spent the time complaining that he had to park in a lot.

She lay still as I entered her darkened room, unaware of my presence until I spoke. "How are you?" I asked quietly.

She turned her head slowly and looked at me, frowning. "Bernie?" she asked in a voice that barely existed.

"How are you?" I repeated.

"Not so good," she said. "They killed me with their x-rays." She squinted past me through the dim light. "Are you alone? Steven isn't with you?"

"I'm alone," I said.

"Good," she said. "I want to talk to you." She shifted her eyes to make sure "they" were not listening on the other side of the room. Assuring her that no one could overhear, I pulled the chair close to her bed. "It looks like instead of getting better it got worse," she said.

I jumped at a crash in the corridor, which she did not seem to notice.

"Bernie," she said, "I want you to do some things that aren't in my will. I know you'll take care of them for me. I trust you."

"Whatever you want," I said.

I knew her will. It was the one she made out when I took her to Cal. The one with 5 percent of her money going to Teller, which, ironically, she now hated. But it was too late. Perhaps her money would buy still more testing equipment so that future medical students could practice on future Dora Sloans.

It was not Teller that bothered her, but the disposition of her possessions. The silver that I had dragged across the country. She named a niece to get it. She designated another niece to get her linens. "Hand-embroidered," she said. "Worth a fortune." And to her favorite niece, the wilted-plant young lady, she bequeathed her greatest treasure, her bedroom set.

She wanted to be assured that Ethel would get none of her valuables.

"She's foxy," she whispered. "I never liked foxy types. She told me her parents had a will. You think I didn't know what she wanted? Oh, the things I could tell you that she said to me. Once she opened a mouth at me, I didn't deserve it. Be careful, Bernie. Nowadays you don't know what people can do when they're angry."

According to the experts on dying, this was the time for my mother to accept death—and that acceptance was supposed to change her. She would release her prejudices, clear her soul, regret her treatment of Ethel. She would tell me that she was happy that she had such a wonderful daughter-in-law and would slip away at peace with the world. ·

My mother had not consulted the authorities.

Her safe-deposit box, she revealed, was crammed with valuables. An Omega watch to go to a nephew, unless I wanted it. Jewelry for the nieces.

I told her they would all most likely be heavily taxed, since she had never given me a key or signed the card permitting me to open the box.

"I didn't sign it?" she gasped, still acting. On the threshold of death, still acting. She was positive, she insisted, that she had signed it, but simply forgot to give it to me. An oversight. I thought the mind "went" as a person neared death. Nature's way of protecting from the terror of the abyss. Not my mother. Far from fading, her mind seemed to sharpen the nearer she came to the end. The weaker her body grew, the more tenaciously her mind clutched its defenses. She was not giving up even if every bone in her body disintegrated. She revealed where she hid the safe-deposit box key and card. In a brown envelope. Somewhere in her apartment.

I told her I needed a power of attorney to pay her bills while she was in the hospital. Her rent, utilities, phone. I did not mention the major expense on my mind. I assured her that the government checked to make sure that any money taken from her account was spent strictly on her needs.

"If I'd only known that," she said. As if I would have stolen her money unless watched. "So bring the papers tomorrow," she said. "I'll sign."

If she could not hold a spoon, I asked, how could she hold a pen?

"So you'll put it in my hand," she said, "and push." She paused, thought for a moment. "I'm tired of taking care of everything anyhow. You do it. You'll give me what I need to live. How much do I need?"

I started. She was talking about living.

"I'm so relieved," she said.

I bend down and kissed her forehead, and left.

In the dark corridor outside her room I walked into Dr. Gordon, who told me that he had just seen my mother's x-rays—the x-rays they broke her bones to take. With each turn on the x-ray table more bones broke in her body, but they ignored her screams until they completed their mission of a complete body x-ray. Now both arms were broken, her leg broken, every remaining bone ready to crumble at a touch, like so many dry crackers. If she were by some miracle to stand, he said, the weight would cause her spine to buckle.

It had won, the multiple myeloma. Nine months. Unstopped by the injections, the chemotherapy, the blood transfusions, the vast resources of the Teller Medical Center. It had neither been frightened by rage nor appeased by prayer.

A giggle erupted from the nurses' station. A TV proclaimed the merits of a Cadillac dealer.

"To prolong her life," Dr. Gordon spoke quietly, "would only prolong her suffering." They could take "heroic measures," he said, naming possibilities, but . . .

I agreed.

He said he would try to get her a better room. With the nicest view they could offer.

He mentioned, as an afterthought, that he had been having far better results with massive doses of Alkeran than with prednisone. "Maybe if we had started on the stronger cycle sooner, . . ." he stopped.

Why hadn't he?

"I thought since Dr. Kraven already began one treatment . . ."

He had succeeded in not offending Dr. Kraven.

42

WHILE THE OTHER MEN of Larchmont were converging on the station, I slipped like a thief into my mother's apartment and searched through her possessions. I found the keys to her safe-deposit box hidden in two different purses, which were in turn hidden in two grocery bags, which were hidden behind shoe boxes on the top shelf of her closet. (How had she done it? Did she scale her walker?) After hours of digging in envelopes I found the authorization card. Unsigned.

I found the power-of-attorney form from the bank. Unsigned.

Both forms had to be signed and notarized. Where was I going to find a notary to come to the hospital?

No problem, said Cal, who was a notary as well as an attorney. He would be glad to witness her signing at the hospital any evening except this one. Temple men's group meeting. What about the next night before the dinner dance of the Guild of the Jewish Deaf?

There might not be a next night, I told him.

Still no megillah, he said, having no intention of missing an event that might produce a client. Most hospitals, he said, had a notary on hand for just such purposes. Teller, undoubtedly . . .

Sorry, a voice rasped, after my usual series of phone calls, holds, and disconnections. Like every other service I sought, this too did not exist—for me. Their notary used to help out patients, I was told, but no more. They had enough lawsuits of their own without getting mixed up in estates.

A neighbor came to my rescue. Kevin O'Gorman. After working a full day, he came with me to the hospital, abandoning his wife and four children. He too was a lawyer and a notary. At that moment I wished he were *my* lawyer.

The sitter, a strikingly attractive young Jamaican woman with a white, miniskirted uniform that ended at her crotch and strained at every protuberance, gently shook my mother awake. Her eyes opened and she squinted at us. She opened her mouth to speak, but no sound emerged. The booming voice would never again be heard asking someone to warm her milk or bring her prune juice.

I explained that Cal could not make it and Kevin was taking his place. "Kevin lives down the block from us," I said. "You probably saw his wife and baby."

"Beautiful baby," my mother whispered with great effort.

Kevin's face was white. "I'm pleased to meet you, Mrs. Sloan," he said quietly.

The rustle of the envelope crackled like lightning as I removed the forms. Pressing buttons carefully, Kevin raised the bed to bring my mother to a near sitting position and placed a pad with the forms on her lap. I inserted a pen between her fingers and, holding her hand, guided it to form a surprisingly legible signature. Kevin signed and stamped.

Make money arrangements ahead of time, advise the magazine articles. Funeral expenses are tremendous. Money is needed quickly. Not many people have enough cash lying around. Let your heirs know where to find your assets. Make sure they have access to your bank accounts and safe-deposit box. Discuss it all frankly with each other. Never wait for the last minute when you can make mistakes. It is not bad taste, the authorities assure us, to discuss finances candidly with the stricken. You are doing them a favor. They want to die with the assurance that they have left everything in good order for their loved ones.

Not my mother.

Simplifying life for her heirs was not top priority in her mind. Not my mother, the fighter, who had no intention of dying. What was the rush to sign anything? With all that she was enduring, why worry about making life easier for somebody else?

A visiting nurse once brought her a chocolate bar. Dr. Spiegelstrauss came with free samples of Mylanta. "You think she gave it to me because she loves me?" my mother said of each. "It's because she wants something from me. Nobody gives anything away for nothing."

"If she feels that way about other people," Ethel said, "she must feel that way about us."

Two smiling nurses stepped through the doorway, like tour-group leaders, and announced they were taking my mother to another room. Before I could stop them they tossed her robe at the foot of her bed; she screamed with pain. As they looked at me, bewildered, I explained her problem. They had not known.

Their new-found knowledge did not prevent them from jostling and banging the bed as they wheeled her away, roaring with each bump.

"You're going into a nicer room," I told her as we moved through the corridor. "Dr. Gordon arranged it."

Dr. Gordon's final achievement for my mother was a big, bright room with enormous windows framing the surviving trees of the neighborhood. The sky was a brilliant purple as the setting sun poured into the room. The weather was predicted to be dazzling for the St. Patrick's Day parade tomorrow.

"Look," I pointed to the window. "A beautiful view."

She tried to lift her head, but it fell back on the pillow.

Dangling over her head was a shamrock taped to the wall, left by the patient with whom she had switched rooms.

"May the luck of the Irish be with you," Kevin said. Bowing his head at the foot of her bed, he moved his lips in silent prayer.

43

ST. PATRICK'S DAY.

At the bank, Vera Hackett, one of the last of the gray-haired ladies, glanced up from the cards and the forms. "If the owner of the
account dies, we freeze it, you know. Government regulations."

"Oh?"

"You won't be able to use it, you know. Of course, if we don't
know and nobody tells us, . . ." she smiled slightly. "What you do is
come prancing in all smiles like nothing happened and draw out
the money . . ."

Like I was doing now.

One of the advantages of dealing with your small community
bank—they are on your side. No eager arm of the IRS, they.

I explained that my mother was sick, and with the power of attorney I planned to draw out money from her account to pay her
bills—rent, housekeeper, phone, utilities. "All she needs," I said,
"is to come back from the hospital and find her electricity shut
off."

"It'd be just like Con Ed to do it, too," she said.

We took a few seconds to be angry with the utility.

"So full of life," Vera said. "I remember when she came in with
her grandson. Such a handsome boy."

Steven.

"He was so concerned about her. The things you hear about
teenagers nowadays. But he was so thoughtful, he worried over every step she took. I kept wishing he was mine. Nothing serious, I
hope?"

I shrugged.

She cautioned me to keep careful records. Once it turned into an
estate, she warned, the government was in like a shot, looking for
every penny. "You can be sure they want to get theirs," she said.

They headed for the safe-deposit box like bloodhounds, she
said. "You should see how fast they're in here. They seal up the

box; and anyone who tampers with it, it's a federal offense. It's easier to get away with murder." She urged me to close out the box at once.

"I think you're right," I said, opening the manila envelope I brought for the purpose.

At the funeral home, Mr. O'Reilly, an earnest young man with just the right flicker of a sympathetic smile on his serious face, assured me that they would handle everything when the time came. The removal of the body from the hospital, all "preparation," shipment in a coffin to Arizona to the proper mortuary with whom they would arrange burial in the plot next to my father. Mr. O'Reilly would even handle the newspaper announcements and contact the Arizona rabbi whom my mother wished to officiate at a simple graveside ceremony.

At last I found the one service that took care of everything.

I had always thought the law required a death notice to be published, until Mr. O'Reilly asked if I would want an announcement in the Larchmont newspaper as well as the one in Arizona. It was my choice. Since the only people in Larchmont other than us who would be concerned about her death were the bank officials, I decided that the city in which she had lived for thirty years would be sufficient.

A decision I later regretted when I was hungry for visitors but few appeared. When the time came most of our friends did not know that my mother had died, just as I did not know the depth of my feelings.

An obituary, I learned too late, was not for the deceased but for the survivors. A means of drawing friends for support. I felt it would be hypocritical playing the role of the grief-stricken son. I had had enough of role-playing. Our friends had a pretty good idea of what we had gone through. Condolences would be far from appropriate. And yet it turned out they were.

After providing Mr. O'Reilly with such data as my mother's Social Security number, birthdate, the name of her parents and close relatives, the hospital, the doctor, I was led through a very discreet door and down a flight of carpeted stairs to a room filled with coffins. It was reassuring to see a Star of David on several.

Sensing my uneasiness at consigning my mother to the hands of an O'Reilly, he hastened to point out a rough pine box. "We use this for the synagogue," he said. "But most temple people," he stepped to a smoothed and varnished version, "choose this one." I selected the temple model.

Let her travel first class for the first time.

Outside, the day was clear and sunny. The drum majorettes would finally make it up Fifth Avenue without goose bumps. Women in warm-up suits dashed in and out of stores and station wagons. In the travel agency in the next block Ethel was arranging trips. In the high school a mile away Paul was hacking his way through his freshman year, questioning the relevance of French and biology to someone destined to fulfill his life playing jazz guitar and skiing. In the same school Steven was deep into his advanced-placement courses, determined to squeeze every bit of knowledge out of every moment of his life even though he had already been accepted by M.I.T., almost by return mail.

I stuffed the manila envelope in a dresser drawer and, following Mr. O'Reilly's instructions, selected one of my mother's long gowns, still in a moving-company wardrobe box, for her burial. It turned out that the Orthodox Jewish Mortuary in Arizona insisted on nothing more worldly than a shroud, which they would provide.

She would have a shroud.

"COMA," SAID THE SITTER, perched on the window ledge reading *People.* Her shapely legs, sheathed in white, dangled freely, disappearing just in time into her tight white miniskirt.

I winced at the figure lying motionless under the sheet, like a mummy. Eyes stared upward from the gray face, air hissed in and out of the gaping mouth. No tubes, no nozzles, no hoses.

Set free at last.

"You're starting up already?" twanged a teenage boy on the other side of the curtain that divided the room. "Willya act like a human bean for a change?" snarled a man. "What'll you make for supper?" asked a woman. "A mess, I suppose."

"We'll eat somethin', don't worry."

"Anything good he don't like."

"What he calls good."

It seemed that every other day I read of the hospices rising across America, sanctuaries for the dying staffed with trained, loving personnel. I read of terminal-care pavilions that offered quiet and tranquility and dignity. But not where we were.

The sitter said she had tried to give my mother juice, inserting a straw in her gaping mouth, but there was no response. My mother, she said, had not moved for hours. Death was taking over without resistance. The blitzkrieg was in full swing. No more teasing. No more game-playing.

The sitter, bending over to display her panties, daubed my mother's forehead with a towel.

No more tests, no more injections, no more transfusions, no more pain, no more terror.

No more x-rays.

No more being strapped to tables, stretchers, beds.

No more freezers. No more hammers. No more screams.

No more plastic pouches emptying blood into a body no longer able to make its own.

No more homemaker to steal her shampoo or sneak a sausage into her suitcase.

No more Shatzi Spiegelstrauss, yah?

No more superintendent to rage at her for her meager Christmas gift.

No more visiting nurses, no more aides, no more physical therapists, no more specialists, no more waves of medical students.

We had decided for her, Dr. Gordon and I. It might be her life, yet we decided what she would do with it. We did not even ask her if she wished to prolong it. No one so much as inquired if she might be willing to pay for a few more days of life with a few more days of suffering. After years of fighting to get what she wanted, no one thought of asking her if she wanted to live a little longer.

A nurse entered, leaned into my mother's face, and shouted, "Mrs. Sloan! Mrs. Sloan!"

She snapped her fingers in front of my mother's eyes. She whipped one finger from side to side. Her eyes did not move. They might have been the stone eyes of a statue. The ball of fire was an ember. Quelled.

A second nurse appeared and slipped a thermometer under the blanket. My mother's body jerked slightly.

"Yesterday she screamed," said the nurse.

Was it really true that the staring eyes could not see, that the brain behind them was not reacting, strongly disapproving of what was occurring? Occasionally her brow jerked into a frown, a spasm, and returned to its motionless state. Reflex, said the nurse. Something about electrical impulses in the body, she learned in a course vaguely remembered.

Supposing it was more than reflex action? Could my mother tell us?

Steven appeared, materializing silently. A moment of pain on his face turned into a nervous giggle, as if he were afraid of being caught feeling. When I was his age I had the same nervous laugh, a laugh that denied feelings, a lubricant to get through life.

My mother was dying.

He cracked his knuckles.

He had provided her with the closest thing to a deep relationship she had with anyone in the months—perhaps years—before she died.

"I fell in love with Steven the first time I met him," she said. "Only a baby, but so intelligent. He had the family look."

"He looks like her," the sitter smiled. "You can tell he's her grandson."

I watched my mother closely for a reaction. If anything would do it, the sitter's words would.

The eyes continued to stare.

"Nothing," the sitter shook her head. She was taking night courses to become a nurse. Intensive care. She required more action than this, she said. Too bad my mother was failing her. "Oh, it isn't her fault," she assured me. "Most families don't get sitters once someone is this far gone."

I glanced uneasily at my mother, hoping she had not overheard. I had the eerie feeling that she could hear everything we said. That she was pretending to be in a coma, just as she pretended to be asleep when she was in our house, hoping to catch us talking about her. I felt I should talk to her. It would be my last chance. But I had nothing to say. What could I tell her? That I was angry? Was I supposed to agree with her that Ethel was foxy? Was I supposed to love her for leaving this world without a kind word for the only person who had really sacrificed for her?

She was rewarding her nieces for doing nothing.

She was crucifying Ethel for doing everything.

I was not about to tell her what I had decided to do. Okay, she did not trust people, she did not trust me; then I was going to justify her lack of trust. She had put me through a turmoil I did not need after nine months of fighting for her life. She had sent me scurrying to banks, digging up a notary, searching through her apartment. Okay, she did not trust me; I was going to prove her right.

There was nothing sacred, I decided, about deathbed wishes. Dying did not give people the right to be cruel or unfair. I was going to do what I thought was right.

Ethel was waiting for me the night my mother spoke about her will. "She wants her bedroom set to go to Diana," I said. "I just hope she wants it. One thing less to worry about."

"Has she ever seen it?" Ethel asked.

I shrugged.

"Gold paws aren't the kind of thing you're neutral about," Ethel said.

I told her that my mother wanted her linens to go to another niece.

Ethel smiled wanly. "She told me she wanted me to have them."

"She's befuddled."

"It's all right, I don't need them. I guess she was particularly grateful that day and forgot herself."

I quickly lied that my mother wanted her to have her mink jacket, a jacket treasured for more than twenty years. "Now you'll be able to join Hadassah," I said.

She knew I was lying.

I told her my mother's wishes for her silver, but I was not planning to carry them out. Not after wrenching my arm out of its socket dragging it across the country. I would save it for Steven and tell him she wanted him to have it.

In the nine months that my mother lived in Larchmont, the niece for whom the linens were destined called once to say she might visit her when she was settled in her apartment. She managed to reach Florida, Mexico, and Israel, but New York was inaccessible. My mother once asked if I would pick up Marcia at the airport should she favor us with a visit. "If she's coming to help you," I said, "but not to be entertained."

"She doesn't help herself," my mother replied. "She has plenty of maids."

"Let her bring a couple to help you."

That set the tone for that night.

As I stared at my mother on the threshold of death, I thought, without guilt and with considerable satisfaction, that I was going to do what I thought was right. She was going to express her gratitude the way it should be expressed, her dying wishes be damned. She was going to show her appreciation to real people she put through hell, not to fantasy nieces whose aid went no further than dialing a phone or licking an envelope.

There was no point in staying and watching her die and crying over what might have been. I felt no need to prove anything, no need to demonstrate the devotion she so craved. If she could understand what was happening, if she could speak, she would probably say, "It's not nice to leave a mother alone while she's dying. What will the sitter say?"

"Don't start with me," cried the teenage son on the other side of the curtain.

"He won't wash a dish; thinks he's a prince," said the father.

"I got homework."

"What homework? You got your nose glued to the television."

"I don't need this, I'm goin' home."

"By yourself? How?"

"Don't worry, I'll manage . . ."

"Wait downstairs, I'm leavin' soon . . ."

"You just got here, Seymour."

"Lousy kid."

After making arrangements for a sitter for the next shift, I left with the kangaroo totebag stuffed with my mother's ledgers and checkbooks. Steven stayed to wait for Ethel and Paul, a plan that delighted the sitter, who bounced back up on the ledge and hiked up her skirt.

45

IT WAS NEARLY TEN O'CLOCK when Ethel and the boys returned from the hospital. While the boys carried MacDonald's bags into the kitchen, Ethel slumped in a chair in the living room and lit a cigarette. Her face was drawn, her eyes red. She had been with my mother since four that afternoon. What had she done in all that time? How had she filled it? My mother was in a coma; what was Ethel trying to prove?

"The sitter said you didn't talk to her," Ethel said.

I winced. Had my mother awakened? Had the glazed eyes moved, had a voice emerged from the mute mouth? Had it all been another test?

"She was in a coma," I said. "The nurses said she couldn't understand a thing."

"They want her to be in a coma," Ethel snapped. "It's less work for them."

It was exactly what my mother would have said.

"She couldn't speak," I protested. "She couldn't hear, she couldn't see, she couldn't move."

"She heard *me*," Ethel said. "She spoke to me."

I looked for help to Steven, who stood in the archway, smiling slightly. His mother, he said, was exaggerating again.

"I am not exaggerating," Ethel said sharply. "Paul?"

Paul, drifting into the room, mumbled something.

"She spoke to me," Ethel repeated. "And I spoke to her. Speaking doesn't have to be words. There are other ways of reaching people. If you want to."

"What did you do?" I asked.

"I took her in my arms," Ethel said. "I told her who I was, and I said if she could hear me to blink. Once for yes, twice for no."

"And?"

"She blinked."

Steven said it was the same frown she made when I was there. The reflex.

"It was no reflex," Ethel said. "She communicated with me. We talked to each other. Didn't we, Paul?"

Paul shrugged.

"Paul was afraid at first," she said. "I made him come close to her so she could see him."

"I wasn't afraid," Paul said.

I told her how the nurse had snapped her finger in front of my mother's eyes and how she whipped it back and forth.

"Who wants to look at a finger?" Ethel cried. "She wanted to look at her family. She wanted to look at her grandchildren. And her son." She looked pointedly at me. "I can't believe you didn't try."

"I tried," I said. "When I came in I tried, but . . ."

"The sitter said that you didn't talk to her."

"She didn't respond," I defended myself.

"They why did she respond to me?" Ethel attacked.

"I don't know if she did," I said.

"I know," Ethel said.

"The nurse said she was definitely in a coma."

"They want her to be in a coma so they don't have to do anything for her. So they can make out with the residents."

"What did you say to her?" I asked.

"I told her she had two beautiful, wonderful grandchildren who loved her. And a fine son. And she could be proud of them."

Could I tell Ethel the reason for my coldness? The reason I did not try to reach my mother during her last hours of life? Was I about to tell her my mother's last words to me?

"The sitter thought that I was her daughter and you were her

son-in-law," Ethel said. "I kept moistening her lips with a washcloth. When you breathe through your mouth they get dry. I asked
her if she liked it. She blinked. Once."

"It was that frown," Steven said. Steven who was born old and
wise and scientific.

"She was talking to me," Ethel said. "No one even bothered to
moisten her lips. The sitter was just sitting there reading magazines."

I asked her what she found to talk about for four hours.

"I told her about Steven and how he was looking forward to going to M.I.T., and what a good school it was, how it accepted only
the best students in the country. I knew she would like to hear that.
I told her that Paul was going to a guitar workshop at a college this
summer—and how they picked only the best. I told her he was on
the freshman tennis team, and he was the best."

"I'm not," Paul said.

"I told her the sitter said that Steven looked like her, and she
smiled."

"She didn't when I was there," I said.

"You had to be close to her," Ethel said.

"You wanted to see her smile," Steven said.

"She licked her lips when I moistened them, didn't she, Paul?"

"I don't know," Paul said.

"You told me you saw her."

"I guess so," Paul said.

"Even Dr. Gordon acted as if she were already dead," Ethel said.
"He stood right next to her bed and started to tell me that she
didn't have much longer to live. I could have killed him. I pulled
him out to the hall."

"What did he say?"

"He thinks it will be sometime tonight."

When they start to go, they go fast, people said.

"She cried when I started to leave," Ethel said. "A quiet cry. A
whimper."

Paul said he had not heard her.

"You had to be very close," Ethel said. "I had my ear to her lips.
I hugged her. She cried. She didn't want me to leave."

"But you left."

"I explained that I was sorry but I had to get home to fix dinner for her son and grandchildren. I promised that we would come back tomorrow, early." Pausing, Ethel pressed her lips together. "I hate to say it, but if it were my mother I would have stayed."

"You did enough for her," I said.

"You could go to see her now," Ethel said. "There's still time."

I told her I saw no reason to sit next to someone in a coma.

"I can't believe that you didn't try," she said.

"I told you I tried . . ."

"But if you really tried."

"I really tried."

Was it possible that as she lay paralyzed, treated by everyone as already dead, she heard us all and was fully aware of everything that was happening? That buried deep within the still body pulsated a mind, sharp to the end, receiving signals? And that she understood Ethel and felt her caring? Helpless, unable to respond as life closed around her, did she sink into death desperate to cry out that she had made a mistake?

Was that, perhaps, the cruelest punishment of all her God had devised for her?

Or a beautiful final revelation?

AT ELEVEN-THIRTY the phone rang in the kitchen, piercing the silence of the house. Like an unwelcome guest the sound entered the darkened living room where we had been sitting, waiting.

I froze in my chair, hoping it was a mistake.

It continued to ring.

Wouldn't it be a joke, I thought, if I answered it and it was my mother's voice calling from Arizona? The past nine months not really having happened.

It continued to ring.

I felt as cold as a cadaver as I walked through the downstairs rooms to stop the sound.

"Mr. Sloan? Dr. Gordon."

After he assured me that the body would show no signs of having been sliced open and ravaged, I gave my permission to perform an autopsy, her final contribution to medical knowledge. Hanging up, I held back the tears until I made it up the stairs and behind the bedroom door.

I wanted no one to step through the door and stand over me and touch my shoulder. I wanted no one to talk about grief and how they understood. No one could understand. I did not want anyone to know that I cared for her. I was astonished at the depth and intensity of my feelings that I thought had long atrophied; they were like the roots of a tree that appears dead—buried but very much alive. Nothing she did could destroy them.

I was bawling at her death, and there was nothing I could do to stop.

I had advanced one step closer to the grave.

At midnight the phone rang again, bringing the voice of a woman from Teller who wished to tape my permission for the autopsy. I repeated the words she gave me without a tremor.

In the living room Ethel sat with Steven. Paul had gone out of the house, as eager to escape her dying as her living. "Well, it's over," I said.

"I wish I'd stayed," Ethel said. She turned to Steven, who sat in silence. "Don't you want to cry?" she asked him. "If you feel like crying, cry. Don't hold it back."

He smiled uncomfortably and mumbled. He was like me, his emotions controlled to the world, churning inside. Later, behind the closed door of his room he would face them. Privately.

"She didn't want me to leave," Ethel said.

"She was in a coma," Steven said.

"Another two hours," Ethel said. "It would have meant so much."

Several months later I read in a book on death that patients in a coma are often fully aware of what is going on, yet even doctors dismiss them as already dead. Sometimes the mind functions even

more sharply than when the entire body is able to respond, because now all perceptions are focused at one point. The doctor
who wrote the article urged that the living make every effort to
speak to the comatose, using signals such as blinking—perhaps one
blink for yes, two for no.

47

UNDER A GREEN CANOPY, as if for a garden party, three rows of
folding chairs faced the coffin, which was covered by a green tar-
paulin and suspended over an unseen grave. Although it was still
morning, and only March, the sun blistered from the absolutely
cloudless blue sky. From the highway outside the cemetery gates
came a steady roar of trucks nosing in and out of a factory.

A dozen or so elderly women arrived in cars, widows with the exception of one lone lady flaunting a barely living husband. While
waiting for the arrival of the rabbi and the beginning of the ceremony, the women drifted among the headstones, visiting one or
more former spouses.

At the head of my mother's grave stood a double stone, one half
blank, the other half etched with my father's name and birthdate,
which had been advanced by an additional two years. Two rows beyond, Cy Raskin lay next to his first wife.

I thought I had been drained of tears in the past four days,
breaking down whenever I spoke to anyone close to me. I had only
to clasp a hand to break into tears. I could handle details without a
tremor—the bank, funeral arrangements, removing documents
from her apartment—but when I spoke to someone involved with
my life I collapsed into tears. At the sight of Pearl stepping toward
me at the cemetery I broke into uncontrollable sobbing, throwing
my arms around her, powerless to contain feelings that had a will
of their own.

Pearl, however, was not too distraught to ask how much I paid
for the coffin, which she pronounced very nice. When I told her

five hundred and seventy dollars her hand flew to her face in amazement. She paid two hundred dollars more for her last husband's, she said, and it wasn't half as nice. My mother would have liked that.

The rabbi, his smile, gestures, and resonance a virtual duplicate of the Larchmont rabbi, as if they were products of the same seminary, gave what I suspect was his basic funeral speech. Wonderful woman. Devoted to Jewish causes. Loving wife. Devoted mother. Beloved grandmother. Would be sorely missed. Peace at last.

He followed his talk by selling me a memorial plaque to be hung on the temple wall. Two hundred dollars.

After the two gravediggers lowered the coffin by a system of ropes and pulleys, the mortician handed me a spade, with which I threw dirt on the coffin below. It was then that I realized our mistake in not bringing our sons. It was they who had shared her fight for life and her dying, it was they whom she had loved as much as she could love. In our haste, and in our concern for the cost, we excluded them. A mistake I could always regret but never undo.

It was Steven and Paul who should have thrown the dirt after I did, and not my Uncle Dave to whom the mortician passed the spade. Uncle Dave, the twice-divorced San Francisco swinger who called once in all the time his sister was dying.

None of the Raskin family came to the funeral.

After the services we drove past the home where my mother and father once lived, the elegant home that no one dared enter without an invitation. "Aren't you moved?" my uncle asked, a tear in his eye.

"By the house?" I asked. "No."

"You must be a very cold person," he said.

I looked at him in amazement. You bastard, I thought. You bought a plane ticket and came to a funeral and shed a tear.

"Where were you these nine months?" I asked. "Where were you when we were taking care of her? Did you come to Arizona and move for her? Did you come to New York and help her in her apartment? You made one phone call. She brought you from Europe, saved you from Hitler, and in nine months you made one damn phone call!"

"I used to come running whenever she called," he said. "All she did was abuse me. So I dropped out of sight."

"We didn't," I said.

On the way to the airport Uncle Dave kept up a steady mono-
logue about his new diet, his disenchantment with humanity, and
the women who snubbed him in previous years now desperate for
his attentions. "I tell them I have nothing against age," he giggled.
"It's what age does to them."

When I called to tell him of my mother's funeral arrangements,
he said, "Just when I'm moving to a new apartment."

"It's a rough life," I said.

"Keep in touch," he said at the airport. There was an unsaid
"please."

We flew back to New York.

THE OMEGA WATCH she was certain the world coveted turned out
to have long since stopped running. The "jewelry" guarded in the
safe-deposit box was an assortment of Swank tie clips and belt
buckles from Raskin's Tecumseh Indian souvenir stores. Her pre-
cious necklaces and rings turned out to be costume jewelry with
broken clasps. The linens packed in her dresser were spotted with
long imbedded stains and yellowed with age. And the silver turned
out to be plated. Like her life, it all looked impressive at a distance
but fell apart on close inspection.

Mrs. Epstein of the management company assured me that giving up her apartment would be no problem. I had merely to write a
letter agreeing to forfeit the month's security, pay an additional
month's rent for breaking the lease, and swear in writing that the
estate would be responsible for the rent until a new tenant was
found. When I protested that the extra month's rent seemed un-
conscionable since my mother had done nothing more destructive
than pay the superintendent twelve dollars to hang a mirror, I was
told that, sorry, it was their policy.

Engraved, apparently, in a stone tablet handed down from a higher authority.

We took a few of my mother's things and gave away others. A friend who owned an antique shop pounced on items from the thirties—saved from the period when my parents worked together in the hardware store and lived simply. A local auctioneer took everything else at a price that would have killed my mother—including the famous bedroom set that turned into a nightmare.

I called my cousin Diana in Boston who, after declaring that she was touched at being remembered by dear Aunt Dora, asked if I would mind sending Polaroids. The prospect of gold claws and griffins among her Swedish modern did not exactly thrill her. Surrounded by an apartment full of furniture that had to be disposed of and a ton of papers to sort through, I offered my apologies but I had no intention of hunting up a camera and taking pictures for anyone. If she had visited my mother in her apartment, I thought, she would not be faced with her current dilemma. I also mentioned the linens for her sister.

She asked for the weekend to think.

A week later she called to say that in the memory of her dear Aunt Dora she would happily accept the set. That was before I told her I had no idea what it would cost her to move it. I could practically hear the silence.

Several days after I made all the moving arrangements with a local company, Diana called to say she was upset at the $400 figure her investigations had turned up. She could not believe that dear Aunt Dora had made no provision for shipping it. Diana's husband was a dermatologist in practice with his father. They had recently bought a $150,000 home.

Diana said she would think about it.

Faced with the need to evacuate the apartment, I sold the set to the auctioneer the following week, a day before a letter arrived from Diana, refusing the set but suggesting that she would be happy to receive the proceeds from its sale so that she could buy something she really liked in memory of dear Aunt Dora.

Her letter was followed by a sympathy note from Uncle Dave's ex-wife in San Francisco, who disclosed that my mother had prom-

ised her bedroom set to her daughter, Dedee, who was eagerly
awaiting it.

Calls came regularly from the superintendent, impatient at our
lack of haste in evacuating the apartment. He accused us of preventing his staff from cleaning it. Since I was expected to continue
paying rent, I informed him, he would have to suffer some inconvenience.

Not enjoying the harassment, we cleared everything out too
quickly. The day after handing him the key I called to ask when I
could come for the roof antenna I had forgotten. He told me it was
now in his workroom and could be had for fifty dollars. "Once you
turn in the key," he said, practically salivating through the phone,
"you give up the apartment and all that goes with it."

"You've got a good business going," I told him.

"We all have to make a buck as best we can," he replied and
hung up.

I understood why some people got reported to the IRS.

Among the items I found in her apartment, among the old envelopes, bank statements, news of 1965 stock splits, and bargain of-
fers from *Barron's*, was a bottle of capsules to be taken for anemia.
They were prescribed by Dr. Greenstone two months before she
was hospitalized in Arizona. I still have it.

And there was her previous year's tax return, which turned out
to be my responsibility after all. The first thing I learned was that
anyone can get a tax extension, especially the dead. Forms came
from the IRS and New York State. I was buried in forms.

There were doctor bills to pay, Medicare forms, and a steady
correspondence with Arizona Blue Cross, which could set a standard for Blue Crosses everywhere. They not only answered my letters with clear, detailed instructions but sent postage-paid envelopes, as if they needed the business. In New York I've had trouble
finding Blue Cross. The woman from the agency called to praise
my mother and ask for the $600 she owed Darlene. Similar invita-
tions (without the praise) came from New York Telephone and
Con Edison.

Two days after the funeral a registered letter arrived from Dr.
Greenstone with a bill for $500 my mother had failed to pay. I re-

turned the bill together with a note saying: "It seems to me that a doctor who prescribes medication for anemia to a patient exhibiting the classic symptoms of multiple myeloma, possibly delaying proper treatment, would be more concerned about expanding his medical knowledge than collecting a bill."

I did not hear from him again.

Social Security, after requiring me to fill out an endless form, informed me that my mother was not entitled to death benefits, since she had never worked under Social Security but had collected only as a widow. Information I could have given them in a second and saved a form, if they had asked.

One day when Ethel was gathering up the last items from my mother's apartment, she was asked in to "tea" by two elderly sisters in an apartment across the hall. Over Bloody Marys they told Ethel how they tried to meet my mother, but her housekeeper always answered the door and held them at bay. Sometimes they heard my mother's voice saying that she was resting, about to bathe, or otherwise indisposed. She seemed like such a nice person, said the sisters, both widows, both Jewish. And wasn't she lucky to have such a concerned family, they said. They noticed that one or the other of us was always coming to see her.

My mother would have liked that.

"They love me so much," I could hear her saying. "They treat me like a queen."

On going through her strong boxes, the opening of which required fitting dozens of keys into heavy padlocks that would have done Fort Knox proud, I found among expired insurance policies and old letters written in Yiddish, photographs of my mother as a girl in Europe. She looks to have been about seventeen as she posed with various people whose identities I did not know. They are all very serious. Having one's picture taken was clearly no laughing matter. There are surprisingly well-preserved photographs of her village. Mud streets and wooden shacks straight out of *Fiddler on the Roof.* A bearded man with flashing eyes and a skullcap may or may not be my grandfather. Any one of the several women could be my grandmother. As for uncles, she had six brothers, take your choice.

They are all a far cry from the snapshots she displayed proudly in a leatherette album. Pages of color snapshots of Cy Raskin and herself in Israel, Italy, Hawaii. Pictures of her beaming proudly in long dresses and fur wraps at weddings and bar mitzvahs with other overweight people with too much jewelry.

There are a great many pictures of her with the Raskin family, who treated her, she used to say, like one of their own. She is beaming among them over birthday and anniversary cakes, in recreation rooms, on lawns under Japanese lanterns, with women in beehive hairdos, one Cadillac or another in the background.

I threw out the photographs in the album and replaced them with the solemn Jews and ramshackle houses and mud streets of the incinerated shtetl, whose ghosts may still hover over the long-buried tracks of Hitler's divisions.

For weeks after my mother's death Ethel had a recurring dream—the phone rang and a voice told her that someone was dead. My mother. Her mother. Her father. An uncle. An aunt. People long dead as well as living. She tried sleeping pills, she returned to Valium, but each night she awakened in a sweat, straining to hear the phone in the hallway outside our bedroom door.

"She's with me all the time," Ethel said. "She follows me into the kitchen and tells me what to do. Sometimes when she wants me to do something for her, she's very sweet. But most of the time she finds fault. Last night she accused me of hiding pork."

Looking over the books in her apartment, all on Jewish themes or the biographies of celebrities such as Mike Douglas, the Duke of Windsor, Golda Meir, Dick Cavett, I found written on a number of flyleafs, "To Nana with love—Ethel, Bernie, Paul, Steven."

She had reached seventy without understanding that the way to get love is simply to give it. It is not for sale.

We are healing now.

We are taking care of our home again. Painting here, repairing there. There is time again. Time to rejoin life. It is as if we have been away on a very long trip.

Steven is eating regularly once more. He smiles a lot, a handsome, dazzling smile that lights up the house. He had a date for the senior prom, which has returned along with Benny Goodman and Woody Herman. Our major problem now is getting him off the phone. He will do well at M.I.T.

Ethel no longer works full time at the travel agency. At my insistence she has become an outside agent, working on her own accounts. Ironically, she is making more money than before and has far more time. And time is what's important. All the money in the world cannot buy the disappearing seconds.

I learned from the experience with my mother. I've changed my attitude about money. I spend *now*. So I'll die with twenty dollars less, I say. A hundred dollars. A thousand dollars. I say that a lot now. I am far more accepting than I ever was. Little things no longer irritate me. I am grateful to be alive.

Would we do it again?

Knowing what we do now?

We accomplished what we set out to do. We gave my mother the chance to know her grandchildren before she died—and let them know her.

But could anyone know her?

Among her possessions was an oil painting of our boys that we had sent her while living in Australia. It was in a carton, still unpacked from her flight from Arizona. It's on our wall now. Paul at nine with an impish grin, Steven at eleven smiling happily. They are in their school uniforms—Paul's tie noticeably askew, Steven's correctly neat.

"Steven, my prince," I can hear her saying. And to Paul, with laughter, "Mark my word, you'll miss me when I'm gone."